CASE STUDIES
FOR TEACHER
DECISION MAKING

CASE STUDIES FOR TEACHER DECISION MAKING

Gordon E. Greenwood
University of Florida

Forrest W. Parkay
University of Florida

RANDOM HOUSE  NEW YORK

This book was developed for Random House by Lane Akers, Inc.

First Edition
98765432
Copyright © 1989 by Random House, Inc.

Library of Congress Cataloging-in-Publication Data

Greenwood, Gordon E., 1935–
   Case studies for teacher decision making/Gordon E. Greenwood,
Forrest W. Parkay.—1st ed.
    p. cm.
   ISBN 0-394-37011-2
   1. Teaching—Decision making—Case studies. 2. Teacher-student
relationships—Case studies. I. Parkay, Forrest W. II. Title.
LB1025.2.G675   1988
371.1'02—dc19   88-11502
                                              CIP

Cover Design: Lisa Polenberg

Cover Art: Paul Klee, *Lenkbarer Grossvater,* 1930, Klee-Stiftung. Copyright ARS N.Y./ADAGP, 1988

Photos: p. 1, Peter Southwick/Stock, Boston; p. 35, Stuart Cohen; p. 73, Billy E. Barnes/Stock, Boston; p. 129, James Holland/Stock, Boston; p. 179, Billy E. Barnes/Stock, Boston; p. 235, Miriam Reinhart/Photo Researchers; and p. 283, Elizabeth Crews.

Manufactured in the United States of America

CONTENTS

PART 3
INSTRUCTION CASES 73

PART 4
GROUP MOTIVATION AND DISCIPLINE CASES 129

PART 5
PUPIL ADJUSTMENT CASES 179

PREFACE

Case Studies for Teacher Decision Making is designed for any education course that has as its goal the application of theoretical knowledge to the practical problems of teaching. This goal, of course, describes just about every course in most teacher education curricula and some courses in the areas of counseling, administration, and the foundations of education. This broad goal can be broken down into two more specific subgoals that provide the rationale for this book. They are:

1. To provide students with an opportunity to strengthen their understanding of theoretical and conceptual knowledge by applying it to the resolution of realistic teaching situations
2. To become metacognitive (i.e., to develop self-awareness) about their professional decision making.

A word about each of these goals.

Applying Conceptual Knowledge. For decades teacher educators have known that their students need to be given immediate and ongoing opportunities to apply the theoretical content of their courses in order to truly learn that content. They have told their students about the theoretical connection between the application of knowledge and the transfer of learning but have given them little opportunity to experience this connection in their own courses. Teachers are the first to criticize themselves for this failure but, too often, have done little to remedy the situation. This book is an attempt to do that. It presents 30 high-frequency teaching situations that have been constructed from survey data supplied by real teachers in six states regarding their "most troublesome" or "most enduring" teaching situations.

In writing each case, the authors have attempted to preserve as much original data as possible. When available, actual quotes are used. All names of people, schools, and places have, of course, been changed. Finally, an attempt has been made to divide the cases as evenly as possible among elementary, middle, and secondary levels and to distribute them among the following decision areas:

1. *Curriculum* Selecting and organizing subject matter
2. *Instruction* Making effective decisions about how to teach
3. *Group Motivation and Discipline* Keeping students involved

4. *Pupil Adjustment*   Dealing with the special problems of individual students
5. *Conditions of Work*   Dealing with the context within which teaching takes place

The resulting cases have intentionally been left open-ended and un-resolved. This permits their analysis using a variety of theoretical or conceptual frameworks. It is important that students understand that there is no correct way for a problem situation to be analyzed. A theory or set of principles fits a situation if the student shows that it does. Different frames of reference may produce different courses of action in dealing with a given situation. Hence, for educational purposes, a theory is the correct one to use if the student shows that it fits the situation by citing evidence, and a decision is correct if it is consistent with the frame of reference used. The goal, quite simply, is to force students into higher-order thinking regarding the knowledge base on which teaching practices rest.

Developing Metacognitive Decision Makers.   Just as teacher training curricula have made too little provision for the application of theoretical knowledge, so too have they all but ignored the development of what some refer to as the most fundamental of all teaching skills—professional decision making. Learning to be systematic in decision making and to be aware of cognitive processing during decision making take just as much practice as acquiring relevant bodies of psychological, sociological, pedagogical, and organizational knowledge. In short, to be an effective decision maker, one needs to practice decision making. Moreover, this practice needs to be distributed over a variety of decision areas.

This book provides typical teaching situations for students to work through thereby developing their analytical and decision-making skills. It provides a manageable decision-making model that students can easily master and apply. Other models can, of course, be applied just as easily. Since the practice cases are distributed across grade levels and decision areas, students will learn that decision making is an ongoing responsibility that permeates every aspect of their professional lives. To be aware that decision making is inevitable and continuous and that the most effective decision making requires ongoing, self-monitoring practice with a systematic model is what this book is all about.

Using this Book.   *Case Studies for Teacher Decision Making* can be used either with another text or texts, or it can be used as the primary course text with the library or teacher handouts serving as the students' primary source of reading materials. As for its integration into existing course syllabi, the following (all based on actual experience) are offered.

1. The cases can be used at the end of a course to provide practical application activities for the previously covered theoretical material.

2. One or more cases can be presented at the beginning of a course to help establish a practical rationale for the ensuing theoretical material.

3. Relevant cases can be mixed into units of theoretical study. For example, a certain theory or set of related principles can be studied for two weeks followed by a week or two of application to relevant cases. Some variation of this pattern is probably the most common method of using such cases.

4. The cases can also be used as the basis of small group decision-making activities. Such procedures have been employed by the senior author and are described in some depth in the Appendix at the end of the book.

5. Role playing activities in which the students act out the roles where the situation ends can also be based on these cases. Video-taping such role-playing activities adds still another dimension to the learning process. For students to see themselves playing, for example, the role of a teacher on video-tape can be both illuminating and motivating.

6. Finally, the cases provide an excellent evaluation device for tapping the upper levels of Bloom's taxonomy, especially the application and analysis levels. The cases can be used in a pre-test, post-test fashion to assess student gains in subject matter mastery or in decision-making. The Appendix offers a practical format for using the cases in this fashion.

As the previous list illustrates, this text can be used in many ways that will add variety and spice to your course and strengthen student learning and decision making.

Acknowledgments. Writing a book of this type, which involves the collection of case material from many teachers, always requires the help and cooperation of friends and colleagues. The authors wish to particularly thank the following persons for their invaluable assistance: Dr. Dan Boyd, Principal of Gainesville High School, Gainesville, Florida; Dr. Sandra Damico, Radie Armstrong, and Delores Durrance of the University of Florida; Dr. Chris Sparks Mann of Stephen Foster Elementary School, Gainesville, Florida; Jane Greenwood of the Vermont Department of Education, Burlington, Vermont; Dr. Howard Ramagli of Memphis State University, and Debbie Riley, Director of the Campus School, Memphis, Tennessee; Dr. Stevie Hoffman of the University of Missouri; Dr. William Bechtol and Dr. Beverly Hardcastle of Southwest Texas State University; Dr. Nathalie Gehrke of the University of Washington; Dr. Katherine Newman and Dr. Jeanne Pfeifer of California State University at Sacramento; and Ann Wilson of the Pinellas County School District, Clearwater, Florida.

The authors especially wish to thank our editor Lane Akers without whose encouragement and knowledge this book would not have been possible.

Dedication. The authors dedicate this book to Dr. David Gliessman of Indiana University, who started the senior author on this path back in 1965, and to our wives, Patti and Arlene, who provided the love and encouragement to sustain our efforts.

PART I

INTRODUCTION

CHAPTER 1

EDUCATIONAL THEORY AND TEACHER DECISION MAKING

Teachers As Decision Makers

Teaching is a highly complex process that many have studied and tried to describe. Questions that are often raised include: (1) What relationship exists between the art of teaching and educational science? (2) How can teachers use the research findings from fields like educational psychology and curriculum and instruction? (3) What are the various sources of professional knowledge that teachers can apply to everyday teaching situations?

One view of teacher knowledge is that of Connelly and Elbaz (1980) who maintain that teachers use their knowledge in a uniquely practical way and that such knowledge consists of five components:

1. Knowledge of the context of a specific situation (e.g., "What is the ability level of my third period class?")
2. Knowledge of various theories of practice (e.g., "What do researchers like Skinner and Piaget have to say about such situations?")
3. Knowledge of social conditions and constraints (e.g., "What are the expectations of parents in this community?")
4. Knowledge of oneself (e.g., What kind of teacher do I see myself to be?")
5. The teacher's experience (e.g., "What have I learned about teaching?")

In other words the teacher's practical knowledge as to how to deal with daily teaching situations consists of a unique blend of the five components of knowledge just described. Educational science would seem to contribute most to the second of the five components: theories of practice.

Take the case of Bill Jones, a high school social studies teacher. During a typical week Bill is constantly making many decisions and draws upon his personal practical knowledge in order to make them. First Bill has to decide what he is going to teach. Thus he spends time before class writing objectives. Second Bill must decide how to teach and what instructional materials to use. In making these decisions, Bill must consider the characteristics of the particular students he is teach-

3

ing. Third, as Bill actually teaches the class, he is continuously making decisions, for example, how to explain more effectively the point he just tried to make or how to respond to Jerry in the third row if he makes another smart remark. Fourth Bill has to decide how to evaluate his instruction and how to interpret and follow up on the results of the evaluation.

As the preceding brief example illustrates, teaching is a complex, multifaceted activity that requires the ability to make decisions before, during, and after face-to-face interactions with students. Regarding the almost limitless number of decisions that teachers must make, the authors of this book hold the following views:

1. Decision making is a critical aspect of a teacher's work.
2. Teachers typically make decisions on the basis of their personal belief systems.
3. Education courses should help teachers examine and clarify their personal belief systems and encourage them to integrate their belief systems with research-based educational theories and principles.
4. Education courses should help teachers develop their decision-making skills by giving them opportunities to make decisions using the theories and principles they are learning. (The case materials presented in this book provide one opportunity for practicing decision making.)

Many researchers view teachers as decision makers (Clark and Peterson, 1986; Good and Brophy, 1986; Gage and Berliner, 1984; Davis, 1983; Dembo, 1977; Brubaker, 1970; McDonald, 1965). One researcher (Shavelson, 1973) maintained that decision making is the basic teaching skill. "What distinguishes the exceptional teacher from his or her colleagues is not the ability to ask, say, a higher-order question, but the ability to decide *when to ask* such a question . . ." (p. 144).

Decision making may be defined as the process of choosing between two or more alternative courses of action. Whether it is based on educational research or not, decision making is inevitable. Even when ignoring a problem, teachers are choosing a course: inaction. Frequently teacher decisions involve choosing between two or more well-known alternatives. For example, "Shall I teach the world history unit on ancient Greece the way I taught it last semester, or shall I teach it the way I taught it the semester before that?" In such cases the teacher may feel that it is not necessary to consider new and unfamiliar courses of action. However, effective teachers are not likely to go for long periods without engaging in some decision making activity. Unless teachers periodically examine and evaluate the effects of their teaching routines, they probably will not remain effective teachers for very long since routine responses rarely apply to all situations.

Some teacher decisions involve the broader context of education. The decisions to go on strike or to become active in politics are obvious examples. Other recognized situations that lie outside the classroom but nevertheless affect the teacher's work are such things as working with an uncooperative principal, handling over-protective parents, and dealing with the problem teacher in the room next door. Today's teachers have to deal with a variety of issues and situations that lie outside the classroom, many of which eventually find their way into the classroom in one form or another.

Teacher Beliefs and Educational Research and Theory

As has been stated, most teachers base their decisions on their personal belief systems. Such systems are influenced by educational research and theory in varying degrees according to the experiences of the individual. A theory may be viewed as "a collection of related statements that are intended to organize and explain a set of observations. But the goal of theorizing goes somewhat beyond explanation: In addition, it involves prediction and control" (Lefrancois, 1987, p. 32). As pointed out earlier, the knowledge base from which the teacher operates may include research-based theories but is likely to include other components as well (Connelly and Elbaz, 1980). The organized set of these components is what we call the belief system, and it is what guides the teacher in making decisions.

For example a teacher may operate from a consciously or unconsciously held set of beliefs like the following: "In order for the kids in my class to learn, they must keep busy and work hard. Other types of behavior are not conducive to learning and therefore are not desirable. I must keep good discipline by being firm and consistent and by keeping enough distance between my kids and me to maintain respect. I must also be fair and not favor certain kids over others."

The preceding set of generalizations contains complex and interrelated psychological and philosophical assumptions. Upon examining more of the teacher's beliefs, we would find still other generalizations relating to curriculum, objectives, teaching methods, and so forth. As you read these beliefs, you probably wished for more specific knowledge of certain words, like "busy," "other types of behavior," and "being firm." Because the teacher's beliefs are unsystematically stated and somewhat vague, he or she might have a hard time communicating them to someone else.

How can teachers learn to integrate the research and theory they study with their personal belief systems? In an educational psychology course, for example, they might:

1. Examine and state their own system of beliefs under the direction of their instructor.
2. Examine the various psychological theories, principles, and concepts

that seem to have relevance to teaching (e.g., Piaget's theory of cognitive development), noting the strengths, weaknesses, and focuses of each.

3. Determine which psychological theory or theories seem to be closest to their own.
4. Compare and contrast their own with others, making any necessary revisions in their own theory while reserving the right to be eclectic.
5. Test their revised or reintegrated theory in the classroom. Testing can be done through their own "action research" as well as by reading about and participating in the research of others.

In order for teachers to begin examining their personal sets of beliefs, they might try answering as honestly and realistically as possible such questions as:

1. What causes students to behave the way they do? To what extent is student behavior a product of learning as opposed to heredity?
2. What is learning and what conditions promote it?
3. What must teachers do to promote learning in the classroom? How can they tell when learning is taking place?
4. What is a discipline problem? At what point does a child become a discipline problem, and what techniques are available to deal with such problems?
5. What can teachers do to prevent such problems from happening again?
6. How can teachers tell when they are doing their job effectively?
7. To what extent should teachers be concerned with student growth outside of academic achievement? What aspects of student growth should be emphasized?

The teacher will find that different theories or organized sets of principles will be emphasized in different courses, depending on whether the course is in educational psychology, curriculum and instruction, social foundations of education, and so forth. In an educational psychology class, for example, a student might study Jean Piaget's theory of cognitive development or a set of measurement and evaluation concepts and principles relating to testing and grading. Similarly, curriculum models such as that of Jerome Bruner and classroom management techniques such as those developed by Jacob Kounin might be taught in curriculum and instruction courses. Whether a formal research-based theory or a curriculum model, any organized set of principles and concepts presented as part of the teacher education curriculum should be examined from the standpoint of the student's own belief system and, when appropriate, interpreted into that belief system and the decisions that flow from it.

Before leaving the topic of personal belief systems and scientific theories, it should be pointed out that scientific theories and principles, like personal belief systems, are constantly growing and changing over time. As a result of research, old theories can change or disappear and new theories are developed. It is important for teachers to be aware of these changes through a continuous program of teacher education.

A Strategy for Attacking Teaching Problems

The purpose of this book is to provide typical teaching situations that preservice and in-service teachers can use to develop their own analysis and decision-making strategies. It is assumed that the teachers have already been exposed to some educational theories and principles or will be learning them as they consider the teaching situations found in this book. Perhaps some will even develop and use their own theories. Whatever the prerequisite learning or course structure, why do so many teachers not learn to use research-based theory and research in their decision-making activities? Part of the answer lies in the fact that many teachers have not developed a process or strategy for making decisions about the kinds of problems they face. It is important for teachers to develop a decision-making strategy for dealing with teaching situations regardless of the theory employed as a framework for analyzing it.

One such strategy, long used by the authors, is presented in the following six-step decision-making model:

1. Examine the situation and decide to deal with it.
2. Gather data to examine further the nature of the situation.
3. Interpret the data.
4. Arrive at a decision by generating alternatives and choosing among them.
5. Examine the decision for consistency, feasibility, and operationality.
6. Execute and evaluate the decision.

The case materials in this book are intended to provide practice in the first five steps of this decision-making model. Videotape materials, such as those used in microteaching, are more suited to step six. Each step will now be examined in greater detail.

Examine the Situation and Decide to Deal with It   The first thing that a teacher must do is to decide that a decision needs to be made. Teachers are sometimes unaware that certain problems result from long-used teaching routines that are not working in a particular situation. In other cases they are aware that their routines are not working but refuse to acknowledge that fact or to do anything about it.

Take the case of Charles Brown, who is now teaching American history for the first time to students in a vocational education program as well as to students in a college prep program. Charles decides to make no changes in his objectives, teaching methods, and evaluation procedures in spite of the differences in student characteristics. To Charles history is history, no matter whom you are teaching. Later when discipline problems begin to arise and students question why they have to take history, Charles grudgingly becomes aware that his third period American history class is more difficult to teach than his other classes. However, he attributes this to the fact that the students are lazy and unwilling to work, so he continues to follow the same course of action rather than to consider alternatives. Originally Charles failed to consider student differences, and when he became aware of them, he chose to ignore them. Eventually when the discipline problems become bad enough, Charles will have to face them and deal with them.

External pressures from parents, principals, other teachers, and even students often cause certain teachers to face problems that they would just as soon avoid. The most obvious internal pressure influencing teacher behavior is their own personal belief system or theory of teaching. Whereas Teacher A may interpret a given student's behavior as quite desirable, Teacher B may interpret the same behavior as a serious problem and decide to do something about it. For example, the teacher who is primarily concerned with good discipline and pupil achievement may not interpret Mary Smith's highly anxious, introverted, and socially withdrawn behavior as a problem. Such behavior may be seen as quite desirable since Mary is a hard worker and never a discipline problem, even when the teacher leaves the room.

Gather Data to Examine Further the Nature of the Situation Once a teacher decides to deal with a situation, he or she then must examine fully and objectively the nature of the problem. Take the case of a teacher named Mrs. Jones who, as far as she is concerned, has two problems: Mary and Johnny. Mary is constantly seeking attention and disrupting class while Johnny is bored and goes to sleep. What can she do about them? First, before doing anything, she probably needs to gather more information.

Suppose that Mrs. Jones has just taken a course in which she learned how to use behavior-modification classroom management techniques and has integrated these techniques into her personal belief system. Such techniques would involve an observer's determining when and how often Mary exhibits her attention-seeking and disruptive behavior and what reinforcement serves as the payoff for Mary. Mrs. Jones might have a teacher aide or parent volunteer collect the appropriate behavioral data. She would then need to examine and interpret the data in order to decide what to do. Perhaps Mrs. Jones is unwittingly reinforcing Mary's behavior by giving her attention or, possibly, it may be maintained by the attention she gets from other students. Mrs. Jones would then have to decide how to change the reinforcement pattern.

On the other hand, suppose that Mrs. Jones takes a different approach to Johnny. She examines Johnny's cumulative record in the counselor's office and finds that he has a high I.Q. and is classified as gifted. Other information indicates that Johnny's parents are divorced and he has to work after school to help support himself and his mother, with whom he lives. Mrs. Jones will have to decide, probably from talking to Johnny and his mother, to what extent he is challenged by classroom activities and to what extent his job and his home life contribute to his listless behavior. Without having this information Mrs. Jones might simply label Johnny lazy and unmotivated. The self-fulfilling prophecy research of Rosenthal and Jacobson (1968) describes how such labeling occurs.

What kind of data might a teacher gather? It all depends on the nature of the situation and the constraints of the educational theory or personal belief system that the teacher is operating from. In the previous example if Mrs. Jones operates from a behavior-modification perspective, she will observe, count, and record Mary's external behavior. On the other hand, in Johnny's case Mrs. Jones's data came from his cumulative record and I.Q. score as well as from discussions with Johnny's mother about his work and sleep habits. These data were then interpreted in terms of psychological principles regarding gifted children and children from single-parent homes. In both cases the theories or principles that were applied determined the kinds of data that were collected. The interpretation of the data, in turn, helped form hypotheses regarding the nature of the two situations.

Interpret the Data   One of the most difficult things for teachers to learn is to be objective about interpreting data they collect. They must learn to distinguish between the data itself—whether an I.Q. score, the comments of a child's parents during a home visit, or the recorded observation that Mary is hitting other children 1.4 times per minute—and the interpretations made from the data. The fact that Johnny often has his eyes closed in class may mean that he is tired, or that he is bored and daydreaming, or that he is ahead of the teacher and is already working out in his head the solution to the math problem. To quickly make any one of these interpretations would be premature. To prematurely decide Johnny is bored and daydreaming and then, further, to make the inference that he is lazy and unmotivated compounds the objectivity problem. Like good attorneys, teachers must learn to cross-examine themselves and ask, "Is that what Johnny actually said, or did I just infer that he said that?"

It is also important for teachers to keep personal biases under control when interpreting data. To illustrate this point, consider George Smith, who has frequently observed two students in his senior civics class, Jean and Shirley, whispering together in the back of the room. He has always ignored this behavior, hoping that it would disappear. The two girls are physically attractive and very popular among their classmates. He wanted to befriend them, but they seemed to make fun of him at times. Once when he tripped over a wastebasket, they seemed to laugh louder and longer at him than anyone else in the room. At other times they would whisper together, look in his direction, and begin to giggle.

One day another teacher hurt Mr. Smith's feelings by criticizing the tie he wore to school, saying "Man, you're never going to be cool as long as you wear square ties like that." During second period civics class on the same day, Jean and Shirley once again whispered together in the back of the room, looked in Mr. Smith's direction, and began to laugh. Mr. Smith inferred from their behavior that they were talking about him. He told them to go to the Dean of Girls' office.

The Dean of Girls later told Mr. Smith that the girls had been telling one another jokes. Mr. Smith did not really believe this story and told the girls in no uncertain terms that he was going to move them away from each other and that the next time they talked he would lower their grades. Both girls had confused and bewildered expressions on their faces, and Jean began to cry. Shirley said, "Why are you treating us this way, Mr. Smith? We always thought you were the one teacher we have who really understands us!"

You can probably think of many things that you would like to find out about Jean, Shirley, Mr. Smith, and others before you begin to analyze this case. A good starting point is to consider Mr. Smith's objectivity. Was he objective in examining the data? From a measurement standpoint, objectivity of this kind refers to the amount of agreement between observers. If two other teachers had observed the same behavior, would they have made the same inferences from the behavior?

If Mr. Smith could remove his perceptual blinders for a moment, what would he have actually observed about Jean's and Shirley's behavior, and what would he have inferred? He has definitely seen the two girls whispering together, glancing at him, and laughing from time to time. He could probably estimate how many times they have engaged in this behavior if it were important. He did hear and see them laugh loud and long when he tripped over the wastebasket. Furthermore, the Dean of Girls said that the girls admitted telling jokes on the day he sent them out of class. Finally we know exactly what the girls said to Mr. Smith when he talked to them later because we have an exact quote. We cannot see the girls' faces or hear the way in which Shirley said what she did to Mr. Smith. Our data have many limitations, but they do provide some clues and suggest the need to collect additional information.

What kinds of inferences did Mr. Smith make from the data, and are there other interpretations that could be made? First he seemed to feel that the girls saw him as an inadequate male. Second he inferred that they were whispering and giggling about him and his inadequacies. After the incident he refused to accept Shirley's statement concerning his adequacy as an understanding teacher. Did Mr. Smith respond to the behavior that he observed or did he respond to the inferences that he drew from the behavior?

Imagine now a future conversation between Mr. Smith and some fellow teachers during their planning period. Imagine another teacher saying, "I have Jean Sinders and Shirley Merrick in my class this semester. Hey, George, didn't you have some trouble with them last semester?" Mr. Smith says, "I sure did! They were always disrupting the class. Every time I turned my back, they were whispering and giggling and making all kinds of noise."

It is unlikely that anyone in the teachers' lounge will ask Mr. Smith to state the evidence on which he is basing his statements. How accurate are his statements? What expectations might they create in the mind of the teacher who asked about the two girls? To summarize, the actual behavior of the girls is not the same thing as inferences made from the behavioral data.

When a teacher interprets data in terms of an educational theory or a set of principles, he or she is obviously interpreting the data in terms of that theory. It is at this point that the principles and concepts taught in theory courses can become relevant.

Arrive at a Decision After collecting and interpreting the data, the teacher must decide whether to gather more data, to continue the present course of action, or to choose a new course of action. The whole decision-making process, from deciding to deal with the situation to arriving at a decision, may take only an instant or, depending on how reflective and systematic the teacher tries to be, it may take considerably longer.

For example, decision making may be relatively simple and quick when a teacher is choosing between two familiar courses of action such as: "Should I develop an essay or multiple-choice exam for this unit?" The case may be quite different, however, when the teacher encounters an unfamiliar and complex situation like: "Somehow I have totally lost control of this class, and I don't understand why it happened or what to do about it!" In such a case it may take considerable time for the teacher to fully analyze the situation, perhaps with help, and to consider and choose among several possible courses of action. A considerable amount of time is likely to be involved when teachers first begin using research-based theories or principles as a basis for analysis and data collection in examining a situation and choose a course of action that follows from such analysis. Eventually, once research-based theory has been integrated into the teacher's personal belief system, its use should become "second nature" and much more rapid.

Examine the Decision for Consistency, Feasibility, and Operationality The courses of action that a teacher chooses in dealing with a situation should have three characteristics. They should be (1) consistent with the teacher's analysis of the situation, (2) feasible or reasonable given the limits of the teaching situation, and (3) operational or clearly "spelled out" with regard to how they are to be executed or carried out.

Consistency is possible only to the extent that a teacher fully understands the theory used to analyze the situation. Assuming, of course, that a teacher is trying to analyze in terms of a research-based theory, it is important that the teacher not only understand the theory's terminology and philosophical underpinnings but also understand its data-collection procedures and applicational techniques.

To illustrate, suppose a third grader named Bobby has been labeled a "problem child" and referred to two different school psychologists, one of whom has been trained in the behavior-modification tradition of B. F. Skinner and the other in the humanistic one (Rogers, 1951). The behavioral-school psychologist begins to analyze the situation in terms of "specific behaviors the child is emitting" and what "teacher and peer reinforcers" might be maintaining such behavior. This psychologist begins to "pinpoint, observe, count, and record" appropriate external behavioral data.

On the other hand, the humanistic psychologist is more concerned with how to enter Bobby's "perceptual field." This psychologist may choose to have a one-on-one conference with Bobby to determine how Bobby sees himself and his world. The focus will be on Bobby's self-report data and not on the observation of external behavior. Getting "inside" Bobby will be seen as the key to dealing with the situation.

With regard to application, the behaviorist is likely to hold a conference with the teacher, not Bobby, show the teacher the summary of the behavioral data collected, and discuss what the teacher can do to "change the reinforcement pattern in the classroom." The humanist, on the other hand, may spend some time counseling the teacher on the importance of being warm, open, and genuine in the classroom, but is more likely to emphasize counseling or small-group therapy procedures for working with Bobby. Such procedures may at times involve taking Bobby out of the classroom rather than dealing with the situation totally within the classroom.

Psychologists who call themselves eclectics may be able to combine two or more psychological perspectives and procedures into one approach that represents the best from each. It should be noted, however, that to be such an eclectic, one must know a lot, not a little, about the theories being combined. Further it has been our experience that teachers often do not have the background to be effective eclectics. A common example is trying to help a child by combining behavior-shaping techniques with nondirective counseling procedures. Teachers would do better to learn one theory well than to try to become eclectic too soon.

How does all this relate to the consistency of teachers' decisions? Using the preceding example, if a teacher analyzes Bobby's problem from a humanistic perspective, he or she should choose humanistic (e.g., nondirective counseling), not behavioristic (e.g., behavior shaping) applicational procedures to deal with the situation. If behavioristic procedures are preferred, then the teacher should analyze the situation from the behavioristic perspective rather than "mix theories." Perhaps later, when the teacher has become sophisticated enough to develop an eclectic view, it would be appropriate to use that view to analyze and to choose courses of action.

A feasible decision is one that is reasonable given the limits of the situation. If, for example, the teacher decides to do such things as change school board opinion, or give each student a Stanford-Binet test and subsequently work with many of them individually after school, he or she had better consider the skills, the time and money, and the amount of effort and dedication required. This is what is meant by feasibility or practicality.

Operationality refers to the process of translating the chosen course of action into concrete operations or procedures. Such theoretical decisions as "helping George see himself in more positive ways," or "using praise and approval as reinforcers to encourage Mary to work harder," must be translated into actual classroom operations. Is the teacher going to use client-centered counseling techniques with Bobby in one-to-one counseling sessions after school? Is Bobby's teacher going to praise him verbally each time he recites in class or sits still and studies for five minutes?

From such examples it should be noted that feasibility and operationality often interact with one another. If an idea is stated in terms that are too general to be operational (e.g., "What the teacher should do is try to meet each child's individual needs"), it is often hard to tell whether it is feasible or not. The difference between the two can sometimes be seen more clearly in ridiculous recommendations such as, "What the teacher should do is walk right up to the student, grab his belt with the left hand and his leg with the right hand, carry him to the nearest window, and throw him out." Although the course of action intended is stated in very operational terms, it is not feasible.

Execute and Evaluate the Decision   Once a course of action has been chosen, the teacher must execute and evaluate it. The evaluation procedures chosen are likely to be influenced by the theory that the teacher uses to analyze the situation. In the example of Bobby, the behavioristic psychologist is likely to continue to observe and record Bobby's "pinpointed external behaviors" to see if Bobby's "desirable" behaviors increase and his undesirable behaviors decrease. The humanistic psychologist, on the other hand, will collect self-report data regarding Bobby. Perhaps he or she will look for a positive change on a self-concept inventory or a more positive evaluation of the classroom situation by Bobby during a counseling session.

In situations involving the broader context of teaching, the selection of evaluation procedures is not always so clear. How does one evaluate a decision regarding how to get along with the building principal or the teacher next door? The essential questions that have to be answered are:

(1) What do I want to have happen in this situation? and (2) How can I check to make sure the course of action I have chosen is bringing about that end?

What ideally do you want the principal or teacher next door to do? How do you want them to behave? Do you want the principal to provide you with new teaching materials? Do you want the teacher next door to begin to handle his own discipline problems and stop asking you for help? When you receive some teaching materials from the principal and when the teacher next door handles his discipline problems alone for one day, you may be willing to accept these as evidence of success. In other words, it is necessary to clarify the goals involved and to use evaluation procedures appropriate to the goals.

This discussion suggests certain criteria that teachers can use in evaluating their decisions. They should ask themselves the following questions:

1. How clearly and accurately stated is the theory or set of principles that I am applying to this situation and how well does it fit and fully cover the situation?
2. How objective and thorough have I been in gathering and examining data?
3. Is my decision *consistent* with my theoretical interpretation of the problem?
4. Is my decision *feasible* and *operational* in its present form? The reader should apply these criteria to the decisions reached in "Joe Defies Authority" in the next chapter.

REFERENCES

Brubaker, D. L. (1970). *The teacher as decision-maker.* Dubuque, Iowa: W. C. Brown.

Clark, C., and Peterson, P. (1986). Teachers thought processes. In M. Wittrock (ed.), *Handbook of research on teaching* (3d ed.). New York: MacMillan.

Connelly, F. M., and Elbaz, F. (1980). Conceptual bases for curriculum thought: A teacher's perspective. In A. W. Foshay (ed.), *Considered action for curriculum improvement.* Alexandria, Va.: Association for Supervision and Curriculum Development.

Davis, G. A. (1983). *Educational psychology-theory and practice.* Reading, Mass.: Addison-Wesley.

Dembo, M. H. (1977). *Teaching for learning.* Santa Monica, Calif.: Goodyear.

Gage, N. L., and Berliner, D. C. (1984). *Educational psychology* (3d ed.). Boston: Houghton-Mifflin.

Good, T. L., and Brophy, J. E. (1986). *Educational psychology: A realistic approach* (3d ed.). New York: Holt, Rinehart & Winston.

Lefrancois, F. R. (1987). *The lifespan* (2d ed.). Belmont, Calif.: Wadsworth.

McDonald, F. J. (1965). *Education psychology* (2d ed.). Belmont, Calif.: Wadsworth.

Rogers, C. R. (1951). *Client-centered therapy.* Boston: Houghton-Mifflin.

Rosenthal, R., and Jacobson, L. (1968). *Pygmalion in the classroom: Teacher expectation and pupils' intellectual development.* New York: Holt, Rinehart & Winston.

Shavelson, R. J. (1973). What is *the* basic teaching skill? *Journal of Teacher Education, 24,* 144–151.

CHAPTER 2

SAMPLE ANALYSES

Having presented a strategy for teacher decision making in Chapter 1, Chapter 2 provides examples in which the strategy is applied to a teaching situation using different theories or sets of principles. The examples are most suited to courses in educational psychology or curriculum and instruction, the disciplines taught by the two authors. However, theories or principles from courses in philosophy of education, introduction to education, and educational administration could be applied just as easily by persons trained in those fields. It should also be noted that the theories and principles applied in the sample case would not be appropriate for some of the other cases contained in this book. We believe, however, that they are applicable to the teaching situation illustrated here.

Finally it should be understood that the analyses and decisions presented are not "correct," "final," or "conclusive." They merely illustrate the teacher decision-making strategy presented in Chapter 1. Only if the courses of action were actually executed and evaluated would there be a basis for judging whether they were good or effective. However, they will be *tentatively* examined in terms of whether or not they meet the criteria presented at the end of Chapter 1.

Joe Defies Authority

The teaching situation Joe Defies Authority represents a real case faced by a student in one of our classes. The ensuing analysis and decision are the product of a group of seven students within that class.

Setting A small, relatively new high school in a rural area of a southeastern state.
Time Lunch period on a warm autumn day.

Mr. Nash, on hall duty, is standing in the doorway because students are not permitted in the building during lunch period.

Joe, a large, muscular, 19-year-old senior, whom Mr. Nash recognizes as one of his students in American history, approaches the door. Mr.

Nash has been warned that Joe is a troublemaker but has experienced no trouble with him to date.

Mr. Nash You can't come in the hall now. You know students aren't allowed in here at this time.
Joe [stalling belligerently] I want some water.
Mr. Nash You have to wait until the bell sounds. [Joe, ignoring Mr. Nash, walks to the water fountain and gets a drink.]
Mr. Nash I told you you couldn't get water.
Joe [insolently] I've already gotten it now. [Mr. Nash says nothing more and Joe walks outside.]

***

Shortly after this incident, Mr. Nash goes to the principal to secure information about Joe. From the disciplinary file, Mr. Nash learns that Joe has been a problem child through the years. He learns that Joe at one time threatened a teacher with a knife, has a reputation for tormenting other children, and shows no respect for authority. The file indicates that Joe has been reprimanded both physically and verbally. Scholastically he appears to be average.

Joe lives with his grandmother. He never knew his father and was abandoned by his mother when he was eight months old. His grandmother is unable to discipline him, but she is concerned and cooperates with the school.

***

A few days later while Mr. Nash is conducting class, Joe loiters in the hall after the last bell rings. He then comes into class late expecting to be sent out according to school policy for tardiness, but he is ignored by Mr. Nash.

Joe takes his assigned seat in the back of the classroom and pulls out a comic book instead of entering into the discussion. He keeps glancing at Mr. Nash as though daring him to say something, but Mr. Nash calmly ignores him and teaches the class.

At the end of the class period, Mr. Nash calls for the papers that have been assigned. All the students but Joe hand them in. Mr. Nash says nothing as Joe walks by without handing in his paper.

***

The next day Joe is on time for class. However, instead of taking his assigned seat, he sits in another student's seat.

Brenda Get out of my seat, Joe! [As Joe looks at her daringly, Brenda goes to Mr. Nash in the front of the room.]
Brenda Joe's in my seat.

Mr. Nash   Joe, you know where your seat is. Will you please sit where you belong?

Joe   I'll sit where I want to.

Mr. Nash   You'll sit where you are supposed to sit or we'll go to see the principal. [Joe grudgingly goes to his seat. An hour later, the class is dismissed.]

Mr. Nash   Joe, will you stay after class for a few minutes? [Joe hesitates, then comes grudgingly.]

Mr. Nash   Joe, what happened to the assignment that was due yesterday?

Joe   I didn't get around to doing it. I'll turn it in later.

Mr. Nash   See to it. Why did you sit in Brenda's seat? I thought you and Brenda got along pretty well.

Joe   I was having a little fun with her, that's all. [Mr. Nash dismisses him.]

***

A week later Mr. Nash is in charge of admitting students to a football game. Joe walks in without paying, and Mr. Nash follows him.

Mr. Nash   Don't you know you are supposed to pay?

Joe   So what?

Mr. Nash   Without a ticket, I can't let you in.

Joe ignores Mr. Nash and bolts into the stadium. The incident is reported to the principal and Joe is escorted from the game.

***

Joe's grandmother is interviewed by the principal the next day. She describes Joe as a problem at home also.

Grandmother   I've always tried to keep him in line. I used to use the strap on him several times a day, but now he's too big. I guess he'll always be a bad boy. I've always said he'd be just like his no-good father.

***

The next day in the teachers' lounge during Mr. Nash's planning period, several teachers are discussing Joe's conduct.

Mr. Nash   I'm concerned about Joe. I think he has a serious problem, and we should do something to help him.

Mr. Evans [the shop teacher]   I haven't had too much trouble with Joe in my class. In fact he's one of my better students.

Mr. King [the math teacher]   He's always late for my class, and I won't let him in. You're just wasting your time on Joe.

Other teachers agree that it is a waste of time to work with Joe.

***

Later Mr. Nash meets Joe in the hall after school.

Mr. Nash Come into my room, Joe, I'd like to talk to you for a minute.
Joe What's the matter? I didn't do anything wrong. You teachers are always picking on me.
Mr. Nash I respect you, Joe. I think you're capable of doing fine work. So what seems to be the problem? Have I done anything to offend you?
Joe No.
Mr. Nash Don't you think I respect you?
Joe [shrugs] I don't know.
Mr. Nash Then what's the problem?
Joe I don't have a problem. Nobody's gonna tell me what to do.
Mr. Nash If you're going to remain a part of this school community, you have to obey the rules, just like everyone else.
Joe I'm not like everyone else. You just don't want me around, that's all. Nobody does.

Joe Defies Authority: A Psychological Analysis and Decision

In this case Joe is presented as a young man who lacks a sense of belonging. ("You just don't want me around, that's all. Nobody does.") He defies rules and the people responsible for enforcing them ("Nobody's gonna tell me what to do"). However, he uses his misbehavior as a plea for recognition from these same representatives of authority. The teacher "should realize that children misbehave not to annoy him but because they do not know of better ways to satisfy their needs; they are simply calling for help. . . . This is especially true of children with an unhappy home background who have to depend that much more on the teacher's understanding and acceptance" (Mouly, 1973, pp. 60–61). Joe, having been left to the care of his grandmother and abandoned by his mother and father, certainly has not had a very happy or satisfying home life. The grandmother's statement to the principal ("I've always said he'd be just like his no-good father") indicates that Joe's childhood was filled with insecurity and the lack of affectionate relationships.

Joe's behavior may be analyzed in terms of Maslow's Hierarchical Theory of Motivation, according to which love and belonging are listed as basic needs (Napoli, Kilbride, and Tebbs, 1985). Maslow developed a hierarchical order of needs required for a healthy, normal, and fully satisfying life. The five categories of needs are listed here beginning with the most basic (lower-level) and progressing to the least basic (higher-order) needs.

1. Body needs—basic tissue needs, food
2. Safety needs—protection from harm or injury
3. Needs for love and belonging—warmth, status, acceptance, approval
4. Needs for adequacy, security, self-esteem, self-enhancement, competency
5. Needs for self-fulfillment, broader understanding

Maslow assumes that physiological needs and safety needs are almost universally met due to the nature of our society. However, if one of these needs was not fulfilled, a person would be dominated by that particular need, for example, hunger or thirst. Someone without anything to drink would place that need above all others. Once the physiological needs were satisfied, an individual would then seek to satisfy the next highest unfulfilled need—safety or security.

Continuing along the hierarchy, we come to the love and belonging needs. If the lower two levels are satisfied, these needs emerge, causing the individual to seek friends and affectionate relationships.

The fourth level contains esteem needs. "We want respect, both from other people and from ourselves. The two types of needs for esteem share something in common, but they also differ. Both are concerned with meeting standards for achievement. However, we gain the respect of others by meeting their standards, while we gain self-respect by meeting *our own* standards. Generally, when we satisfy our needs for esteem, we feel good about ourselves and are confident that we can do whatever we choose to do. When we do not satisfy these needs, we feel frustrated, discouraged, inferior, and helpless" (Napoli, Kilbridge, and Tebbs, 1985, p. 49).

If the previous four levels of needs are fulfilled, then the individual can satisfy the need for self-actualization. As Maslow says, "A musician must make music, an artist must paint, a poet must write, if he is ultimately to be at peace with himself. What a man *can* be, he *must* be. This need we may call self-actualization" (Maslow, 1954, p. 91). Maslow states that most of us are seeking the fulfillment of the lower-order needs. Not many of us are able to reach this self-actualizing state.

According to Maslow's hierarchy of needs, Joe's first-category (physiological) needs are being filled. Moreover, there does not seem to be an immediate need for safety despite the fact that his grandmother used to whip him. There is evidence, however, that Joe is in need of love and a sense of belonging. ("You just don't want me around. Nobody does.") Joe never knew his father and was abandoned by his mother as a baby. The only home he has known is his grandmother's, and she seems to be annoyed by his presence and expresses openly her low opinion of him. ("I guess he'll always be a bad boy. I've always said he'd be just like his no-good father.")

Joe shows a distrust of authority when he says: "What's the matter? I didn't do anything wrong. You teachers are always picking on me."

Children establish an attitude toward authority during their first five years of life. The grandmother has been Joe's only symbol of authority at home. ("I have always tried to keep him in line. I used to use the strap on him several times a day, but now he's too big.") Given her method of approaching Joe, it is no great surprise to see that he has formed a negative attitude toward authority. "Some [parents] reject their children openly and brutally, even to the point of abandoning them. . . . These children build up hate and hostility which they vent through retaliation against people and their property" (Mouly, 1973, p. 449). Joe has demonstrated hostility and defiance with his disregard of school rules. Such defiance is demonstrated by Joe's actions in three incidents.

1. **Mr. Nash** I told you you couldn't get water.
   Joe [insolently] I've already gotten it now.
2. **Mr. Nash** Joe, you know where your seat is. Will you please sit where you belong?
   Joe I'll sit where I want to.
3. **Mr. Nash** Don't you know you are supposed to pay?
   Joe So what?

The fourth and fifth levels of need, those of self-esteem and self-actualization, receive less attention since Joe is lacking in the third-level need, that of love and belonging. According to Maslow an individual concentrates all efforts on the satisfaction of the lowest-order need that remains unsatisfied. As Napoli et al. (1985) point out: "In Maslow's view, we can attend to only one level of need at a time, so the needs cannot conflict. The person with unsatisfied needs for love and belongingness must attend to them before needs for esteem can be satisfied" (p. 50). Until his needs for love and belonging are sufficiently satisfied, Joe will continue to seek the satisfaction of these needs in undesirable ways, such as his defiance of authority.

Jersild (1975) summarizes possible causes of Joe's type of behavior in this way: "Studies of the backgrounds of persons regarded as overaggressive, antisocial individuals have quite consistently disclosed an early environment characterized by the following factors: parental rejection; family discord; the use of physically painful punishment or threats of physical punishment; inconsistent treatment; parental permissiveness of aggression; a low level of parental expectation; a lack of parental supervision; parental examples of social deviance; and parental dissatisfaction with the child's role in life" (p. 364).

Decision

Having analyzed Joe's constant misbehavior at school as a need for love and belonging, the following three general courses of action seem to follow consistently from the analysis and are therefore recommended to Mr. Nash.

1. He should develop and display a warm and accepting manner toward Joe. "A warm, accepting attitude is especially important for pupils who have already come to think of the world as hostile, critical, and exacting. And there are many children who acquire this unfortunate attitude early in life and who come to school with all the apprehension, fearfulness, and even defiance which such an attitude engenders. For this child, who has had to accept more criticism than he can absorb, or who has had to face standards which he does not know how to meet, the teacher should be especially generous in his acceptance" (Stephens, 1965, p. 380).

Assuming that Mr. Nash is emotionally secure, he will then be able to give Joe this acceptance. "Specifically this basic acceptance or liking may be shown by the frequent and ungrudging use of praise. This need not be expressed in the form of a fulsome speech or in a sugary manner. A frequent enthusiastic exclamation, interjected sincerely and under conditions that are reasonably appropriate, would seem more natural and more effective. . . . Older pupils may suspect the sincerity of praise that bubbles continuously. Here the most useful test would probably be that of sincerity. If you do feel an admiration for the student's performance, give free vent to your feeling. . . . Praise, certainly solemn praise, is not the only means of providing an atmosphere of acceptance. Many teachers can be hearty, jovial, or even rough, and yet give the child a feeling of acceptance and belonging" (Stephens, 1965, p. 379).

Also in the water incident Joe approaches Mr. Nash intent on defying the teacher's authority. Mr. Nash denies Joe permission to enter the hall, but he does not give Joe any reason for denying him a drink other than that it is a school rule. ("You know you can't come in the hall now. You know students aren't allowed in here at this time.") Mr. Nash might have displayed a more warm and accepting manner with a comment such as: "Hi, Joe, I'm afraid I can't allow you in the building now. It would be chaos if everyone were in here running around while the teachers are at lunch. If you can't wait until the bell rings, I'll bring you a drink, okay?"

2. He should offer Joe opportunities to accept responsibility within the school, showing confidence in him. Mr. Nash should give Joe daily responsibility to make him feel closer and more "special" to his teacher. Possibly Joe could take attendance and see that every student is in his or her seat. (As a by-product of this action, Joe would also make it to class on time and see the reasons for punctuality.) He would receive attention and gain a feeling of belonging by helping Mr. Nash. Instead of opposing certain rules to gain attention, he could help uphold them. Gradually, as time allowed, Mr. Nash could place more emphasis on giving Joe certain responsibilities that required an amount of trust and affection on both Joe and Mr. Nash's part, such as running Mr. Nash's errands. After Joe fulfilled these duties, he could see Mr. Nash as a *person* in a role of authority not just an authority. This association could eventually transfer to other people in authority positions.

3. He should improve Joe's social relationships with his peers by arranging group interactions. Group relationships could help Joe by providing love and a sense of belonging which are lacking in his home environment. Mr. Nash could give Joe a position of leadership and peer recognition by allowing him to moderate a panel concerned with current events. Or, at the appropriate time, he could allow Joe to supervise the construction of a project concerned with his area of study.

To give Joe further experiences and opportunities for developing a sense of belonging, Mr. Nash should contact the shop teacher, Mr. Evans. Mr. Evans pointed out that he had experienced little trouble with Joe, and in fact Joe was one of his better students. Perhaps the two teachers could design a history project to be constructed in shop class. Such concern shown by two teachers would help Joe develop a sense of belonging and trust of authority.

After Mr. Nash has displayed a warm and accepting manner, offered opportunities for responsibility, and improved Joe's social relationships, we would expect Joe's attitude toward authority to improve. Thereafter Joe should find socially acceptable methods for meeting his needs.

Critique of the Analysis and Decision

After examining the preceding analysis and decision, one might ask, "Well, is that the right answer?" Whether the decision reached is the right one or not depends, in the last analysis, on what happens when it is executed. The decision makers would have to answer the question, "How could the teacher check to make sure that the recommended courses of action are working?" Only after this question has been answered is it possible to evaluate the effects of the decision.

However, without actually testing the consequences of the decision, it is still possible to examine the analysis and decision in terms of the criteria stated earlier. Although a panel of experts might quibble with the students' recommendations, an examination of their work indicates that they have done a fairly good job overall.

How clearly and accurately stated is the theory that is applied to this problem, and how well does it fit and cover the problem? The theory used is primarily Maslow's motivational or need hierarchy theory along with some supporting principles drawn from adolescent development. The students seem to have an adequate grasp of the theory, since they use its language correctly and avoid errors of interpretation. Their use of the theory offers a rather full explanation of Joe's behavior and its causes. In general a theory can be said to "fit" a problem situation if it fully explains the problem in terms of the behavioral evidence that is cited. The students do this rather well.

How objective and thorough has the gathering and examination of the data been? The students do a good job of citing behavioral events to objectively support their application of the theory. Although some of the supporting data cited are lacking in objectivity (for example, the data relating to home life and the cumulative record), it should be remembered that the students were looking back on a problem situation and could not reconstruct or obtain as much data as they would have liked.

Is the decision consistent with the theoretical interpretation of the problem? If one examines the courses of action suggested, it is apparent that the students have done a fairly good job. Each course of action seems to follow from the psychological principles used to analyze the problem situation.

Is the decision feasible and operational in its present form? Probably the weakest aspect of the decision involves the criteria of operationality and feasibility. For example, one wonders how (operationality) Mr. Nash is going to arrange things so that he can bestow sincere warmth, acceptance, and praise upon Joe and whether or not peer approval of Joe is a possibility (feasibility). Obviously these two criteria interact with one another since judgments about the feasibility of peer approval depend on making the plan fully operational. On the basis of available evidence, it may be far more feasible to make Joe chairman of the history project to be constructed in shop class, where he is doing well, than to make him moderator of a current events panel. More information would have to be given about the operation of the current events panel for it to become an operational and feasible course of action.

Some educational psychologists reading the preceding analysis and decision might suggest that this teaching situation could be better interpreted in terms of some other psychological theory or set of principles. Whether one theory is better than another many come down to debates regarding the nature, currency, and research support for competing theories. Another important consideration that was mentioned in the first chapter is that teachers may find one theory more compatible with their personal belief systems than another. For example, some may prefer humanistic to behavioristic theories. To make the point that different theories (in this case, psychological) can be applied to the same problem situation, the Joe Defies Authority problem situation is now analyzed and resolved from a behavior-modification perspective.

Joe Defies Authority: A Behavioral Analysis

Joe, described as a "large, muscular, 19-year-old senior," has been socially reinforced for emitting socially aggressive operants (belligerence, trouble making, defiance). His undesirable behavior persists because verbal and physical reprimands, intended as punishers, have not functioned to decrease his behavior and may actually be maintaining it. Joe also appears to have been exposed to socially aggressive models at home and does not appear to receive much reinforcement for his socially appropriate responses.

First, let us examine the evidence. Evidence that Joe is emitting socially aggressive operants includes the following:

1. Joe "belligerently" ignores Mr. Nash's prohibition and procedes to get a drink of water.
2. From the disciplinary file, Mr. Nash "learns that Joe once threatened a teacher with a knife, has a reputation for tormenting other children, and shows no respect for authority."
3. Joe "comes into class late" and "pulls out a comic book instead of entering into class discussion."
4. Joe "takes Brenda's seat" instead of his own and moves only when Mr. Nash threatens to take him to see the principal.
5. Joe ignores Mr. Nash's attempt to collect his ticket "and bolts into the stadium."

Second, evidence that aversive stimuli, intended as punishers, are not effective and may instead be maintaining the behavior is as follows:

1. Mr. Nash learns from the disciplinary file "that Joe had been reprimanded both physically and verbally."
2. Joe's grandmother says that she "used to use the strap on him several times a day."
3. Mr. King indicates that he won't let Joe in class when he's late.
4. "Joe is escorted from the game."

Third, the following is evidence that Joe's aggressive responses are often ignored.

1. Mr. Nash does not punish Joe when he goes ahead and gets a drink of water but instead says, "I told you you couldn't get water." He says nothing more to Joe's response that he has "already gotten it now."
2. Joe's grandmother is concerned but is "unable to discipline him" and says that "now he's too big. I guess he'll always be a bad boy."
3. Mr. Nash ignores Joe's coming to class late and "pulling out a comic book instead of entering into the discussion."
4. Mr. Nash says nothing when "Joe walks by without handing in his paper."

Fourth, Joe was presented with an aggressive model when his grandmother "used to use the strap on him several times a day." She also adds "I've always said that he'd be just like his no-good father." Her constant use of the strap may have also caused Joe to become desensitized to physical punishment.

Fifth, shop seems to be self-reinforcing for Joe. Mr. Evans says, "I haven't had too much trouble with Joe in my class. In fact, Joe's one of my better students." In the disciplinary file, Joe is described as "average" scholastically.

Becker, Engelmann, and Thomas (1975) suggest the following procedures for eliminating aggressive behavior:

1. Do not give attention to the aggressive behavior. Do not let the aggression produce a consequence favorable to the aggressor.
2. If punishment is used, do not be a model of aggression yourself. Use withdrawal of reinforcement as your punishment and provide a way of earning the reinforcers back through cooperative behavior.
3. Reinforce cooperative behavior directly.
4. Use rules and prompts to teach behavior incompatible with fighting (p. 304).

To these procedures Clarizio (1980) adds the following. "Research shows that reinforcement of academic behavior is more likely to positively influence both academic and disruptive behavior than is reinforcement of off-task behavior. Thus, we are more apt to 'kill two birds with one stone' if we reinforce the daily percentage of problems completed correctly than if we focus on the elimination of disruptive behaviors . . ." (p. 9).

It should be noticed that when Mr. Nash is able to ignore Joe (e.g., the water-drinking situation, coming to class late, not handing in his paper), Joe is unable to get the attention that he seeks. However, neither ignoring Joe nor punishing him is an effective deterrent when used alone. To be effective these courses of action must be combined with positive reinforcement of appropriate behavior. As if to support Clarizio's point, Mr. Evans has little difficulty with Joe probably because Joe's academic behavior is reinforced in shop. However, no evidence is presented to suggest that Joe is receiving any positive reinforcement for his academic efforts elsewhere.

Decision

If the other teachers agree with Mr. Nash when he says, "I think he has a serious problem and we should do something to help him," then a behavior-modification program might work which consists of (1) reinforcing Joe's appropriate academic behavior as well as his socially cooperative behavior, (2) using rules and prompts to cue appropriate responses, and (3) ignoring aggressive responses when possible and using withdrawal of reinforcers when responses cannot be ignored. Joe's behavioral responses should also be pinpointed, observed, and charted both before reconditioning begins (baseline data) and after (intervention data) (Vargas, 1977, ch. 6). Since Joe's problems stem from his responses to social stimuli, social reinforcers should be employed in efforts to shape Joe's behavior in the direction of academic success and social cooperation. It is recommended, therefore, that Mr. Nash take the following steps in dealing with the problem.

1. He should determine what courses Joe is currently taking and try to solicit the help of Joe's teachers. Perhaps Mr. Nash could talk with them in the teachers' lounge. Together they should try to pinpoint both Joe's disruptive and socially cooperative behaviors as well as his effective and ineffective academic performances. While the reinforcement program should focus on academic objectives, socially cooperative behavior should also be reinforced, observed, and recorded. If the teachers do not want to collect baseline and intervention data on Joe's academic and disruptive behavior, perhaps a school counselor or school psychologist would do so. Another possibility would be to train an aide or parent volunteer to record the data.

In the case of Mr. Nash's American history class, Joe's behavior appears to be mostly off task (e.g., reading a comic book) and defiant (e.g., getting a drink of water, entering class late, sitting in Brenda's seat, not turning his paper in on time). Such behaviors and their consequences should be recorded both on a baseline and intervention basis.

At the same time, Mr. Nash should ask himself what kinds of on-task and socially cooperative behavior he would like to see from Joe and how he might reinforce it using social reinforcers. Additionally Mr. Nash should make a list of Joe's academic strong points in American history and begin to think of procedures for reinforcing those. Mr. Nash's general strategy should be to put Joe in situations in which he can experience academic success and emit socially cooperative behavior. Mr. Nash should then reinforce such behavior using sincere and clearly merited social reinforcers (e.g., attention, approval, praise) and ignore inappropriate aggressive behaviors when possible. If the aggressive behavior cannot be ignored, Mr. Nash should withdraw social reinforcers in a calm and unemotional manner.

2. He should have a private one-on-one conference with Joe in which he tells Joe that he has been thinking matters over since their last talk and that maybe he has not been showing Joe enough respect. Mr. Nash should mention that Mr. Evans told him that Joe was one of his best students in shop and that obviously Joe has the ability to do good work in school. Mr. Nash should then tell Joe that he would appreciate his help at the beginning of class by taking attendance and seeing if every student is in his or her seat. Mr. Nash could then explain to Joe how difficult it is to be responsible for the enforcement of school rules even though such rules are needed in order for people to get along with one another.

3. He should initially reinforce Joe's assistance on a regular basis and gradually expand Joe's socially cooperative activities. When papers are passed in, for example, Mr. Nash could ask that they be passed to Joe and ask Joe that he check them to see if everyone turned one in. When Mr. Nash forms the students into small groups, he can let Joe be the group leader from time to time. Mr. Nash should also look for everyday opportunities to provide Joe with social reinforcement, such as helping another student, picking something up off the floor, or turning in a reasonably good paper. Without being conspicuous about it, Mr. Nash should be sure that Joe gets reinforced on a regular basis, especially for his academic improvement.

4. He should be calm and unemotional. When Joe emits aggressive responses that cannot be ignored, such as the ticket incident or his taking Brenda's seat, Mr. Nash needs to respond in a calm and unemotional manner by (1) explaining to Joe the reasons why he must enforce the rules and (2) by calmly and consistently withdrawing the reinforcers involved. In the ticket situation, for example, Mr. Nash could have said something like, "Joe, if we let everyone in without buying a ticket first, then we wouldn't have enough money to have a football team. Won't you be a good fan and support the football team by buying a ticket?" If Joe insists on entering without paying, then Mr. Nash should have Joe removed as quickly and quietly as possible.

5. He should explain what he is doing to Joe's other teachers and encourage them to try something similar in their classrooms. If Mr. Nash can show them Joe's improved grades and behavioral data indicating a positive attitude change, he might be able to strengthen his argument. If the teachers argue that it is not fair for them to spend that much time and energy on one student, Mr. Nash can point out, hopefully, that he is now spending less time and energy worrying about Joe than he did before and consequently has more time to spend on the rest of the class.

6. He should meet with Joe's grandmother after he has evidence that a positive change has occurred in Joe's academic and social behavior. The purpose of the visit would be to enlist the grandmother's aid in providing more positive social reinforcement for Joe. Mr. Nash should encourage Joe's grandmother to "brag on him a bit," and he should keep in touch with her to reinforce Joe's "new image." However, Mr. Nash should be careful not to say anything to her that might get back to Joe and lead him to believe that he is "being manipulated" by Mr. Nash. Perhaps after the reinforcement program has been in effect for a while, Mr. Nash could explain to Joe's grandmother what he has done and encourage her to experiment with similar procedures at home.

7. He should examine his intervention data. Mr. Nash must do this to see if Joe's academic performance and socially cooperative behaviors are increasing and his off-task and defiant behaviors are decreasing. If not, Mr. Nash will have to determine whether or not he needs to choose different reinforcers or a different set of reinforcement procedures.

Joe Defies Authority: An Analysis Based on Classroom-Management Theories

A final analysis of the teaching situation that confronts Mr. Nash will be made from the perspective of classroom-management principles that are often taught in curriculum and instruction courses. Though the data we have in this case say little about the events Mr. Nash had to "manage" at any given time, principles of classroom management can suggest an appropriate course of action for him.

Classroom management refers to "the provisions and procedures necessary to establish and maintain an environment in which instruction and learning can occur" (Duke, 1979, p. xii). In short, management refers to what teachers do (or, in some cases, do not do) in order to keep students focused on the learning tasks at hand. The events that teachers must manage in the classroom can be overwhelming in regard to their number, complexity, and the rapidity with which they occur. Walter Doyle (1986) has described these events in this way: "A classroom is a crowded place in which many people with different preferences and abilities must use a restricted supply of resources to accomplish a broad range of social and personal objectives. Many events must be planned and orchestrated to meet special interests of members and changing circumstances throughout the year. Records must be kept, schedules met, supplies organized and stored, and student work collected and evaluated. In addition, a single event can have multiple consequences: Waiting a few extra moments for a student to answer a question can affect that student's motivation to learn as well as the pace of the lesson and the attention of other students in the class. Choices, therefore, are never simple" (p. 394).

Unlike the first two analyses, which presented psychological explanations of why Joe might have behaved as he did, this analysis is most concerned with the behavior of Mr. Nash and the steps he took (or might have taken) to prevent Joe's behavior from interfering with either his own learning or the learning of other students. This classroom-management analysis and the two psychological analyses presented earlier merely represent different approaches to resolving the same problem. Each has its own framework for problem analysis, validity in terms of research support, and set of applications or procedures for problem resolution.

If we concern ourselves only with Joe's behavior while in Mr. Nash's classroom, we find ample evidence that Joe is a management problem. We learn that Joe:

1. Comes into class late
2. Pulls out a comic book instead of entering into the discussion
3. [Glances] at Mr. Nash as though daring him to say something
4. Walks by without handing in his paper
5. Takes Brenda's seat at the start of class

6. Defies Mr. Nash, at least momentarily, saying, "I'll sit where I want to."

From a management standpoint, Mr. Nash's main concern is to keep Joe and the rest of the class engaged in the learning tasks at hand. Most likely Mr. Nash is aware of the "ripple effect" and how it operates in his classroom. This theory, based on the work of Jacob Kounin (1970), holds that the way in which a teacher handles a particular instance of misbehavior has a considerable effect on other pupils who observe the incident. If students observe that Mr. Nash is consistently firm and even-tempered in handling discipline problems, they will be inclined to act appropriately. If, on the other hand, students note that Mr. Nash angrily tries to correct Joe, they will not be motivated to behave better or to attend to the task; rather they will become anxious, restless, or uninvolved. Finally if Mr. Nash fails to correct Joe's misbehavior altogether, other students will be encouraged to misbehave also.

If we evaluate Mr. Nash's response to Joe's misbehavior in light of the "ripple effect," we note that on three occasions Mr. Nash did not move to correct Joe. (1) He ignored Joe's tardiness to class; (2) he ignored the fact that Joe pulled out a comic book instead of taking part in the class discussion; and (3) he said nothing (until the next day) when Joe failed to turn in an assigned paper. On the other hand, Mr. Nash firmly corrected Joe when he took Brenda's seat, saying, "Joe, you know where your seat is."

It is possible that Mr. Nash "ignored" Joe's misbehavior on these three occasions because to have corrected Joe at those particular moments might have disrupted the positive momentum of the class. In effect Mr. Nash made a professional judgment that the tradeoff for correcting Joe would be to detract other students from their task-oriented, conforming behavior. At those times, at least, he was unwilling to make that tradeoff. When Mr. Nash corrected Joe for taking Brenda's seat, he did so in part for several possible reasons. (1) In this instance Joe's misbehavior has disrupted another student, Brenda. (2) The rest of the students have not yet begun their work, and a desist aimed at Joe at this moment would be less disruptive than later in the period. (3) The situation presents Mr. Nash with an opportunity to reconfirm, in front of the entire class, his position as a firm but fair group leader.

Kounin (1970) proposed another basic principle of effective classroom management—one that, on the surface at least, Mr. Nash appears to have violated. Kounin found that effective managers display *withitness*, a continuous awareness of what is going on in the classroom. Teachers who have withitness regularly scan the classroom so that they can respond quickly to problems and prevent them from spreading or increasing. Teachers who lack withitness often give desists only after a problem has spread or has become significantly disruptive. While we said earlier that Mr. Nash may have had good reason for not correcting

Joe, the withitness concept suggests that Mr. Nash may have communicated to his students that he was unaware of Joe's misbehavior. If so, other students were probably tempted to misbehave believing that their teacher was unaware of what was happening in the classroom.

When Mr. Nash does correct Joe's misbehavior in a classroom situation, his directions are short and to the point: "Joe, you know where your seat is. Will you please sit where you belong." Mr. Nash identifies the misbehaving student by name and clearly indicates what Joe should be doing. Moreover Mr. Nash avoids two behaviors that Good and Brophy (1984) suggest are inappropriate responses to easily interpretable misbehavior. First he does not ask questions about what is obvious misbehavior on Joe's part. His immediate aim is to get Joe to take his proper seat; he does not need to interrogate Joe. Such questions would be counterproductive and would increase the conflict between Mr. Nash and Joe. Joe might have reacted with anger, embarrassment, or fear if Mr. Nash had asked questions such as: "Why can't you do what you're supposed to do?" Or, "How many times do I have to remind you that you sit over there?" Students view such rhetorical questions not as legitimate requests for information but as attacks on them. After class, when Mr. Nash does ask Joe why he sat in Brenda's seat, he requests the information for a good reason—because Joe's behavior seems to conflict with the relationship he knows the two students have ("I thought you and Brenda got along fairly well").

Second Mr. Nash avoids "overdwelling" on, or nagging about, Joe's misbehavior. For example, he does not bring up Joe's previous misbehavior—Joe's encounter with Mr. Nash at the water fountain, his threatening another teacher with a knife, tormenting other children, and so on. Nor does Mr. Nash go into an exhaustive, detailed analysis of Joe's present misbehavior. To have done either would have placed Joe in even greater conflict with him and perhaps tempted him to misbehave at a later time to see if he could elicit an even greater overreaction from Mr. Nash.

While he avoids pointless, rhetorical questions and overdwelling on Joe's misbehavior, Mr. Nash fails to avoid a third behavior that Good and Brophy's research found characteristic of inappropriate teacher responses to misbehavior. He does not avoid unnecessary threats or appeals to his own position of authority. When Joe shows his open defiance of Mr. Nash's request that he take his proper seat ("I'll sit where I want to."), Mr. Nash responds with a threat ("You'll sit where you are supposed to sit or we'll go to see the principal."). Fortunately Mr. Nash is not forced to carry out his threat. But it is not hard to imagine Joe on another day refusing to take his seat, thereby *daring* Mr. Nash to carry out his threat. This would have increased the level of conflict between the two and made it even more unlikely that Mr. Nash would ever be successful in his attempts to help Joe.

A Management-Based Decision

Two basic principles should be kept in mind when formulating a management-based decision for the problem situation that confronts Mr. Nash. First, the key to effective management lies in using classroom techniques that will *prevent* management problems from occurring (Evertson and Emmer, 1982a, 1982b). Mr. Nash will be able to devote more of his time and energies to teaching if he can minimize or prevent altogether Joe's misbehavior. Once Joe has misbehaved, Mr. Nash is forced into a reactive stance, and he runs the risk of unforeseen negative consequences when he corrects Joe. Second, the primary aim of classroom management is to maintain order and to keep the group on task and moving ahead, not to spot and punish those students who are misbehaving (Doyle, 1986). This does not mean, of course, that Mr. Nash should allow Joe to misbehave in the future; it does mean that he will have to balance the consequences of disciplining Joe or any other student with the larger purpose of teaching all students in the group. The following two general recommendations, then, would allow for Mr. Nash to take a management-based approach to the problem.

1. He should see that Joe continues to realize that his teacher is "with it," that is, aware of what is happening in the classroom. Mr. Nash can accomplish this by positioning himself so that he can see Joe at all times and monitor his behavior regardless of what he might be doing at the moment. Furthermore, Mr. Nash should evaluate carefully any future decisions to ignore Joe's misbehavior. Mr. Nash apparently recognizes that to intervene in response to student misbehavior does have some possible negative consequences. Mr. Nash might try out some strategies for correcting Joe's misbehavior that are less "disruptive" than direct interventions. These techniques would enable him to keep the rest of the class on task and moving ahead. For example, when Joe pulled out a comic book instead of taking part in the discussion, Mr. Nash might have unobtrusively corrected Joe by making direct eye contact and perhaps nodding in disapproval. Or if Mr. Nash had been moving about the room during the discussion, he might have moved to the section of the room where Joe was sitting. The actual physical presence of his teacher might have motivated Joe to join the discussion. Finally Mr. Nash might have drawn Joe into the discussion by asking him a question related to the topic being discussed. In this way Joe would have been compelled to participate, and Mr. Nash would not have had to mention Joe's misbehavior.

2. He should also continue to convey to Joe what he expects of him (and indeed of all students) and what he will not tolerate. In this regard Mr. Nash should emphasize appropriate student conduct as opposed to dwelling on misconduct. Students are more likely to respond appropriately if they are told what to do rather than what not to do. Mr. Nash should also be alert to signs that Joe does not know what he is supposed to do. It is possible, for example, that Joe failed to turn in his assignment not because he wished to defy his teacher but because he did not know what he was supposed to do. Finally if Joe misbehaves in the future, Mr. Nash should give him corrective feedback rather than threaten or nag him.

A Final Note

The cases that comprise the remainder of this book represent a wide range of problem situations frequently encountered in teaching. These teaching situations are offered as a means of sharpening your own analytic and decision-making skills. First, however, a word about how they were developed.

Twenty-five of the 30 cases presented in this book were selected from 375 problem descriptions obtained from teachers in six states who represent a wide range of teaching experience. First the teachers were asked to look back over their teaching careers, identify, and describe either the "most difficult" or "most enduring" teaching situations they faced. Second after the descriptions of the teaching situations were obtained, they were categorized by type. Third we then selected several specific problem situations that they felt best represented each category. Finally the resulting cases have intentionally been left open-ended and unresolved to permit their analysis using a variety of theoretical and conceptual frameworks.

When the cases were categorized by type, they were then organized into the five following categories:

1. **Curriculum**   Selecting and organizing subject matter—Cases 1 through 4
2. **Instruction**   Making effective decisions regarding how to teach—Cases 5 through 9
3. **Group Motivation and Discipline**   Keeping students involved—Cases 10 through 14
4. **Pupil Adjustment**   Dealing with adjustment problems of individual students—Cases 15 through 20
5. **Conditions of Work**   Dealing with the context in which teaching takes place—Cases 21 through 25

Five other cases (26 through 30), which were developed earlier and have been tested in the classroom, have been added, bringing the total to 30 cases. These additional five cases were developed using the same procedures as with the first 25.

In writing each case, we have attempted to preserve as much of the original data as possible. When available actual quotes are used. All names of people, schools, and places have, of course, been changed.

Finally an attempt was made to divide the cases as equally as possible between elementary, middle, and secondary school levels.

After most of the cases, you will find data that may be of use to you, such as information from a child's cumulative record or data compiled by the teacher. You will then find a series of questions intended to stimulate your thinking about the case in the event that you are having difficulty beginning your analysis. Since the authors' backgrounds represent the areas of educational psychology and curriculum and instruction, the questions will primarily represent those two perspectives. Other questions, such as those relating to educational philosophy or educational administration, could also be raised just as validly as the ones that have been included. Of course, your instructor may specify that you use a particular theory (e.g., observational learning theory, Ausubel's cognitive theory, etc.) as the framework for doing your analysis.

REFERENCES

Becker, W. C., Engelmann, S., and Thomas, D. R. (1975). *Teaching 1: Classroom management.* Chicago: Science Research Associates.

Clarizio, H. F. (1980). *Toward positive classroom discipline.* New York: Wiley & Sons.

Doyle, W. (1986). Classroom organization and management. In M. Wittrock (ed.), *Handbook of research on teaching* (3d ed.). New York: Macmillan.

Duke, D. L. (1979). *Classroom management* (Part 2). Chicago: University of Chicago Press.

Evertson, C., and Emmer, E. (1982a). Effective management at the beginning of the school year in junior high classes. *Journal of Educational Psychology, 74,* 485–98.

———. (1982b). Preventive classroom management. In D. Duke (ed.), *Helping teachers manage classrooms.* Alexandria, Va.: Association for Supervision and Curriculum Development.

Good, T. L., and Brophy, J. E. (1984). *Looking in classrooms* (3d ed.). New York: Harper & Row.

Jersild, A. T. (1975). *Child psychology.* Engelwood Cliffs, N.J.: Prentice-Hall.

Kounin, J. (1970). *Discipline and group management in classrooms.* New York: Holt, Rinehart & Winston.

Maslow, A. H. (1954). *Motivation and personality.* New York: Harper & Row.

Mouly, G. J. (1973). *Psychology for effective teaching.* New York: Holt, Rinehart & Winston.

Napoli, V., Kilbride, J. M., and Tebbs, D. E. (1985). *Adjustment and growth in a changing world.* St. Paul, Minn.: West.

Stephens, J. M. (1965). *The psychology of classroom learning.* New York: Holt, Rinehart & Winston.

Vargas, J. S. (1977). *Behavioral psychology for teachers.* New York: Harper & Row.

PART II

CURRICULUM CASES

CASE 1

A CLASS DIVIDED

Central Elementary School is in a working class neighborhood in a midwestern city of about 75,000. Built in the early 1970s, the school was designed to handle a K–6 student body of about 600. Before the end of the decade, however, Central experienced a large influx of students whose parents had taken jobs at three new plants that had opened on the edge of the city. To handle the enrollment that had now mushroomed to over 800 students, a new wing for fifth and sixth grade students was added in the early 1980s. The school's student body is approximately 80 percent white, 15 percent black, and 5 percent Hispanic.

Karen Ellison has been teaching sixth grade reading and language arts at Central Elementary for eight years. She is 30 years old and a graduate of the state's major university. At this moment she is seated at her desk, spending the remaining minutes of her lunch period reviewing materials for her next class—a group of 27 students two-thirds of whom are reading at or near grade level, the remaining one-third two to three years below grade level. This latter group of low-ability students has been especially difficult to work with during the last few class meetings. Karen knows that they are frustrated by having to read materials that are beyond their independent reading levels.

Two days ago Karen introduced a unit from the new district-adopted reading text organized around the theme of courage. She announced to the class that they would spend about a week reading several short stories dealing with that theme and exploring what it means to be courageous. Almost immediately her lower ability students began to grumble about having to read stories that were "boring" and "stupid." They wanted to continue doing the exercises in the reading workbooks they had been using.

Karen has just finished skimming today's story—about an Eskimo boy who kills his first polar bear—when the passing bell rings. She gets up from her desk and moves out into the hallway to stand next to her classroom door. Throngs of noisy, excited fifth and sixth graders have already poured out into the hallway. There is a lot of good-natured kidding and shoving as the youngsters work their way to their next class.

Karen notices two of her students who are getting too excited as they wrestle playfully, each trying to prevent the other from getting into his locker.

Karen [loudly]   Come on, Kevin and David. You can play around all you want after school. Right now, though, you've got reading, and you both better be in your seats by the time the bell rings. [She motions them into the room.]

Kevin [in a voice filled with exaggerated despair]   But, Miss Ellison, he won't let me in my locker. This creep just keeps messing with me. [He takes another playful swipe at David who is fumbling with the key to his padlock.]

Karen senses that the two boys will get to class faster if she ignores them and does not give them an opportunity to draw her further into their harmless squabbling. She gives both boys a stern, authoritative frown and then turns to direct a trio of girls just entering the room to take a reading book from the stack on her desk.

***

About five minutes into the class period—after students have finished getting their books and papers organized, sharpening pencils, and generally winding down from the hustle and bustle of the passing period—Karen stands in front of the group ready to begin the lesson.

Karen   Everyone open your books to page 99. We're going to read a story about a boy who lives in the Arctic and shows a very special kind of courage. Remember we said yesterday that a person can show courage in many different ways. Who remembers how we defined courage? [Beth and Mary raise their hands.]

Billy [blurting out]   Hey, I ain't got no book.

Karen [with irritation]   I told you to take one off the desk as soon as you came into the room, Billy. Now hurry up and get one. [She motions with her left hand toward the few books that remain on her desk.] Mary, what did we say courage is?

Mary   It means being able to do something without being afraid of getting hurt.

Karen   That's part of it, Mary. Can you give us an example?

Mary   Like that guy that jumped in the river last week and saved that little girl who was drowning. He wasn't afraid.

Karen   Good example, Mary. But you mean jumped *into* the river, don't you? Beth, what were you going to say?

Beth [loudly and clearly]   Well, sometimes being courageous means that you're willing to stand by what you believe. Even though other people might criticize you, you do what's right.

Suddenly Billy who is returning to his seat with his reading book engages in a brief bit of horseplay with Wally who has stuck his foot out in a half-hearted attempt to trip Billy. Everyone's attention momentarily turns to the two boys.

Karen [angrily]   Get back to your seat immediately, Billy. If I have any more problems from either of you, you're staying after school. [Before proceeding she looks around the entire room to make certain that all eyes are on her.] Now, Beth, you've said that someone can be courageous without necessarily facing physical danger? [Beth gives an affirmative nod.] Can you give us an example?

Beth   Well [hesitating] I remember this basketball coach on T.V. who made his team give up the state championship it had won because one of his players was ineligible. [Several of the boys break into exaggerated expressions of disbelief at what their classmate says.]

Karen   That certainly took courage, didn't it? Well, the story that we're going to read now involves an Eskimo boy who shows that kind of courage. As we read be thinking about how today's story shows a different kind of courage from what we saw in yesterday's story. Okay, who'd like to begin reading on page 99?

About seven students raise their hands; another five or so stare off into space or fidget restlessly. The rest appear ready to follow along as soon as someone else begins reading aloud. Karen is surprised to see John, one of her poorer readers, with his hand held aloft, urgently waving it back and forth. She hesitates for a moment, considering whether to call on John or Judy, perhaps the best reader in the class. Karen decides to let John begin reading.

Karen   Okay, John.

John   Miss Ellison, do we have to read these stories again? I don't like these stories. They're dumb.

Several other students [echoing]   Yeah!

John   These stories are boring. Why can't we do more of the vocabulary worksheets and the stuff in the workbooks?

Karen   Now wait a minute. [She gestures with her right hand to calm her students.] We've spent two weeks in the workbooks, and now it's time to read and put into practice the things we've learned.

Scott   Yeah, I don't want to work in the workbooks again; that's *really* boring.

Michael   Right, these stories give us something to talk about. We learn how different people live and stuff. When we're in the workbooks, we just fill in the blanks, check your work, fill in the blanks, check your work.

Karen realizes that her students are divided—about one-third want to return to the drill-and-practice exercises in the workbooks, another third want to get on with reading the story, and the remaining third are seemingly content to do either one. She also notices that those who do not want to read the story are all reading well below grade level. Because she believes that her students will not learn to read better by working exclusively on exercises pertaining to prefixes, suffixes, and so on, Karen resolves that all her students are going to read the stories in the unit.

Karen [firmly] We *are* going to read and then discuss the stories in this unit on courage. When you get to junior high, and definitely by high school, you will have to read and talk about different kinds of literature. Now, Judy, I believe you were ready to read. [A few resistant students scowl and slouch down provocatively low in their seats making every effort to use body language to express their disagreement with the teacher.)

Judy [in a sing-song voice] "The polar bear is the king of the Arctic. Among land animals, it is the largest predator in the world. For the people who live in the Arctic, hunting the polar bear is the truest test of a man's courage. . . ."

After Judy reads about four paragraphs, Karen calls on Michael who she knows reads well. After Michael, she calls on Elizabeth, also a good reader. In order to keep the class moving ahead and to build up some interest in the story, Karen has her stronger readers read before calling on those who do not read as well.

Karen Okay, John, now would you like to read a bit from the top of page 102?

John Okay. [Stumbling and in a low voice.] "Though a . . . polar bear might look . . . white, its skin . . . is really black . . . and its hair has no color at all. Each hair is really a hanging . . . uh, a hollow tub . . . uh, a hollow tube. Sunlit . . . ah, sunlight . . . reflects . . . off the hair, and this makes the bear . . . white . . . ah, look white.

As John is reading, several students are becoming noticeably restless and fidgety. Three students are looking around the room. One boy is writing something on his desk. A girl seated in the row by the window is reading a magazine. Four students are whispering in low tones at the back of the room. Suddenly the four begin laughing. Nearly all the students turn to the back of the room. John, however, continues with his slow, labored reading.

Karen [irritated] John, stop right there. We've got some people who can't seem to follow along. [She walks to the back of the room.] What seems to be the problem here? [All four students stare at the open books on their desks avoiding eye contact with the teacher.] Is there any reason you can't follow along? [Three of the students shake their heads; the fourth, Allen, begins to speak.]

Allen It's just when some people read you can't hear them, and they go *so* slowly. [Several students nearby giggle.] It's really hard to follow along.
Karen Well, you'll just have to concentrate. [She points down to the open book on Allen's desk.] You never know when I might call on one of you to read. All right, John, would you continue, please.
John I don't want to read any more of this. It's a dumb story. Why can't I work in the workbook?
Karen [obviously frustrated] Listen, everybody, we *are* going to finish this story *and* this unit together. [She begins to move to the front of the room to be easily visible to everyone in the class.] I know that most of you are eager and ready to move ahead. If you're not, be patient and do your best to follow along. It won't be long before we start doing something in class that you like and maybe some other people won't. [Before returning to the story, she surveys the class carefully to make certain that each student is paying attention.] All right, everyone, we're right in the middle of page 102. I'll read to the top of page 104, and then I'll have someone else read from there.

For the remainder of the period, the atmosphere in Karen's room is tense. To avoid the risk of another disruption, Karen only calls on her better students to read. She walks up and down the aisles, carefully checking to see that each student is paying attention. After finishing the story, Karen conducts a brief discussion that focuses on several questions she prepared beforehand. Her better students respond enthusiastically and animatedly, while her slower readers sit silently with blank expressions on their faces. During the final 10 minutes of class, Karen has her students write a paragraph on "My Most Courageous Moment."

***

Two days later, just after the students have left for home, Karen decides to drop by the office of Claudia Jenkins, the school's curriculum coordinator. Claudia has just hung up her phone when Karen arrives.

Karen Do you have a minute, Claudia? I'd like to get your advice about one of my sixth grade classes.
Claudia Sure. My husband's not picking me up until four. Come on in. Have a seat. Is this about your sixth period class?
Karen You've got it; that's the one. They're really good kids—all of them. It's just that I don't know if I'm giving all of them the right curriculum. My real problem is that I've actually got two classes in there. The kids who read at or near grade level, and then those who are two or more years behind. I can't seem to come up with a curriculum that suits both groups.
Claudia I know what you mean.
Karen For a few weeks we did workbook exercises—you know, phon-

ics drills, word attack skills, and so on. The kids were staying together pretty well, though I sensed that the kids at grade level were getting a bit bored. Well, I figured their turn would come when we started reading in the new readers that just came in.

Claudia   I know the book you're talking about. It's a good one; it's got some excellent stories.

Karen   Right, it's really a swell book. No book is perfect, but this one is close. So ever since we started in the readers—I put together a unit on courage—my low-ability kids don't want to read. They want to keep doing the workbooks! I guess the structure and always having to look for the *right* answer to fill in the blank with gives them security. But their comprehension scores aren't going to improve unless they actually start reading.

Claudia [with concern]   It's hard to work with a group of kids if some of them want to be doing something else. Have you thought about grouping them?

Karen   I thought you might suggest that. And to be honest, that was my first reaction. But I really don't believe in tracking or grouping; there's enough research out there to show that it doesn't work. And, darn it, someone's got to wean these kids from always doing worksheets and filling in the blanks. That's not reading, but some of the kids seem to think it is. [With determination.] But I'm not going to teach in a certain way just because it'll make some of the kids happier. If I don't push them to read now, they're just going to get further and further behind.

Claudia [nodding her head]   I agree with what you're saying. I think it's important that all students get beyond drill and practice exercises.

Karen   Also I think it's important for my kids to learn to function in a group situation—where the group focuses on something that *everyone* has read. I think that's the best way for them to learn higher-order thinking skills. [Sighing.] But oh it's certainly not easy. Sometimes I wish I could design a separate curriculum for each child, but that's not realistic.

Claudia   What I hear you asking then is how can you develop a curriculum that challenges your more able students and doesn't turn off the less-able ones. Right?

Karen   Yes, I guess that's what it comes down to. Really, how do you meet the needs of all students? It's a real dilemma, because no two kids are at the same place.

Claudia   I think you've done a good job clarifying your problem. It seems to me that the logical thing to do now is to ask, given all the facts and given your views about what an effective teacher does, what are you going to do? What options are open to you?

CENTRAL ELEMENTARY SCHOOL
Reading Comprehension and Vocabulary Grade Equivalent Scores

Class: Sixth Grade Reading
Teacher: Karen Ellison
Period: Sixth

Name	Reading Comprehension*	Vocabulary Grade Equivalent*
1. Ahrens, Kevin	5.6	5.8
2. Anderson, Jan	5.5	5.6
3. Baker, David	5.7	5.8
4. Becker, Hannah	4.5	4.5
5. Boyer, Mary	5.0	4.9
6. Byrne, Ann	5.1	5.0
7. Dukes, Walter	3.4	3.5
8. Green, John	3.5	3.6
9. Gunn, Amy	5.2	5.6
10. Hahn, Elizabeth	5.4	5.7
11. Harrison, William	3.8	3.9
12. Herring, Lynn	3.4	3.6
13. Holt, Anita	3.7	4.0
14. Jarvis, Nicki	5.8	6.0
15. Jennings, Judy	6.5	6.7
16. Munson, John	6.2	6.7
17. Murray, Michael	6.5	7.0
18. Newberry, Scott	5.7	5.7
19. Neff, Rachel	3.1	3.3
20. Payne, Cyndi	3.9	4.1
21. Peacock, Beth	4.8	5.1
22. Reynolds, Annie	5.7	5.7
23. Rodriguez, Alfredo	4.7	4.9
24. Schmidt, Carol	5.7	5.6
25. Sontag, Allen	5.9	6.2
26. Yang, Ming	5.5	5.8
27. Zimmerman, Martha	6.0	6.4

*Scores are for the Test of Academic Progress given during the fifth month of the fifth grade. Decimal scores refer to months; e.g., 5.9 = fifth year, ninth month.

QUESTIONS

1. Is a teacher with a group of students of varying ability levels justified in giving better students more opportunities to participate in class in order to avoid disruptions?

2. What are the possible advantages and disadvantages of grouping students according to ability? Does educational research generally support or refute the practice of grouping? What procedures can be used to form and work with ability groups?

3. Are there techniques—such as small-group instruction, peer tutoring, learning centers, individualized instruction, or mastery learning—that might be effective for Karen's situation? How realistic would it be for Karen to implement each of these strategies?

4. Should the slow readers in Karen's class be in a remedial reading class?

5. What is the role of drill and practice in teaching students higher-order thinking skills?

6. Is it possible for Karen to design a curriculum that would motivate her more able students *and* meet the needs of her less-able students? Describe that curriculum.

7. Are Karen's more able students motivated intrinsically or extrinsically? Her less-able students?

8. From the standpoint of a motivational theory like Maslow's need hierarchy, what needs seem to be operating? Can the differing reactions of the students to the use of the courage theme be explained by their different need levels? Do frustration and aggression help explain such disruptive behavior as Kevin and David wrestling? How might Karen lessen the tension between the two groups of students?

9. How would you explain Karen's attempt to have her stronger readers read first in terms of observational learning? Does this strategy seem to be working? Why or why not?

10. Explain the disruptive behavior in the classroom, such as the horseplay between Wally and Billy, in operant conditioning terms. What reinforcers seem to be maintaining the behavior? Can behavior modification techniques be used to modify the behaviors being emitted?

11. What instructional objectives does Karen seem to be pursuing? To what levels of Bloom's Cognitive Taxonomy do Karen's objectives relate? What recommendations would you give Karen regarding her instructional objectives?

12. What are some of the ways that individual students in the class might view the reading material Karen is using? How do some of the individual students view themselves (self-concept)? What criteria do

individuals among the two groups of students use to determine whether an activity is meaningful and worthwhile?

13. Can Karen's students be analyzed in terms of their being field-dependent or field-independent learners? What instructional procedures work best with the two types of learners?

14. What is the best interpretation that Karen can make of the reading comprehension and vocabulary scores?

CASE 2

THE GLORY THAT WAS GREECE

Santa Zorro Junior High School is located in a mid-sized, West Coast city of approximately 50,000 people. Its student body is primarily white with minority groups consisting of approximately 10 percent black, 10 percent Chicano, and 3 percent Asian origins. The school's physical plant is only three years old and is well equipped. It is situated among many palm trees not far from the Pacific Ocean. All the classrooms are well furnished with the latest equipment and supplies.

It is early in a new school year. Charlene Dutton, a social studies teacher with five years' teaching experience, is introducing a new unit in her fourth period world history class of 31 ninth graders.

Charlene   Today we're going to start a new unit in your text on ancient Greece called "The Glory That Was Greece." I can't emphasize enough our heritage from the ancient Greeks in terms of art, theater, philosophy, science, even the idea of democracy itself. How many of you knew that the Olympic Games began in Greece? [Many hands go up.] Good. Now remember that both the unit exam and the quizzes will be objective: multiple choice, matching, and fill-in-the-blank like before. It isn't enough just to read the material—you need to underline important names, dates, battles, and key terms. Then go back over them just before the exam. [Sees a student's hand raised.] Yes, Anna?
Anna   Will we have the quizzes on Friday like before?
Charlene   Yes. [Picking up papers from her desk and starting to hand them out.] Also, please take a copy of this outline map of ancient Greece. Begin to put city-states, important battles, and so forth on it as we talk about them. It will be due on the day you take the unit exam. [A few students groan.] It is also important that you keep bringing in items for our current events bulletin board each Monday. I'll let a few of you read some of your contributions in just a minute. First open your notebooks and make some notes as I give a little introduction, including some material that's not in your text, as to how the Greek civilization began. [Students open their notebooks, some try to borrow paper, and others search for pencils. Two students, Barry and Bill, whisper to one another as Barry borrows a sheet of paper from Bill.]
Barry [whispering]   You coming over tonight?

Bill You better believe it! We gotta get that bike of yours working so we can go party with Mitzi and Yvonne!
Barry [excitedly] You mean Yvonne Simmons?
Bill [smiling wisely] In the flesh! I think she's got a thing for you!
Charlene [looking at Barry and Bill] I'd very much appreciate it if you two would stop talking so I can begin! [Barry and Bill stop talking and look down at the floor.] Now—to really understand where the Greeks originally came from, we need to go back to the year 1500 B.C. and the island of Crete. Let's all get our outline maps out now and find the island of Crete.

***

It is one week later and Charlene is leading a discussion of the Persian invasion of Greece.

Charlene The Persian Great King, Darius, was succeeded by his son Xerxes. Xerxes, like his father, tried to invade Greece. Even though they knew the Persians were coming, the Greek city-states still could not unite to form a common defense. In the year 480 B.C., one of the two Spartan kings named Leonidas led his personal bodyguard of 300 soldiers to a narrow mountain pass at Thermopylae to try to slow the Persians down until the Greek city-states could unite. [Pause.] Now let's all get our outline maps out and locate the pass of Thermopylae. [Sees a hand raised.] Yes, Anna?
Anna [pointing to the map] Is it here or here, Miss Dutton?
Charlene [walking to Anna's seat and pointing to her map] Here, Anna. [Pause.] Now, class, why did Leonidas think he could stop a Persian army a thousand times the size of his at Thermopylae? Yes, Bill?
Bill Because the pass was narrow. Only a few soldiers could get into the pass at a time to fight.
Charlene Right, Bill. Jerry?
Jerry Also the Spartans were tougher than the average soldiers and they had bigger shields and longer spears.
Charlene Very good, Jerry! So by choosing to hold a narrow mountain pass, Leonidas took advantage of his small army's strengths and didn't allow the Persians to use their advantage in terms of size. [Pause.] So what happened? [Looks at Barry who stares down at the floor.] Barry, you haven't had much to say about this important battle—what happened?
Barry [frowning] Oh, I don't know. I suppose the Spartans won.
Charlene [frowning] Didn't you read the assignment?
Barry [in a sullen tone] No.
Charlene [with a slight edge in her voice] May I ask why not?
Barry It's hard for me to read this stuff. It's a real pain!
Charlene [shocked] Why what do you mean, Barry? Don't you enjoy reading about the heroism of the Spartans at Thermopylae?

Barry [sullenly] I don't enjoy reading history—any kind! I mean, I'm going to be a mechanic and I don't see how knowing how a bunch of soldiers who carried shields like Captain America fought a battle two thousand years ago is going to help me! [Smiling.] Can you imagine how long the Spartans would hold that pass today against a division of Marines carrying machine guns? [Several students laugh and a few voice their agreement.]

Charlene [angrily] Now just a minute, Barry! I didn't ask for any cute remarks! [Pause.] Do you mean that you don't see any connection at all between what has happened in the past and what is happening today?

Barry [testily.] No! Not that makes any difference. [Several hands go up.]

Charlene Yes, Anna?

Anna [hesitantly] Well, I sort of agree, Miss Dutton. I mean, well, my mother is always telling me what things were like when she was my age. But things today aren't like they were back then. . . .

Charlene [somewhat shaken] Thanks, Anna. I guess I'm a bit surprised at what some of you are saying! Let me ask the entire class a question. How many of you feel there is some value in studying history? [About one-third of the class raise their hands. Others hesitate as though deciding.] This is such an important issue that I think we need to spend the next class meeting discussing it. All of you come prepared with your arguments and we'll sort of debate both sides of the issue and then see how people feel.

***

It is the next day and Charlene leads the debate on the value of history as the fourth period begins.

Charlene The way we'll proceed is I'll make a few opening comments and then I'll call on people one at a time. First I'll call on a person who feels that history has some value and then someone who takes the opposite side until everyone has had a chance to state his or her position. Then at the end, we'll vote by secret ballot to see how the class stands on the issue. Yes, Anna?

Anna Should we take notes?

Charlene No—well, maybe on my introductory remarks. [Pause.] Of course, as a history teacher I'm biased. I think that a knowledge of history is very important. I believe it was George Santayana who wrote that "a nation that does not know history is fated to repeat it." Harry Truman once said, "There is nothing new in the world except the history you do not know." Someone else, I don't remember who, said that we need to study history so we won't get traveling so fast that we fail to look back and make sure we're traveling forward. In short, students, history repeats itself and, as a nation, we need to profit from past mistakes. We can use history as a basis for making decisions about the future. History is a summary of our cultural heritage. Not to bother to learn history is to throw out our cultural heritage that so many have struggled to build and to die for. [Pause.] But then that's a choice that each of us must make. Now since I've given affirmative arguments, who'd like to go first for the negative side. [Barry and Bill look at one another and raise their hands.] Yes, Bill? Why don't you begin.

Bill Well, it's a little hard to argue against a teacher, but I still think it's a waste of time and has nothing to do with today. Our textbook doesn't even go up to the present. And another thing—you said history repeats itself. Well, my Dad says that we hated the Japanese and the Germans in World War II. And today we are friends with the Japanese and Germans. See? Past history has nothing to do with what's happening now.

Charlene Now somebody for the affirmative side. Yes, Marsha?

Marsha Well I think we'd better know history or we just might blow ourselves up with atomic bombs and all. Our leaders had better know what mistakes we've made in the past so we don't repeat them or we'll all end up paying for it!

Charlene Yes, Barry?

Barry [with slight sarcasm] No offense, Miss Dutton, but no matter what arguments anyone gives about how wonderful history is, there is one fact they can't argue down: It's just plain uninteresting and boring. One thing's for sure—it's not for me. I've got more important things to do and to worry about.

Charlene [shocked] Scott?

Scott I agree with Barry. History is boring. And it doesn't help us find records for the Hi-Y dance next Friday night. [Pleading in a clowning manner.] Please, guys, help us! We're desperate!

Bill Yes, Miss Dutton. How's history going to help poor old Scott?!

Charlene [angrily] All right, you guys! Cut it out! Now who wants to go next? [Pause.] No one? No one at all? [Pause.] Well tear out a slip of paper then and vote "yes" if you think that history has some value and "no" if you don't. Don't sign your names. Pass them up to Anna. Yes, Barry?

Barry Are you gonna tell us the vote?

Charlene Yes, I will. Now, open your books to "Athens' Golden Age" on page 71. [Looking at Barry.] You too Barry—page 71. Now. . . .

***

It is two weeks later and Charlene is returning the unit exams to the fourth period class. Out of 31 students, there were no A's, three B's, eight C's, eleven D's, and nine F's using a 90–100–A, 80–89–B, 70–79–C, and 60–69–D grading scale with a 100-item objective exam.

Charlene Needless to say I was disappointed that we had no A's and so many D's and F's. I don't know whether that means people are not studying or that they don't know how to study. Remember I told you at the beginning that you have to underline when you read and go over the material again just before the exam. Yes, Barry?

Barry Miss Dutton, how can I keep going over some of this stuff again and again?! Like the Delian League and "ostracism" and guys like Aeschylus. I mean how much of all this junk can a guy remember?

Charlene I'll bet you don't have any trouble remembering spark plug gap sizes.

Barry Well, no—hey, how do you know about spark plug gapping, Miss Dutton?

Charlene I took a basic engine tune-up course in adult education about a year ago.

Barry Hey, that's great! But it's not the same thing. I gap spark plugs all the time, but I never use history.

Charlene Learning is hard work! Auto mechanics and history are not exceptions to that rule. All some of you need to do is work a little harder. The rest of you need to examine the way that you study. I'll be glad to work with any of you in any way that I can. If some of you don't have anyone to study with before the next unit exam, I'd be glad to schedule a study session with you. All you need do is ask! [Pause.] Now it's time to begin a new unit—"The Grandeur That Was Rome." [Several students groan.] The contributions of the Greek civilization were many, but they might have been lost forever if what started out as a small city-state— what's now Italy—had not conquered the world and preserved it. [Students begin to take notes.]

***

It is one week later and Charlene is trying to lead a discussion on the rise of the Roman Empire.

Charlene Our topic today is the change of the Roman government from a republic to an empire. What is the difference between those two forms of government? [Only one hand goes up.] Anna?

Anna I think a republic is like a democracy and an empire is like, well, where they have a king.

Charlene That's a good start. Now—can anyone add to Anna's definitions? [No hands go up.] No one? How about you, Barry?

Barry I don't know. All I know is the Romans used to have a lot of really wild parties! [The class laughs.]

Charlene [icily] That may or may not be historical fact, Barry, but it has nothing to do with the question.

Barry [smiling mischievously] I know. I'm sorry, but I think their party habits are the most interesting part of their culture. [Several students laugh.]

Charlene [angrily] That's enough, Barry! [Pause.] Now let's get back to the subject. What is an empire and how does it differ from a kingdom? [No hands go up.] Well I guarantee you it will be on the quiz on Friday,

so you'd better be finding out! [Pause.] Now, who can tell me who the first real Roman emperor was? [Nods to Anna.]
Anna Julius Caesar?
Charlene No. He wasn't the first real emperor, although he might have been. Anyone else? [No response.] Well I guess we'd better use the rest of the period to read the assignment. Get busy and I'll walk around to see how you're doing.

***

It is after school on Monday of the next week, and Charlene sits in the office of Jack Lymans, social studies curriculum coordinator for the Santa Zorro School System.

Charlene It is very good of you to see me. I know how busy you are.
Jack Charlene, it's my pleasure! I can't imagine, though, what one of our best social studies teachers wants to see me about!
Charlene [sheepishly] Thanks for the compliment, Jack! Maybe I should leave while I'm ahead! I sure don't feel like one of the best teachers in the system right now.
Jack What's the problem?
Charlene It's my fourth period world history class—no, that's not true! I think that my fourth period class has just served as a catalyst to make me question the way I've been teaching.
Jack I'm really surprised, Charlene! Both the principals you've worked under have given you top ratings. They've said you're organized, well prepared, relate well to the students—
Charlene [interrupting] I know! On the surface everything looks fine . . .
Jack Now you've got me intrigued. Tell me about your fourth period class.
Charlene Well they're a bunch of average-ability ninth graders who are well behaved for the most part and relate well to me as a teacher and a person. But they are bored out of their skulls with history. Their attention wanders and occasionally a student or two will misbehave. They just don't see how what they're learning in class will be of much value to them in the future. [Pause.] Their grades on unit tests and quizzes reflect their lack of interest. I just returned a quiz on the Roman Republic today and the grades were the worst yet! [Pause.] Jack, I've been giving it a lot of thought and I've come to the conclusion that it's the way I've been teaching history. I've got to change things, to do something to make history more interesting. The problem is I really don't know what I'm doing wrong. Have you got any advice, Jack?

A Sample of Items from Charlene Dutton's Unit Exam on Ancient Greece

I. Matching   Match the names of the people listed in the right-hand column with the important roles they played in ancient Greece. Write the letter identifying the person's name in the blank to the left of the role that he played. Some of the people's names will not be used.

_____1. The commander of the 300 Spartans at Thermopylae.

_____2. Macedonian king who conquered Asia Minor, Persia, the Fertile Crescent, Egypt, and parts of India.

_____3. Alexandrian scientist who claimed that the earth rotated and revolved around the sun.

_____4. The Father of History who wrote the history of the Persian War.

_____5. The leader of Athens from 460 to 429 B.C. during its Golden Age.

A. Solon
B. Aristarchus
C. Pericles
D. Hippocrates
E. Aeschylus
F. Philip of Macedon
G. Alexander the Great
H. Herodotus
I. Leonidas
J. Plato

II. Multiple Choice   For each question select the one best answer and write the letter preceding your choice in the blank to the left of the question.

_____1. In what year did the Spartans end the Peloponnesian War by forcing Athens to surrender?
A. 490 B.C.   B. 480 B.C.   C. 431 B.C.   D. 404 B.C.

_____2. Geographically Greece is about the size of which American state?
A. Florida   B. Maine   C. Texas   D. Delaware

_____3. At what battle did the Greeks finally defeat the Persians on land in 479 B.C. and end the Persian invasion?
A. Plataea   B. Salamis   C. Marathon   D. Thermopylae

_____4. In which Greek city-state did democracy first develop?
A. Corinth   B. Thebes   C. Sparta   D. Athens

_____5. Which of the following types of columns found on Greek buildings is the most elaborate in design?
A. Doric   B. Ionic   C. Corinthian   D. Delian

III. Completion   Fill in the blank by writing in the correct term or name as required.

1. The 300-year period after Alexander the Great is called the _____ Age.

2. The lowest class of citizen in Sparta who acted as slaves were called the _____.

3. The famous temple dedicated to Athena that was located atop the Acropolis was called the _____.

4. In the seventh century B.C., Athens was governed by a council of nobles called _____, who were elected annually from among the nobles.

5. Prior to 338 B.C. the Greeks, who had the same language and religion although they lived in different city-states, called their land _____. Today we call it Greece.

QUESTIONS

1. Review Charlene's introduction to the unit on ancient Greece. Could she have been more effective? Describe how you would have introduced the unit.

2. When Charlene learned that Barry has not read the assignment, was her response appropriate? Explain.

3. What are the advantages of allowing students to express their true feelings about the content of the curriculum in an open debate? Disadvantages? What does a teacher risk in arranging such an activity? What might a teacher gain?

4. When Charlene learned that about one-third of her students doubted the value of studying history, how else might she have responded?

5. In terms of motivational theory, what different needs are operating among Charlene and her students? For example, at what levels of Maslow's need hierarchy do they seem to be operating? Particularly contrast Anna, Barry, Bill, and Charlene. To what extent do immediate drives like girlfriends and sports cars take precedence over long-range needs like making a certain grade in history? What needs relate to appreciating and valuing history? To what extent is Charlene's approach to teaching history responsible for some of her students finding the subject "just plain uninteresting and boring?" How might she change her teaching to take advantage of her students' needs and interests?

6. Contrast the values of Charlene and Anna with those of Bill and Barry regarding history. For example how do their value systems differ in terms of the Affective Taxonomy of Krathwohl and others? How do values change? Could Charlene use any of the values clarification activities of Simon and others to increase her students' valuing of history?

7. From the standpoint of observational learning, to what extent does Barry serve as a model in terms of his valuing history? What are inhibition and disinhibition, and how do they apply to Barry and Charlene's reactions to his comments? What could Charlene do to take advantage of the principles of observational learning to change her students' behavior?

8. What are Charlene's objectives, both cognitive and affective? What levels of Bloom's Cognitive Taxonomy and Krathwohl's Affective Taxonomy is she aiming for? Write two of Charlene's objectives that exemplify both taxonomies.

9. How do the sample test items at the end of the case reflect Charlene's cognitive objectives? How could a test be written to measure higher-order cognitive objectives? Write examples of such test items. Write examples of affective objectives. What are the advantages and disadvantages of objective tests as compared to essay tests? What other

means of evaluation and learning activities might Charlene have used beside objective tests?

10. From the perspective of cognitive theory, particularly information processing theory, metacognitive theory, or Ausubel's meaningful learning theory, how might Charlene have organized and presented the material so that a student like Barry would not have so much trouble remembering "all this junk?"

CASE 3

THE GREAT WINE CONTROVERSY

It is a hot, sticky August day in Jonesville, a small midwestern rural community of approximately 2,000 people. The 100 percent white population of Jonesville primarily earns its living through farming and coal mining. Jonesville High School has a new, modern physical plant that is the product of the consolidation of three small-town school districts five years ago. Gary Cash, the product of a nearby small town and a 22-year-old beginning teacher, enters the building and walks into the office of George Gardner, the thin, 53-year-old, building principal. George, sitting at his desk in his inner office, spots Gary, smiles, and walks out to warmly shake Gary's hand.

George   Gary, it's good to see you again! I can't tell you how happy I am that you are beginning your teaching career at JHS! [Motions to a chair for Gary to sit down.] Has your mother ever told you that she and I attended high school at the same time? Of course, my class was three grades ahead of hers, but we were still good friends.

Gary   Yes, Mom's told me what a great person you are and that she knew you when she was in school.

George [looking around his office]   Of course, the old building wasn't nearly as nice as this one. [Pause.] And the students have changed a lot since those days. [Smiling.] But being a graduate of State and taking all those psychology courses, I guess you already know all that!

Gary [smiling]   I don't kid myself, Mr. Gardner. I know that I'm wet behind the ears and have a lot to learn. All I can say is I'm going to give teaching my best shot.

George   That's all anyone can ask, Gary. Graduates of State generally are well trained, and Dr. Sharp there told me that you had a very good internship experience.

Gary   Yes, I really enjoyed my student teaching at Midville. My supervising teacher got sick the second day I was there, and they asked me to take over her American literature class instead of hiring a sub. I loved it! I think I did well!

George   Yes, Dr. Sharp told me about that. I'd say that means you're a natural. You'll be a fine teacher, Gary, I'm sure! [Pauses and looks at a sheet of paper on his desk.] I think I've fixed a good schedule for you,

Gary—three American literature and two English literature classes with only two preparations. [Smiling.] I understand that American literature is your favorite.

Gary [smiling]   Fantastic! I couldn't ask for more, Mr. Gardner! I think this is going to be a very good first year! [Stands up and shakes George's hand.] Thanks so much, Mr. Gardner. I know that you're busy and I want to go down and work in my room a while.

George [standing up and smiling]   Let me know if I can help in any way. One of these years I want you to take over the journalism class—Mr. Simpson is getting close to retirement. We'll work you in as soon as we can. I know from your credentials that journalism is also one of your strong points.

Gary   Yes, it is—and the sooner the better! I really don't know which I enjoy more: journalism or American literature. But I really do want a chance to teach both.

George   We'll make sure you do!

***

One month later Gary is leading a discussion in his second period American literature class. There are 31 juniors in the class.

Gary   Now tell me this, class—what is the reason the author gives for the colonists' coming to this country? [Several hands go up. Gary points to a girl in the second row.] Yes, Judy.

Judy   Because of religious freedom—they didn't have it in Europe and came to the new world to get it.

Gary   Right! Bill, what is a dissenter?

Bill   Well, someone who rebels—like against the government or something—like the hippies used to do.

Gary [smiling]   Yes, well, that's one kind of dissenter, but what does it mean in the context of this story? [Points to a girl with her hand up in the back row.] Yes, Sue.

Sue   I looked it up at home [smiling] 'cause I knew you'd ask that, Mr. Cash. It means a person who disagrees with the established church.

Gary   Very good, Sue! But what is an established church?

Sue   I didn't look that up, but I think it means one that the government makes everyone go to. I mean it's not like here where everyone can choose their own church, but everyone has to go to the one the government picks.

Gary   Sue, that's excellent! It's great your doing all that research! [Pause.] To add a bit to what you said, church and state were not separate in countries like England in those days. The official or established church in a country could force people by law to attend and give money. People who rebelled against the official church and perhaps formed their own were called dissenters. Because a number of our forefathers were dissenters, our constitution specifically forbids the government to establish an official church. Yes, Jerry?

Jerry   You mean like if the government decided that the Baptist Church was right then everyone had to belong to it?

Gary   Yes, that's the idea—but what was the established church in this case? [Many hands go up.] Well, I guess several of you were shrewd enough to spot it. Yes, Jack.

Jack   The Church of England.

Gary   Right. Yes, Jerry?

Jerry   What does the Eucharist mean?

Gary   That's an excellent question! What does the author mean when he says that they refused to participate in the Eucharist? Yes, Yvonne?

Yvonne   I looked that one up. [Good naturedly sticks her tongue out at Sue.] It means the Lord's Supper or Holy Communion where they take the bread and the wine.

Gary   Right, Yvonne. How many of you have taken communion at your church? [Every hand goes up.] Yes, Jerry?

Jerry   Well, what does she mean bread and wine? They used grape juice at the Last Supper.

Gary   That all depends on how you interpret the Bible. Some churches, including the Church of England, use wine. Others, like the Baptists and Methodists, use grape juice. Yes, Maria?

Maria   I don't know why anyone would use grape juice when the Bible clearly says they used wine. It doesn't say that Jesus took grape juice and passed it to his disciples. It clearly says wine.

Gary   [with a mischievous smile and a gleam in his eye]   Is that the way you understand it, Jerry?

Jerry   No! It says the fruit of the vine. It's grape juice until it ferments. Look at all the damage that alcohol does! Jesus wouldn't have used real alcohol at the Last Supper!

Gary   [bell rings]   Well, gang, we're not going to settle this today. Let's all do our research and we'll continue this discussion tomorrow. [Several students protest having to leave and go reluctantly.]

***

Just prior to the beginning of second period the next morning, Jerry walks up to Gary at his desk and hands him a piece of paper.

Gary   What's this, Jerry?

Jerry   This is from my grandfather. I told him what we were talking about in class, and he said to give you this note with all the Bible passages marked on it. He said that if you'll look them up they prove that Jesus and his apostles used grape juice.

Gary   Thank you, Jerry, and tell your grandfather I said thanks. [Bell rings.] All right, class! Let's settle down and get started! [Looks at Jack and Yvonne who continue to talk.] Am I talking too loud for you two?

[They stop talking.] Now let's get into a little leftover business from yesterday's story. [Several students titter.] Yes, Jerry?

Jerry   Are we going to finish the discussion about the grape juice?

Maria   You mean wine, don't you?

Gary [smiling conspiratorially]   Don't you just love discussing controversial issues?!

Jack   Yes! This is the most fun I've ever had in any of my classes! [Several students nod and voice agreement.]

Gary   Well my mother used to tell me not to discuss sex, politics, and religion because it always ends up in an argument. But I just love discussions when they're based on research and rational argument! Now how many of you did your research about whether wine or grape juice was used at the Last Supper? [27 of 31 hands go up.] Good! Now before we begin let me make a comment or two. [Several students open their notebooks and begin to take notes.] Man has been searching for the Truth with a capital T for a long time. One of the issues in the search is what kind of evidence do you accept when you look into a situation. Some accept divine revelation as the source of truth. For example, some of you [looking at Jerry] use quotations from the Bible to support your arguments. Others will appeal to expert opinion or logic or science. Still others will say that only direct experience is real evidence. I'll be interested to see what kind of evidence you used for your research. Yes, Jerry?

Jerry   Are you saying that the Bible is wrong?

Gary   No, Jerry. I'm just saying that some people will base their arguments on the Bible and some won't. The Bible isn't the only source we can go to for information on this subject. Now, let's get started. Who wants to begin the debate?! [Twenty hands go up.]

***

It is the beginning of the next week. Gary sits in George Gardner's office after school.

George [smiling]   Gary, tell me about the religious discussion that you had in your second period class last week. I was contacted by several upset parents over the weekend.

Gary [with a serious, surprised expression]   You were? All we were doing, Mr. Gardner, was discussing a story about the early colonists' escaping to America to gain religious freedom. The story refers to some of the dissenters refusing to take communion in the Church of England. It mentioned that they refused the bread and wine. Some of the kids said that they must have used grape juice instead of wine because the Bible says so. That started the whole argument.

George   All that is fine, Gary, but didn't you then tell them to do research on the subject and have a debate in class on it?

Gary   Yes, I did. I thought it would be a good way to help them learn about the sources of evidence and that other people are entitled to their opinions even on religious subjects. And boy did they get excited and get into it! I've never seen a class so involved!

George Gary, don't you know that you can never win a religious debate? Even if you win, you lose. You have to put down the loser's religious beliefs, and he isn't going to thank you for it. [Pause.] Now several of the parents are accusing you of attacking their religious beliefs in the classroom.

Gary [dismayed] I don't know what to say, Mr. Gardner. That wasn't my intention. I was just getting the kids to discuss the issues—not take sides. I—

George [smiling] Gary, you've got to realize that you live in a very conservative area. I told the parents that you are a young, bright man who is going to become a very good teacher. But, Gary, you've got to avoid controversial issues. Go into your class tomorrow and tell them that you've already spent too much time on that story and that you're moving on to the next one. You do that and I'll assure the parents that the whole matter's been straightened out. Okay?

Gary [with humility] I'm sorry, Mr. Gardner. I had no intention of stirring up this kind of mess!

George Don't worry about it, Gary! Just view it as a learning experience and let me smooth things over. That's my job.

***

It is the beginning of second period the next morning. Gary begins the lesson.

Gary I know that we were going to continue sharing the research on the grape juice issue, but we absolutely have to move on to the next story. Since I haven't assigned it, I'm going to give you the rest of this period to read it and to begin answering these questions. [Gary starts to hand out some papers but stops when pandemonium breaks out.] Hey, whoa! Yes, Jack?

Jack That's not fair, Mr. Cash! You gave us an assignment and we went out and did all that research for nothing! You said we'd get extra credit! [Several students shout agreement.]

Gary And so you shall. Just turn in the work you've done and I'll give you extra credit like I promised.

Yvonne But a lot of it isn't written down! It's up here. [Pointing to her head. Several students voice agreement.]

Gary [pause, then speaking slowly] Look, guys, I'll be honest with you. Some parents complained about what we're doing in here. I have to move on whether I want to or not.

Jack What parents? Don't let them spoil our discussion, Mr. Cash! They must be a bunch of religious fanatics! This is the most interesting thing

I've done since I kissed the girl sitting in front of me in the first grade! [Students laugh, then several voice agreement.]

Gary   Look, guys, I've enjoyed it too, but well it's not worth my getting fired over, and some people just can't discuss a religious topic without getting upset. I guess my mother was right after all.

Yvonne   Can't we at least finish our discussion?

Gary [pause]   Well, I'll tell you what. I'll let those of you who want extra credit write up your research and turn it in to me, but there will be no further discussion of the grape juice issue in class, and we're moving on to the next story.

Jack [angrily]   Just when things were starting to get interesting. It never fails!

***

It is after school on Monday of the next week and Gary again sits in George Gardner's office.

George [in a serious tone]   Gary, I thought we agreed that you'd end the discussion of the wine issue.

Gary [with surprise]   I did, Mr. Gardner. The very next day I went on to the next story. Why? Has something happened?

George   Yes. Some of the parents went to the superintendent of schools and said that you called them religious fanatics in class. They also say you had your students continue on with the topic after you were told to stop. The superintendent wants to know why he shouldn't fire you for insubordination. What should I tell him, Gary?

Gary   Mr. Gardner, I didn't call anyone a fanatic—one of the students who was disappointed that we were not going to discuss the topic any further did. The kids felt they should get credit for their work so I told them they could write it up and turn it in for extra credit. But I told them we weren't going to discuss it any further in class.

George   What reason did you give them for stopping class discussion?

Gary [hesitantly]   Well I told them that I had upset some of their parents. . . .

George [handing Gary a copy of the school paper]   Look at this headline. [Front page banner headline reads "Parents Silence Teacher."] I'll bet you didn't know that Jack Purcell in your second period class is editor of the school paper. I don't know how this story slipped by Mr. Simpson—guess it's evidence that he does need to retire.

Gary   Oh boy!

George   That's not all. It seems that some of your students decided to do more research for their extra credit papers and went around interviewing a sample of parents on their opinions about the grape juice issue. You've really stirred up quite a hornet's nest, Gary. [Pause.] I'm sure you know that as a nontenured teacher the superintendent can fire you without giving a reason. If that happens you might find it difficult to get another teaching position anywhere. Prospective employers usually want a recommendation from your previous employer.

Gary [in shock]   I just don't know what to say or do, Mr. Gardner! I was just trying to motivate students! I certainly didn't intend for any of this to happen!

George   The sad thing is though, Gary, it has. The worst part is that it's out of my hands now—the superintendent is just asking me for my opinion. He'll make the decision himself. [Pause.] He's asked me to hire a sub for you for tomorrow and to tell you to be in his office at nine o'clock sharp. Some of the members of the school board may be there also, but none of the parents accusing you will be.

Gary [pleadingly]   What am I going to do, Mr. Gardner?

George   You'll put on your best suit and you'll defend yourself if you want to remain a teacher. You'll explain what happened and promise to do your best not to let it happen again.

Gary   Isn't there anything you can do to help me, Mr. Gardner? I was just trying to get the students interested in American literature!

George   Yes, Gary, there is something I can do. I want you to pretend that I'm the superintendent and that there are three members of the school board sitting here. I want you to defend yourself right now, just like you're going to have to do tomorrow morning. Now tell me what you're going to say to them when they ask you why you are teaching religion in your English class.

QUESTIONS

1.   Do you agree with Gary's principal that teachers should avoid dealing with controversial issues in the classroom? Defend your position.

2.   What should a teacher do when parents raise objections to the material he or she is teaching?

3.   Imagine that you are Gary; how would you explain your actions to your superintendent and the school board?

4.   What is academic freedom? Is Gary's academic freedom being violated? What are the legal limits of academic freedom?

5.   What guidelines should a teacher follow in deciding whether to address controversial issues in the classroom? What does the law say about what topics a teacher may or may not address in the classroom?

6.   What other actions might Gary have taken in response to the objections raised by parents? What would have been the likely outcome of each action?

7.   What are Gary's instructional objectives in his American literature class? Write two or three objectives that you would recommend Gary follow with regard to the controversial American literature

story. To what levels of Krathwohl's Affective Taxonomy do your objectives relate?

8. At what stages of moral development do Gary, Mr. Gardner, and the parents seem to be operating? What about students like Jack and Jerry? How, from a moral-education perspective, might Gary have handled the debate differently?

9. From a motivational perspective, which different needs are operating? For example, at what levels of Maslow's need hierarchy are Gary, Mr. Gardner, the superintendent, the parents, and the students operating?

10. What is values clarification from the position of Simon and others, and could any values-clarification activities have been used instead of the debate?

11. What is conformity with reference to the work that has been done in social psychology? What kinds of sanctions do small communities like Jonesville employ to exact conformity? What is teacher tenure, and would it have helped protect Gary in this situation?

12. What is adolescent idealism from the frame of reference of adolescent psychology? What are some of the adolescent ideals of Jerry, Jack, and Maria with regard to religion? How might Gary have taken such adolescent characteristics into consideration in dealing with the controversy?

CASE 4

THE TYRANNY OF TESTING

Washington High School is located just off a busy expressway in a metropolitan area on the West Coast. The school has over 2,000 pupils, with about 50 percent black, 40 percent Hispanic, 5 percent Asian, and 5 percent white. A few decades ago the neighborhood surrounding Washington High was predominantly middle income. Since the early 1960s, however, the more upwardly mobile families, both black and white, began to move out of the area and into the suburbs. Today, the families that remain are largely low income.

While urban schools such as Washington High frequently have below-average student achievement, the school's performance on the annual state-mandated test of reading, writing, and mathematics skills for all eleventh graders has been close to the mean score for all schools in the state. And when compared to that of the other 11 high schools in the city, the achievement of Washington High students is slightly above average. As a result, the school has a reputation throughout the city for providing low-income students with a better education than they would receive at many other urban high schools.

Although Washington High was built just before World War II, the physical plant has been well maintained. Freshly painted white windows provide a pleasing accent to the three-story brick exterior, which was sandblasted just two years ago. Inside the hallways are regularly mopped and waxed by a custodial staff that takes pride in making an old building sparkle.

It is Monday morning, two days before students return from their summer vacations. Over 100 teachers and other school personnel are seated in the library waiting for their new principal, Mrs. Manning, to begin addressing them at a brief orientation meeting.

Darrell Wilson, a 37-year-old mathematics teacher beginning his tenth year at Washington High, is seated next to his good friend, Steve Neff, a 28-year-old English teacher who came to the school three years ago. Darrell, who is also chairman of the mathematics department, is highly regarded by his colleagues and by his students. For the last four years students voted him Teacher of the Year.

Darrell [in a low voice]   I understand that Mrs. Manning is a real go-getter. She's not afraid to make changes if she thinks they'll improve student achievement.

Steve [leaning toward his friend]   That's what I've heard, too. I'm a bit worried though. A friend of mine from Manning's last school told me something I don't like.

Darrell   What was that?

Steve   She said Manning places a lot of emphasis on test scores. [At the sound of feedback on the portable amplifier being adjusted at the front of the library, he turns in that direction.]

Darrell   Let's hear what she has to say.

After being introduced by Mr. Hawkins, the assistant principal in charge of curriculum, Mrs. Manning welcomes the teachers and staff back from summer vacation and then announces the names of four new teachers. Next she goes over a few details related to the schedule for the remainder of the day. Finally she turns to her goals for the new year.

Mrs. Manning [in a loud clear voice]   When I knew I was coming to Washington High, I was pleased. This school is known for giving students a good, solid education, and all of you are to be congratulated. [A slight pitter of applause spreads throughout the library.] I truly look forward to working with each and every one of you so that we can make a good educational program even better. [She pauses a moment, smiling.] Therefore our primary goal this year will be to increase the basic skills achievement of every eleventh grade student on the state's annual assessment test in March. Each teacher, regardless of subject, must stress the basics. [Several of the teachers stir noticeably in their seats. Darrell leans toward Steve in order to make a comment.]

Darrell [whispering]   You were right. It didn't take her long to zero in on test scores.

Mrs. Manning   As you may recall, last year 73 percent of our eleventh graders reached mastery on the reading section of the test. On the writing portion, 71 percent achieved mastery. And on the mathematics portion, 72 percent were at the mastery level. While some might feel that this level of performance is acceptable for an urban school such as Washington High, it could be better. To improve our scores, then, I am initiating several new procedures this year. Everyone must do his or her part to increase the basic skills achievement of our students. [She clears her throat before continuing.] At tomorrow's departmental meetings, you will receive a list of the specific skills for which less than 75 percent of our students achieved mastery. I want each department to develop an action plan for raising the levels of mastery for those skills. [Several teachers in the audience stir noticeably and whisper to one another at the mention of the action plan. Mrs. Manning continues with a renewed authoritative ring to her voice.] I know it means an effort on our part, but it must be made if we are to raise test scores. Furthermore, I want you to know that *I am* serious about this. Like it or not, our school's effectiveness is judged by how well our students do on the state's test. [She pauses as if to give teachers a moment to reflect on her remarks.] Now let me tell you about *my* action plan. I am requiring several things. First of all, weekly lesson plans that must include basic skills instruction. Also each of you will give monthly practice tests to prepare our students for the state's test in March. Furthermore, we will begin a schoolwide campaign to stress to students the importance of increasing test scores. Finally, I am lining up a couple of in-service workshops later in the year to improve students' test-taking skills.

***

Following Mrs. Manning's meeting with the teachers, Darrell and Steve are walking to their classrooms.

Darrell   I understand that she wants to make the school better; there's always room for improvement. It's just that there's more to a good school than having kids score high on a basic skills test.

Steve [nods his head in agreement]   Yeah, it misses the whole point of education.

Darrell [stopping for a moment near the entrance to the gymnasium]   Also it doesn't seem right to place all that emphasis on a test that just the eleventh graders take. But I guess if you're a principal the name of the game is to make the school look good on paper. If you can go from the seventy-third percentile to the seventy-fifth percentile on a single skill, that makes you look good.

Steve [with determination]   Exactly. [He stops at the doorway to his room.] Say, why don't you see how the people in your department feel about this testing business. If a lot of them feel like us, then maybe, as a department chairman, you could meet with Manning and express some of our concerns.

Darrell [chuckling and with sarcasm]   Thanks, pal. I appreciate your endorsement of my professional abilities.

Steve [with a broad grin]   Not only are you professional, you've got tact. For that, you get an A+. [Placing his hand on Darrell's shoulder.] Come on, Darrell, you're a leader in this school. What better person could we pick to express our position?

Darrell   Hmm. I don't think I should let you off that easy. How about if you survey the English teachers and I survey the math teachers, and then we *both* meet with Mrs. Manning?

Steve [dropping his hands to his side]   What can I say. You math teachers are so darned logical. [He pauses.] Okay, I'll do it. But you know I'll have to work around Dorothy Hamilton. As department chair, she's likely to think I'm trying to stir things up. I know she's a real advocate of testing.

Darrell [grins broadly and slaps Steve on the back]   I know you can handle it!

***

It is the following day, and Darrell is meeting in an empty classroom with the six other mathematics teachers in his department. At this moment the group is reviewing the mathematics skills that fewer than 75 percent of the eleventh graders have mastered. Darrell has written the 10 skills on the board.

The student will:

1. Round a number less than 10 with no more than two decimal places to the nearest whole number.
2. Round a mixed number with a whole number component less than 100 to the nearest whole number.
3. Put in order three whole numbers less than ten million.
4. Identify an improper fraction that is equivalent to a mixed number less than 100.
5. Identify a decimal or percent that is equivalent to a proper fraction having a denominator of 2, 3, 4, 5, 20, 25, 50, or 100.
6. Multiply two three-digit numbers.
7. Divide a five-digit number by a two-digit number.
8. Divide two numbers, each having no more than two decimal places.
9. Estimate capacity in liters, cups, or quarts.
10. Solve real-world problems by finding simple interest.

Darrell stands just to the left of the skills he has written on the board. The teachers are seated in a semicircle a few feet from him.

Darrell [gesturing toward the material on the board]   These are the ten math skills, then, that we're supposed to emphasize in our classes.
Mrs. Wilkins [pointing to what Darrell has written on the board]   I can go along with those, Darrell, but what I want to know is what are we supposed to do about the reading and writing skills? [Shaking her head.] I'm a math teacher, not an English teacher.
Darrell   Remember, Mrs. Manning said *every* teacher is to be a teacher of the basics. But let's decide what we're going to do about the math skills first, then we'll turn to the other areas.
Mr. Montgomery [sarcastically and with a smirk on his face]   I want to see what the folks in physical education do about this. [A few of the teachers chuckle.]
Miss Sides [with obvious irritation]   She wants *all* of us to emphasize these skills to *all* of our students?
Darrell   That's my understanding.
Miss Sides [frowning]   Well with the exception of estimating capacity

and computing simple interest, it would be a waste of my time to stress these skills in my classes. My kids usually know that stuff.

Mr. Montgomery   I'll have the same situation as Dorothy. I'd be using up valuable class time to stress a few skills that a few students have a problem with. Why don't we just set up a remedial class of some sort for those kids who need it?

Darrell   That's a good idea. But my hunch is Mrs. Manning wants all of us to stress these skills so the scores of *all* our students will increase.

Miss Sides   There's a fundamental problem here that bothers me. If we aim our teaching at the test, the kids will just master the lower-order skills those tests measure.

Mrs. Payne [shaking her head and turning in her seat to face Miss Sides]   No, the tests just measure the minimum things the kids are to learn. We don't teach *only* what's on the test.

Miss Sides   That may be the case, but unless we're careful, the minimum becomes the maximum.

Darrell [thoughtfully]   I've seen it happen before. Tests like the one in our state can pressure teachers to teach only what the test measures. And what most of these tests focus on are lower-order cognitive skills.

Mr. Montgomery [emphatically]   He's right. The test ends up determining the curriculum. Whatever's tested—that's what's taught. Somewhere in the process higher-order thinking skills, problem-solving skills, and so on get lost.

Darrell   Related to that, Steve Neff in the English department pointed out something I wasn't aware of: The writing portion of the test doesn't ask kids to write. They just bubble in answers to multiple-choice questions.

Miss Sides   That's sure not writing.

Darrell [speaking slowly and choosing his words carefully]   Let me try this out on you . . . Many of us seem to have some doubts about the influence that the state assessment test is having on our curriculum. Nobody here is against testing; we just want it kept in proper perspective. [A few teachers nod in assent; others murmur their agreement.] How does it sound if we make a list right here on the board of our concerns, and then I meet with Mrs. Manning and tell her about our reservations?

Miss Sides   That's a good idea. We owe it to ourselves to make our views known.

Mr. Montgomery [hesitantly]   Maybe we should find out how teachers in some of the other departments feel.

Darrell   I know Steve Neff is discussing the same thing with the English teachers.

Mr. Montgomery   Good. Maybe the two of you could go talk to Mrs. Manning. It would have more of an impact if she knew that the math and English departments had the same concerns. Do you think you could get Steve to go with you?

Darrell [smiling]   I suppose I could try. But I'm not too sure Steve'd want to go around Dorothy Hamilton. I know she's really in favor of testing.

Mr. Montgomery Well maybe you can convince him. It seems to me that if a lot of English teachers feel the same as we do, someone has a right to represent them.

***

Three days later Steve and Darrell enter Mrs. Manning's office. Mrs. Manning, a trim, well-dressed woman in her middle fifties, meets them at the door and shakes hands with each of them before motioning them into the two brown leather chairs in front of her desk.

Mrs. Manning Can I get either of you a cup of coffee?

Darrell and Steve [in unison] No, thank you.

Mrs. Manning [smiling as she sits in her chair] Mr. Wilson, you said earlier that some of the teachers in your department have concerns about our basic skills program?

Darrell [leaning forward in his chair] That's right, Mrs. Manning. None of us are against basic skills or testing per se. It's just that we're concerned that too much emphasis is being placed on the tests.

Steve [hesitantly at first] The English teachers have the same concerns. Actually the state's test covers only a fraction of our total eleventh grade curriculum. The rest of our curriculum, really, is ignored.

Darrell Basically we're concerned that if we place too much emphasis on the state's assessment test, we'll restrict the curriculum that we present the kids. What's tested will be what's taught. One of my teachers even referred to the current push to increase test scores as "the tyranny of testing."

Mrs. Manning [seriously] I understand your concerns, but you must remember that the minimum standards covered by the test don't reflect the higher-order skills that individual teachers may hold students accountable for.

Darrell That's all well and good, in theory at least. In practice some teachers and most students get the idea that if it's not tested, then it's not important.

Steve Minimum-competency tests like ours really have a limiting effect on the English curriculum.

Mrs. Manning What do you mean, Mr. Neff?

Steve Test scores have become so powerful that the teacher's attention is turned toward the easy-to-measure bits of information that these tests usually assess. Creativity and imagination in the curriculum are gradually phased out. The tests don't measure the kind of growth we want our kids to make.

Mrs. Manning I think you're being overly critical of these tests. They're simply tools for us to use in order to see how effective we are at ensuring that *all* our students get the basics. These are skills that are required for everyday living, and we need to have a systematic way of guaranteeing that every student acquires them.

Darrell   I think Steve's English teachers are right. These tests stifle teacher and student creativity and self-direction. If students see that we place so much emphasis on discrete bits of knowledge, they're not going to be inclined to learn to solve problems, think logically, communicate clearly, and so on.

Mrs. Manning [with some irritation]   Now, Mr. Wilson, you're forgetting that the discrete bits of knowledge are necessary for anyone to be able to do the things you've mentioned. In effect we have to establish the ability of kids to engage in lower-order thinking before there can be higher-order thinking. Right?

Darrell [tersely]   I follow what you're saying.

Steve   There's another area that these tests ignore completely, and that's the affective area. In English we feel it's very important for students to develop appreciation for good literature. When you look at the state's test, though, it doesn't address such goals.

Mrs. Manning [sighing]   Gentlemen, I have to go back to what I've said before. Our state's test only outlines the minimum objectives for our curriculum. Each teacher is entirely free to go beyond those objectives.

Darrell   I guess the point we're trying to make is that if we start giving monthly practice tests, working basic skills instruction into our weekly lesson plans and all the rest, there won't be that much time left for the rest of the curriculum. The kids will be spending most of their time with rote learning.

Mrs. Manning   I understand your concern. However, I want you to know that I feel a tremendous responsibility to the students who have failed to master certain parts of the test. [With determination.] I truly believe that 100 percent of our students can achieve mastery on every skill covered by the test.

Darrell and Steve nod in agreement with what their principal has just said. The three then sit in silence for a few moments. Steve glances at Darrell as though looking for a cue as to what to say next.

Mrs. Manning   I have an idea. [She pushes her swivel chair back from her desk and twirls a quarter turn to the right.] I appreciate your willingness to be candid with me about how you and the other teachers feel. I know we all have our students' best interests at heart. [She turns her chair back to the left and makes direct eye contact with Darrell.] I'd like to create a basic skills task force with the two of you as co-chairs. Select one teacher from each department to be on the task force. Your job would be to study the problem from all angles. Then develop a plan for increasing the scores of those students who have mastered less than 80 percent of the reading, writing, or math objectives. What do you think about that?

Darrell Hmm . . . I appreciate your openness to our input, Mrs. Manning. Frankly I'm not sure what to say. I wasn't expecting this.

Mrs. Manning Well I believe that both of you are truly committed to our students' learning. If you and a group of teachers can come up with a better plan for guaranteeing that all our students learn the basics, then you've got my support. [Turning toward Steve.] What do you think? Are you up to the challenge?

Steve I'm like Darrell, I guess. I'm not sure how to respond. Could we think about it for a day or two and then get back to you?

Mrs. Manning [getting up] Sure. That's all right. Talk it over. Get back to me in a couple of days.

Mrs. Manning smoothly and graciously escorts them to her doorway and once again shakes their hands. A few moments later Darrell and Steve are climbing the stairs to their classrooms.

Steve [excitedly] Wow, was I surprised when she came up with the idea of us heading up a basic skills task force.

Darrell You're not the only one. [Sighs, then continues slowly.] She's right. It's a real challenge, developing a basic skills program that won't end up weakening or watering down the rest of the curriculum.

Steve Darrell, do you really think it's possible to develop a program like that? What do you think it would look like?

WASHINGTON HIGH SCHOOL
Basic Skills Objectives with Less Than 75 Percent of Students Achieving Mastery

OBJECTIVES	Percentage Mastery

Reading

	Percentage Mastery
1. Identify frequently used words by sight.	74
2. Determine the main idea stated in a paragraph.	69
3. Identify the order of events in a paragraph.	70
4. Identify the cause or effect stated in a paragraph.	68
5. Follow written directions.	73
6. Identify the pronoun referent in a sentence or paragraph.	69
7. Identify the main idea implied in a paragraph.	59
8. Identify the cause or effect implied in a paragraph.	60
9. Obtain appropriate information from pictures, maps, or signs.	71

Writing

1. Write the plural forms of nouns correctly.	71
2. Write declarative sentences having compound subjects and/or verbs.	69
3. Make subjects and verbs agree.	65
4. Use the appropriate forms of common irregular verbs in writing.	64
5. Generate headings for groups of words or phrases.	72
6. Organize information related to a single topic.	68
7. Proofread for spelling.	71
8. Spell months of the year, days of the week, and numbers from 1 to 121.	74
9. Spell commonly used "survival" words.	73
10. Use a comma between names of cities and states and between the day of the month and the year.	72
11. Use an apostrophe to form contractions.	69
12. Use an apostrophe and s to show the possessive of singular and plural nouns that do not end in s.	65
13. Capitalize appropriate words in titles.	68

Mathematics

1. Round a number less than 10 with no more than two decimal places to the nearest whole number.	74
2. Round a mixed number with a whole number component less than 100 to the nearest whole number.	72
3. Put in order three whole numbers less than 10 million.	70
4. Identify an improper fraction that is equivalent to a mixed number less than 100.	67
5. Identify a decimal or percent that is equivalent to a proper fraction having a denominator of 2, 3, 4, 5, 20, 25, 50, or 100.	65
6. Multiply two three-digit numbers.	69
7. Divide a five-digit number by a two-digit number.	67
8. Divide two numbers, each having no more than two decimal places.	70
9. Estimate capacity in liters, cups, or quarts.	68
10. Solve real-world problems by finding simple interest.	61

QUESTIONS

1. In addition to scores on achievement tests, what are some indicators of a school's effectiveness? What has educational research identified as the characteristics of effective schools?

2. To what extent should *every* teacher be a teacher of the basics?

3. Has your state mandated a basic skills achievement test for students? If so, what are the reported strengths and weaknesses of that test?

4. Imagine that you were made a member of Darrell's and Steve's basic skills task force. What action would you recommend?

5. To what extent do standardized student achievement tests represent the goals of education? How many of the levels of Bloom's Cognitive Taxonomy do they measure? Do they measure other goals of education, such as those related to creativity and problem solving? Do they measure affective goals, such as those related to motivation to achieve, self-esteem, human-relations skills, and locus of control? What about physical education?

6. Should schools "teach to the test?" What are the arguments for and against such a procedure?

7. What are the basic skills? Does emphasizing them on tests create the danger of "minimums becoming maximums?" Is it possible to develop a program that emphasizes both minimums and maximums? How else might Mrs. Manning have tried to improve basic skills other than by emphasizing basic skills testing?

8. Are most standardized achievement tests of the multiple-choice variety? What are the strengths and weaknesses of multiple-choice items?

9. What are test norms and how are they used to interpret test results? What norms should be used in the case of Washington High School? Would criterion-referenced evaluation procedures make more sense than norm-referenced procedures in this situation?

10. How can the school take into consideration the home, social class, and racial and ethnic backgrounds of its students in developing its instructional and testing programs? What kinds of and how much influence can the home and parents have on the achievement of students in school? What can the school do to take such influence into consideration?

PART III

INSTRUCTION CASES

CASE 5

LIFE IN AN ELEMENTARY CLASSROOM

Lincoln Elementary School is located on a quiet tree-lined street in Mountainview, a city of about 50,000 in a northwestern state. It is early in the fall, and the morning air is filled with the sweet smell of pine. Within a two-block radius of the school, several children can be seen as they slowly make their way to school. Like children the world over, they are easily diverted by objects attractive to the young eye—a strange insect on a tree stump or perhaps a shiny piece of metal on the sidewalk.

Mountainview is the home of one of the regional campuses of the state university, and most faculty children of elementary age attend Lincoln. The school, which spans kindergarten through fifth grade, has an enrollment of just over 450.

Linda Walker graduated from the university last June and began teaching second grade this year at Lincoln. Though she had a high grade-point average at the university and received a very favorable recommendation for student teaching from her cooperating teacher at another elementary school in Mountainview, Linda feels lucky to have begun her teaching career at Lincoln. The school is generally regarded as the best in the city. Parents take an active role in school functions and try to support the teacher's efforts at home. Real estate agents make it known to potential home buyers with elementary-age children that homes in the Lincoln area are more desirable.

As Linda nears the main entrance to the school this morning, a small boy dressed in blue jeans and a red shirt calls to her from high atop the jungle gym.

Timmy [calling out]   Hey, Miss Walker, come over here and see what I got.
Linda [stopping]   What is it, Timmy? [She leaves the sidewalk and begins to walk across the playground toward Timmy.]
Timmy [climbing down]   You'll never guess. [He runs the few steps to his books and lunch box which are stacked on a window ledge of the school building.]
Linda   I don't have the slightest idea, Timmy.

Timmy opens his lunch box and pulls out a small white cardboard box. He removes the lid and then, smiling, looks up at his teacher.

Timmy   It's a meteorite. I got it from my uncle.
Linda [touching the small orelike rock in the box with her right index finger]   This is wonderful, Timmy! Do you know what a meteorite is?
Timmy   Yeah, it's from outer space.
Linda   Right.
Timmy [excitedly]   My uncle, he lives in California!
Linda   He does? [Pausing.] Timmy, why don't you show your meteorite to the class today during our science lesson?
Timmy [agreeably]   Okay. [He replaces the lid and then tosses it back in his lunch box.] I gotta get back to the monkey bars. [He looks over toward the jungle gym.]
Linda [smiling warmly]   Okay, Timmy, I'll see you inside real soon.
Timmy   Bye. [He turns and runs back to the jungle gym.]

As Linda walks the remaining 50 feet to the main entrance of the building, she encounters three more of her students.

Linda [waving to the three girls who are busy writing something on a sheet of notebook paper]   Hi, Mary. Hi, Cathy. Hi, Heather. What are you girls up to this morning?
Heather [excitedly]   Hi, Miss Walker. We're writing a secret code so the boys can't get into our club.
Linda   Oh, that sounds like a good idea! What's the name of your club?
Mary   We're the Power Dreamer Girls, and we've got magic powers.
Linda [continuing to walk toward the main entrance]   Well, it sounds like the boys better be careful. I'll see you girls soon. Bye-bye.
Three girls in unison   Bye-bye, Miss Walker.

Inside the building, Linda first stops in the main office to sign in and check her mailbox. Mrs. Flanigan, the principal, stands at the counter and greets the teachers as they sign in.

Mrs. Flanigan   Good morning, Linda.
Linda   Morning, Mrs. Flanigan. Isn't it a beautiful morning?
Mrs. Flanigan   The prettiest we've had in a long while. I was beginning to wonder if that drizzle would ever stop. [Clearing her throat.] I put a note in your box, Linda, as a reminder that I'll be coming by first thing this morning to observe a reading lesson. We set up the time and date at our preobservation conference, remember?
Linda [enthusiastically]   Oh, I haven't forgotten! I'll be working with the children in their reading groups.

Mrs. Flanigan Good. I'll be down there in just a few minutes. I'll be using the same observation form I used last time.
Linda Good. See you soon.

***

A short time later Mrs. Flanigan arrives at Linda's classroom as her students are filing into the room. Linda is standing behind her desk arranging papers.

Linda [looking up] Hello, Mrs. Flanigan. [She points to a full-sized student desk at the back of the room.] You can sit there. It's right next to the table we use for the reading groups.
Mrs. Flanigan Thank you, Linda. That'll be just perfect.

As Linda's students continue to enter the room they take their seats obediently. The room holds 30 desks that are arranged in five rows of 6 desks each. Only a few students seem to notice Mrs. Flanigan who is now seated at her desk. Within a few moments Linda's 24 students are at their desks, waiting for her to begin. Linda moves around in front of her desk; she smiles at a blond-haired girl who sits directly in front of her.

Linda Okay, children, today we have a visitor. Mrs. Flanigan, our principal, will be observing us during reading.

Nearly every child turns to look at Mrs. Flanigan who looks up from her notebook and smiles broadly. Almost immediately the boys and girls turn back toward their teacher.

Linda [in a sweet, bubbly voice] Is everyone here today?
Class in unison Yes.
Linda Good. [She writes the attendance figure on the small yellow pad she holds in her left hand.] Does anyone know what day it is? [Several students' hands go up.] Mary?
Mary The tenth?
Linda The tenth is the date. What day of the week is it? Carol?
Carol [proudly] Monday.
Linda That's right. Today is Monday the tenth, the first day of the week. And everyone's here. [She enters the date on the yellow pad.] How many are not eating in the cafeteria today . . . you either brought your lunch or you're going home? [Four students raise their hands.] Okay, that's four. Twenty-four minus four is how many? [Three students raise their hands.] Timmy, do you know?
Timmy Twenty.
Linda Very good, Timmy. Twenty-four minus four is twenty. [She en-

ters this number on the yellow pad.] By the way, boys and girls, Timmy has something very special that he wants to show us during our science lesson. Right, Timmy? [She smiles at him.]

Timmy [with energy]   Right! It came from way far away!

Linda [chuckling]   Now don't give it away, Timmy. [Continuing.] Paul, would you put this lunch count outside on the door?

She tears off a page from the pad and hands it to Paul who does as requested. Linda places the pad on the corner of her desk, picks up a stack of papers, and then turns to her class.

Linda   This morning, boys and girls, I have three stories that I want you to read. Read them very carefully. At the end of each story are several questions. They check to see how well you understand the story. [Moving over to the first row on her left.] I'll hand out the three stories now. You may read them in any order you want. Everybody will need a pencil. When you're finished answering the questions for all three stories, you may color the picture that goes with each story.

Linda counts out enough papers for the children in the first row. She hands them to the first student, a black girl, in the row.

Linda [whispering to the girl]   Take one and pass the rest back, please. [She moves on to the next row.]

Within a minute or two, each student is busily at work. Linda moves up and down the rows checking on each student's progress. She stops to help a boy in a green plaid shirt.

Linda [softly]   Let's read it together. [Pointing with her pencil.] "The boy wanted to take a boat and a pail and shovel to the beach. But his mother could not find the boat. 'Maybe you will find a friend at the beach who has a boat,' said his mother. So the boy just took his pail and shovel to the beach." Now, the question here asks "What did the boy take to the beach?"

Gary   A boat and a pail and a shovel?

Linda   No, Gary. Remember, his mother couldn't find the boat. So he just took his pail and shovel. See, in the picture he just has his pail and shovel. Now you try the next question, and I'll come back to help you if you need me. [Addressing the entire class.] Okay, boys and girls, would Group 1 go back to the reading table, please. Everyone else keep working on your stories until it's time for your group to go to the reading table.

At Linda's instructions eight children get up from their desks and walk to the large round table at the back of the room. Two boys at the front of the room and behind Linda also get out of their seats momentarily, pretending as though they are going to join the group at the back of the room. When Linda happens to turn in their direction, however, they dart back into their seats. Linda sees this but does not comment on their behavior.

Meanwhile at the back of the room, a boy hands out hardcover dictionaries as the children take their seats. Linda scans the 16 students who are working on the three stories, and, satisfied that they are on task, she joins the 8 children at the round table.

Linda [taking her seat] Does everybody have a dictionary? Okay. Gwen, do you want to scoot over here so everyone can see the flannel board? [Gwen moves her chair closer to her teacher.] Everybody sit up nice and straight. Let's say the days of the week beginning with Monday. [Beginning slowly until all eight children are responding in unison.] Monday, Tuesday, Wednesday, Thursday, Friday, Saturday, and Sunday. Very good. Now, who remembers which day of the week starts with one of the consonant digraphs we've been studying? Beth?

Beth Thursday.

Linda Thursday. And which consonant digraph does it begin with? Bill?

Bill [softly] T H.

Linda Very good. Now this morning, boys and girls, we're going to begin with the four consonant digraphs we've been studying. As I put them on the flannel board, would you say them with me.

Children in unison C H. [Linda places the letters on the flannel board.] S H. T H. and W H.

Linda Okay, as we all know, a consonant digraph is when we take two consonants and put them together so they make a brand new sound. It doesn't sound like either one of the consonants usually sounds. All right, I'm going to call out several groups of words and you're not going to know whether they have a C H, an S H, a T H, or a W H. Listen carefully. [Slowly, emphasizing the consonant digraphs.] Children. Champ. Church. Chirp. Checkers. Chair. And Cheese. Who knows the answer? Raise your hand. Cathy, which two letters? The C H, the S H, the T H, or the W H? [As Cathy begins to formulate her answer, Linda glances quickly at the rest of her class. Satisfied that they are all busy, she turns back to Cathy.]

Cathy The C H.

Linda Good. Every one of those words began with a C H. Now sometimes a consonant digraph comes where? At the beginning of a word. [Several children try to provide the answers along with their teacher.] Sometimes it comes at the middle. And sometimes . . . at the end. Now we're going to use our magic hat. [From a shelf to her right, Linda takes a large black top hat made out of construction paper. She places the hat in the middle of the table.] In the hat, boys and girls, are words that have the C H in them. Some are at the beginning of the word. Some are at the middle of the word. And some are at the end. Also some words may even have more than one C H. I'm going to shake up the words, and then each of you will draw a word and tell us where the C H is: at the beginning, the middle, or the end. Okay, Timmy, you look ready. You go first. Read the word and then tell us where the consonant digraph is.

Linda pushes the hat over toward Timmy who gingerly sticks his hand in the hat and pulls out a word. Linda again glances back at the rest of her students to check their progress.

Timmy   Church.
Linda   Where's the consonant digraph?
Timmy [softly]   At the beginning . . . and at the end.
Linda   Very good, Timmy. At the beginning and at the end. Let's put your word right up here on the flannel board. [Moving from left to right Linda slowly scans the small group of children.] I like the way Beth is sitting . . . would you like to choose next, Beth?
Beth   Okay. [She reaches in the hat and pulls out a word.] Cherry.
Linda   Cherry. And where's the consonant digraph in cherry?

At this moment, one of the two boys who earlier had started to join this first reading group appears at Linda's side.

Linda   Frank, what do you want? You're in the next reading group.
Frank [lethargically]   I'm tired, Miss Walker.
Linda   Well, go back to your desk and finish your work, and then you can rest.
Frank [insolently]   All right. [With greatly exaggerated fatigue, he walks back to his desk.]
Linda   Okay, let's see . . .
Beth   At the beginning.
Linda   Very good, Beth. The digraph's at the beginning. Let's put your word up here next to Timmy's. Bill, why don't you choose a word. [She pushes the hat toward Bill.]
Bill [weakly]   Peach.
Linda   Peach. How many of you like peaches? [Five children raise their hands.] Okay, where is the consonant digraph in your peach, Bill?
Bill [tentatively]   At the end.
Linda   Yes at the end. [She places the word peach on the flannel board.] All right, Mary, do you want to take a word out of the hat?
Mary   Yes.
Linda   Take a word out and read it to us, and then tell us where the consonant digraph is.
Mary   Chicken.
Linda   Yes, Mary pulled a chicken out of the hat. [Several children giggle.] And where's the consonant digraph?

Mary The beginning.

Linda Good, Mary. Let's put your word right here. [Pausing.] Annie, why don't you take a word out of the hat.

Annie [trying to pronounce ketchup] Ker . . .

Linda Sound it out. It's something we like to put on hot dogs and hamburgers.

Annie [suddenly] Ketchup.

Linda Good, now where's the consonant digraph?

Annie At the end?

Linda No. It's in the middle. See? [She points to the letters.] Okay, let's put Annie's ketchup right here. Gwen, why don't you take a word now. [Pushing the hat toward Gwen.]

Gwen [in a strong voice] Chief.

Linda Right. Chief. Where's the consonant digraph?

Gwen At the beginning.

Linda Right, Gwen, at the beginning. And let's put your word right here on the board. Rusty, you get to take the next to last word out of the hat. [Linda once again glances at the rest of her students. She notices that Frank has his head on his desk and is not doing anything.]

Rusty [with a surprised look on his face] Champ. It's at the beginning.

Linda Right. Champ. Let's put Rusty's word here. Now, Cathy, you get to read the very last word in the hat. What is that word?

Cathy [proudly] It's chair.

Linda Right. And where is the consonant digraph in the word chair?

Cathy At the beginning.

Linda Very good, Cathy. [She places Cathy's word on the flannel board.] Now we have all eight words on the board. Okay, I have a silly tongue twister here. [She takes a one-by-two-foot piece of poster board from the shelf to her right. She is careful not to let the children see what is written on it.] Do you know what a tongue twister is?

Children in unison Yes.

Linda It's when a group of words in a sentence all start with the same letters. Close your eyes, I want you to count the number of C H's you hear in this tongue twister. Raise your hand when you know. Are your eyes all closed?

Children in unison Yes.

Linda [slowly] After church, Charles had a lunch of cheeseburgers and cherries. How many C H's do you hear? [With emphasis.] *Everyone's* hand went up. Timmy?

Timmy Five.

Linda Well, let's see if Timmy's right. Open your eyes, and let's read the sentence together.

All in unison After church, Charles had a lunch of cheeseburgers and cherries.

Linda Let's count the C H's.

All in unison One, two, three, four, five, six.

Linda   There are six C H's. Church had two, and that was hard to catch, wasn't it? Very good. [She removes the words from the flannel board.] Okay. Now we're going to work with another pair of letters that we met last week. The O and the A. Remember, there's a rule for when two vowels go side-by-side in a word. Can anyone remember that rule? [Silence.] When two vowels go walking, the first one does the talking. Let's all say that together.

All in unison   When two vowels go walking, the first one does the talking.

Linda   What does that mean when two vowels go walking, the first one does the talking? Mary?

Mary   You hear the sound of the first one.

Linda   Very good. You hear the sound of the first vowel. The O says its name. The O is first, so that's what you hear. You don't hear the A. All right, all of the words that we're going to look at today say O. The O and the A go together, but we just hear the O. Now, look at these words on this chart. [She takes a two-foot by three-foot piece of poster board from the shelf and holds it so her students can see.] Let's read the words on this chart. [She begins pointing with her pencil.] Timmy, what's this word?

Timmy   Boat.

Linda   Good. Gwen, what's this one?

Gwen   Float.

Linda   Good, Gwen. Cathy, what's this word?

Cathy   Road.

Linda   Yes, that's road. Let's see. Annie, can you read this word?

Annie   Toad.

Linda   Very good, Annie. Okay, Mary, can you read this word?

Mary   Goat.

Linda   Good, Mary. That's goat. All right, Bill, can you read this last word?

Bill   Load.

Linda   Very good, Bill. Now let's all say the words together.

All in unison   Boat. Float. Road. Toad. Goat. Load.

Linda   Okay. Very good, children. The next thing we're going to do this morning is work with some vocabulary words. Each of you has a dictionary in front of you, right?

Children in unison   Yes, Miss Walker.

Linda   Now dictionaries can be used for several different things. Can somebody tell me what we use dictionaries for? Gwen?

Gwen   To find out things.

Linda   Okay, we can find out things. What kind of things can we find out? Gwen?

Gwen   The meaning.

Linda   All right, the meaning of what?

Gwen   The meaning of words.

Linda   Right. If you want to know the meaning of a word, you can look up that word in the dictionary and find out what it means. Can a dictionary do anything else? Rusty?
Rusty   How to spell a word.
Linda   Right. If you know the first couple of letters of a word you can find out how it is spelled. Mary?
Mary   How many syllables.
Linda   Good, Mary. The dictionary will tell you how many syllables or how many parts a word has. Also the dictionary will tell you where the accent mark goes. What does that tell you? [No response.] Well it tells you what part of the word you pronounce the loudest. Very good. Now can a word have more than one meaning?
Children in unison   More than one.
Linda   Okay, it can have more than one meaning. It could have several meanings; it just depends on how the word is used. [Holding up her dictionary.] This is a thick book, isn't it? [Students murmur their agreement.] Is there a quick way to find a word in the dictionary? If I give you a word to find, do you have to look at *every* page in the dictionary in order to find the word? Is there a quick way to do it?
Beth [tentatively]   Maybe.
Linda   Well, you're right, Beth, there is a quick way. What is that?
Timmy   Use the guide words at the top.
Linda   Okay, how do you use those guide words? Cathy?
Cathy   They show you . . . Like if you're looking up the word *boat,* you find B O and then . . .
Linda [interrupting]   All right. The first guide word on a page is the first word on that page, isn't it? [Students murmur in agreement.] What's the last guide word on that page?
Timmy and Annie in unison   The last word.
Linda   All right. It's the last word. So the guide words tell you what word that page is going to begin with and what word it'll end with. Now I'm going to give you each a sheet with five new words on it. These are words that we haven't seen. And I want you to see if you can find them in the dictionary, okay? When you find the word, write down the page number that the word is on in the dictionary. Then we'll talk about those words.

Linda gives each child a sheet with the words on it. After making certain that the children have started their work, Linda leaves the round table and begins to walk up and down the rows checking on the progress of her other students. She notices that Frank now appears to be working on his assignment. Satisfied that all her students are on task, Linda walks over to Mrs. Flanigan's desk.

Linda [whispering]   I'll be finished with this reading group in just a few minutes. Then I'll take the second group and we'll go over the same material. And if I have enough time before science, I'll work with the third group.

Mrs. Flanigan [softly]   That's fine, Linda. I've seen enough. [She begins to return her papers to her notebook.] The children seemed to respond well. I would like to talk to you though about the lesson. Could you come by tomorrow for a postobservation conference during your preparation time?

Linda   Sure, that'd be fine. [Hesitating.] I always get so anxious. . . . Could I ask you what you thought about the lesson? How do you feel things went?

Teacher Summary Evaluation Report

Name _____

College _____

School _____ Date _____

Grade or   Period of   Period of   Period of

Subject _____ Sept.–Dec. ☐   Jan.–March ☐   Apr.–Dec. ☐

Observation Time _____ Conference Time _____

Check on March and Dec. Report	Check on March Report Only	Contract Status
☐ Outstanding ☐ Satisfactory ☐ Unsatisfactory	☐ Recommended for first one-year contract ☐ Recommended for second one-year contract ☐ Recommended for initial four-year contract ☐ Recommended for third one-year contract ☐ Not recommended for reappointment	☐ First year contract ☐ Second year contract ☐ Four-year contract ☐ One-year contract ☐ Continuing contract ☐ Long term substitute (60 or more days)

*OUTSTANDING: Performance shows exceptional professional qualities and growth.

SATISFACTORY: Performance at expected and desired professional qualities and growth.

*UNSATISFACTORY: Performance shows serious weaknesses or deficiencies.

*For more complete definition refer to page 12 in The Toledo Plan.

*Unsatisfactories and/or outstandings must have a written supportive statement.

	Out-standing	Satis-factory	Unsatis-factory
I. TEACHING PROCEDURES			
A. Skill in planning			
B. Skill in assessment and evaluation			
C. Skill in making assignments			
D. Skill in developing good work-study habits			
E. Resourceful use of instructional materials			
F. Skill in using motivating techniques			
G. Skill in questioning techniques			
H. Ability to recognize and provide for individual differences			

I. Oral and written communication skills			
J. Speech, articulation and voice quality			
II. CLASSROOM MANAGEMENT			
A. Effective classroom facilitation and control			
B. Effective interaction with pupils			
C. Efficient classroom routine			
D. Appropriate interaction with pupils			
E. Is reasonable, fair and impartial in dealing with students			
III. KNOWLEDGE OF SUBJECT— ACADEMIC PREPARATION			
IV. PERSONAL CHARACTERISTICS AND PROFESSIONAL RESPONSIBILITY			
A. Shows a genuine interest in teaching			
B. Personal appearance			
C. Skill in adapting to change			
D. Adheres to accepted policies and procedures of Toledo Public Schools			
E. Accepts responsibility both inside and outside the classroom			
F. Has a cooperative approach toward parents and school personnel			
G. Is punctual and regular in attendance			

Evaluator's Signature   Teacher's Signature   Principal's Signature
(when required)   (when required)

Evaluator's Position

Date of Conference _____

DIRECTIONS

1. Rate all categories, bold face and subcategories.
2. Attach all supporting documents that have been signed or initiated.

SOURCE: *The Toledo Plan: Intern, Intervention, Evaluation.* Toledo Public Schools, 1986, p. 13. Reprinted by permission.

QUESTIONS

1. How effective was Linda at beginning class on that Monday morning? What specific things did she do that were effective? Ineffective?
2. Just after Linda gives instructions to students in Group 1 to go to the reading table at the back of the room, two boys not in Group 1 pretend they are going to join the group. When Linda turns in their direction, however, they return to their seats. Why do you suppose Linda does not comment on their behavior?
3. What steps does a teacher need to take in order to work with a small group while the rest of the class works independently?
4. What strengths does Linda have as a teacher? In what areas might she try to improve?
5. If you were to observe Linda's teaching using the Teacher Summary Evaluation Report at the end of this case, how would you rate her performance?
6. If you were to use a systematic observation schedule, such as Flanders' Interaction Analysis, to observe Linda's interactions with her students, what conclusions would you draw about the interactions? For example, what conclusions would you draw about the amount of teacher talk and student talk? About the amount of teacher direct and teacher indirect behavior? How do such interaction patterns relate to student outcomes such as achievement? What are some other systematic observation instruments that could be used to observe teacher-pupil interactions?
7. What kinds of classroom questions does Linda ask? How do the questions distribute themselves in terms of Bloom's Cognitive Taxonomy? To what kinds of student outcomes (for example, achievement or creativity) do such questions relate? How effectively does Linda question her students in the small reading group? For which specific interactions might she have been more effective?
8. How well does Linda's teaching style take into consideration the backgrounds and characteristics of her students, especially in terms of socioeconomic status and grade level?
9. What instructional objectives does Linda seem to be pursuing? State two or three of her objectives in behavioral terms. How well do her instructional strategies fit her objectives?

CASE 6

LIFE IN A HIGH SCHOOL CLASSROOM

After being let out at the curb by the driver of a newer model pickup, two boys dash up the sidewalk to McKinley High School trying to escape the bitter early morning cold. The hard-packed snow makes a squeaking sound under their feet. With hardly a pause in their mad charge, they burst through the green double doors and then slide to a halt in the hallway, laughing wildly and stamping the snow from their feet.

Mr. Swenson, the school's only assistant principal, is standing nearby. During bad weather he monitors students who may wait in the hall by the entranceway until the first period bell. About 25 students stand around in clusters of two to four talking animatedly about the things that matter most to young people in this rural area of a midwestern state—sports, cars, and, depending upon their sex, girls or boys.

Mr. Swenson   Cold enough for you fellas?
Two boys in unison   Yeah!

McKinley High has an enrollment of 670 students, most of whom live on the farms that surround Centerville. The town has a population of 4,500 and is the hub of most of the newsworthy events that happen in the county. All of McKinley's students are white, with almost equal proportions from families with German or Scandinavian ancestry.

After a hotly debated school bond issue was passed in the early 1980s, the school was built at the north end of town, two blocks east of the state highway. The school grounds cover just under four acres which appear exceptionally barren after the previous day's four-inch snowfall.

***

Later that day John Andrews, a 35-year-old mathematics teacher who has been at McKinley for seven years, walks into the main office for his 12:20 P.M. appointment with Mr. Swenson. He places both his hands on the counter and leans over to speak to Brenda, a clerical worker.

John   Hi Brenda. Is Mr. Swenson in? He said he wanted to see me at 12:20.

Brenda [picking up the telephone]   Let me see. I'll give him a buzz. [After a moment, she speaks to Mr. Swenson.] Mr. Andrews is here to see you . . . Okay . . . I'll send him in. [Hanging up the receiver and gesturing toward Mr. Swenson's office.] Go on in, Mr. Andrews, he's expecting you.
John [turning toward Mr. Swenson's office]   Thanks.

A moment later John enters Mr. Swenson's office. On the wall behind Mr. Swenson's desk is a red-and-white banner that reads **"McKinley Wildcats."** Mr. Swenson is seated behind a moderately cluttered desk.

Mr. Swenson [noticing that John is about to close the door]   No, that's all right. This'll only take a minute. Besides it gets darn cold in here when that door's closed. [He motions to John to sit in one of the two chairs on the other side of his desk.]
John [sitting down]   You wouldn't think a building this new would have cold spots in it.
Mr. Swenson   Well when it gets below zero like it is today . . . [Clearing his throat.] I just wanted to let you know that some time next week I'll be dropping by to make this semester's observation. Is there a class that you'd like me to visit?
John   Well really any one's fine. [Pausing.] You might like to see my third period general math, though. They're a good bunch of kids.
Mr. Swenson   That sounds fine. So I'll make it some day third period next week. Remember, nothing special—just business as usual.
John [getting up to leave]   Oh don't worry about that. This group of kids wouldn't let me get away with doing something out of the ordinary to impress you. [Chuckling.] They'll let you see them and me, warts and all.
Mr. Swenson [smiling]   That's good.

***

That next Wednesday Mr. Swenson arrives at John's classroom just as his third period students are filing into the room. He nods and smiles at John who stands in the hallway by his door. Mr. Swenson enters and takes a seat at the back of the room. He removes a district observation form from the manila folder he has with him and begins to enter John's name, the period, date, and other standard identifying information at the top.

The bell rings and two boys run up and squeeze through the door just as John is about to close it.

John [sternly]   I've told you fellas you're gonna have to get here on time.
Paul [breathlessly]   Coach Walker didn't let us out of gym on time.
Cecil   Yeah, he didn't.

John   Well, all I know is I can't have you guys waltzing in late like this. Go ahead, take your seats.

John walks over to his desk and flips open the record book that lies on top of his desk. Pointing with his right index finger he scans the list of the 28 ninth graders in his class, looking up occasionally to determine whether a student is present. As he takes attendance about half the students are arranging their materials—snapping and unsnapping three-ring binders, shuffling papers, thumbing through pages in the math text, or pulling all the contents out of a purse in order to find the right pencil. Another eight students scattered about the room in pairs talk and giggle in low tones. The students seated at the front of the four rows of desks sit and wait silently for the lesson to begin.

John [looking up]   What about Molly? Has anyone seen Molly? She's been out three days now.
Barbara   She rides my bus. Haven't seen her since last Friday.
Patricia   I talked to her last night. She's got the flu. She said she'd try to come today or tomorrow.
John [continuing with the attendance]   Thanks, Patricia.

Two boys on opposite sides of the room nod to one another and then get up in unison and walk over to the pencil sharpener mounted on a bookcase at the back of the room. One of them inserts his pencil in the sharpener and begins turning the crank lazily while he chats softly with the other. After a few moments, he makes a furtive glance over his left shoulder at his teacher and at Mr. Swenson who is seated nearby. Satisfied that neither is paying attention to them, he returns to his conversation.

John [looking up]   Hey, Sam and Dale, sit down right now. We're going to get started.
Sam [with irritation]   Okay, okay. I was just sharpening my pencil. [He and Dale walk slowly back to their desks.]
John [moving around in front of his desk]   All right, before we learn how to figure out the volume of different objects, I think we should review how we figure out the area of plane figures. I'm not sure all of you know that, and you'll need to know it for next week's test.

At the mention of a test, several students make various noises of protest and exhibit a variety of pained expressions for their teacher.

Sherman   Aah, Mr. Andrews, we don't want no test again. We had one last week.
John   That was two weeks ago. [With irritation.] We *are* going to have a test on areas and volume next Friday. Now let's get with it.
Kevin   Couldn't we just use our homework grades?

John [rapidly]   No. No. No. [Walking up to the blackboard.] Now every-one look up here. You should know every one of these formulas.

He quickly writes the following on the board, reading each statement aloud as he writes it:

Area of rectangle =
Area of square =
Area of parallelogram =
Area of triangle =
Area of circle =

John   Okay. Who knows the area of a rectangle? [He stands ready with the chalk to write in the correct answer. About seven students raise their hands.] Come on now. Everyone should know this. [Another four hands go up.] Ray, what is it?
Ray [loudly]   You multiply the length by the width.
John [writing the correct answer on the board]   Good. Length times width. [Turning to face his students.] So what is the area of a square? Robert, do you know? [Robert sits erect and stares straight ahead, but he does not answer.] If the area of a rectangle is the length times the width, what's the area of a square? [Robert still does not answer, though he eventually shakes his head.]
Annie [calling out]   Length times width.
John   Okay. Length times width. [He writes this answer on the board.] Is there another way to write it? [He turns toward his students.]
Carol [calling out]   The side squared.

Suddenly a female student appears at the door and knocks loudly. John walks over to the door, opens it, and standing in the open doorway, begins speaking to the girl. A moment later he turns toward his students.

John   Did anyone find a pink purse from last period?

Several students blurt out that they have not. A few others slide back their chairs so they can get a good look at the bookshelf beneath their desks. Still others look on the floor around their desks. When these efforts fail to turn up the missing purse, John turns back to the student.

John   Maybe you'd better try the lost and found. Sorry. [He closes the door and walks back to the blackboard.] Let's see, Carol, you said it was the side squared?
Carol   Yeah.

John adds this answer to the one he has already written on the board and then turns toward his class.

John Actually the formula for finding the area of a square is the same as finding the area of a rectangle. A square is just a special kind of rectangle. Now what about a parallelogram? [Two students, Paul and Jim, raise their hands.] Oh, come on, you know this. What is a parallelogram? Do you remember that? Karen? [No response.] Agnes? [No response. By now four more students hold their hands aloft.] Okay, Cecil, what is it?

Cecil [softly and without assurance]   It's a four-sided figure that's parallel . . . uh, no . . . that's got opposite sides that are parallel.

John Are you asking me or telling me?

Cecil That's it. It's got parallel sides.

John Good. Cecil got part of it. Besides opposite sides that are parallel, what else does a parallelogram have? [Several students blurt out answers simultaneously.]

Lucy Equal sides.

Jim The opposite angles are equal.

John Great. Now we've got it. The opposite sides are equal *and* the opposite angles are equal. Hmm . . . who could come up here and draw one on the board for us? [He surveys the room. Three students have their hands raised.] All right, Dale, you try it. [He holds out his piece of chalk and motions Dale to come up to the board. Dale gets out of his chair and begins walking to the front of the room. Just then a heavyset boy at the back of the room turns to say something to the girl behind him.] Henry, you'd better pay attention here. I might have you up here next. [Several students laugh.]

Dale takes the piece of chalk from his teacher's hand and swiftly draws a parallelogram with remarkably even parallel sides.

John Good. Thanks Dale. [Dale returns the chalk and walks back to his seat.] See, the sides are parallel . . . [He traces the sides with his right index finger.] And the opposite angles are equal . . . [He also outlines the two pair of equal angles.] Now how do we figure out the area of a figure like this? [Three students raise their hands. John ignores the students' hands and continues.] Suppose we let the base of this figure be 12 inches. [He writes this number beneath the base of the parallelogram.] And suppose we let the height be 10 inches. [He draws a dotted line from the base to the top of the figure and labels this 10 inches.] How do we figure out the area? [Three more students raise their hands. John surveys the room for a moment before deciding to call on a student whose hand is not raised.] Ron, you look like you've got the answer.

Alan He don't know nothing.

John [sharply]   All right, Alan, zip it up. Ron?

Ron [quickly]   It'd be the base times the height.

John Absolutely. [He writes this answer on the board.] It'd be the base times the height. [Pausing.] Does everyone see that? [Continuing.] Okay, now that we know how to find the area of a parallelogram, it should be easy to figure out how to find the area of a triangle. [He points to the statement "Area of triangle = " and then looks out at his students.] Who knows how to find the area of a triangle? [Four students blurt out different answers simultaneously.]

Perry Base times height.

Judy You add the sides and then take half of that.

Louis You multiply the sides.

Jim Half the base times the height.

John Attaboy, Jim. [He writes this on the board.] I don't know where you other guys got those strange answers. [Several students laugh, and two point accusing fingers at the three who gave incorrect answers.] That's enough of that; everybody makes mistakes. [Pausing.] Now we've got one more plane figure, a circle. Who remembers the formula for that?

Miriam [waving her hand excitedly] Oh I know.

John Let's see, everyone's hand should be up. [Pausing.] I think I'll call on someone whose hand is not raised. [Several more hands shoot up.] Kevin, what's the area of a circle?

Kevin But my hand is up.

John [smiling] I know.

Kevin You weren't supposed to call on me.

John I thought if you had your hand raised you'd know the answer. You wouldn't raise your hand if you didn't know the answer, would you? [Several students laugh.]

Kevin Uh, I don't know what it is.

John Well know it by next week. [To the entire class.] What's the area of a circle? [Nearly all the students blurt out something. John cups his hand to his ear as though he cannot quite make out the correct answer.] What was that? [Again the students blurt out answers.] I think I heard pi r squared, but I'm not sure what that other stuff was. [He moves a few steps and writes this final formula on the board.] What is the value of pi? Who knows that? [He turns toward the class.] Dale, what is it?

Dale Uh, 3.1416.

John Good. Everyone remember that. [He then steps back and makes a sweeping gesture to take in the five formulas he has written on the board.] You all better know these by next week. Okay? Now let's turn in our books to page 88 and find out how to figure out the volume of objects. [He picks up a text on his desk and opens it.] Who'd like to begin reading near the bottom of page 88, right where it says "the volume of objects"? [Two students raise their hands.] All right, Beth. Read to the top of page 90. [Beth reads.]

As Beth reads John walks up and down the aisles making sure that each student is following along. He stops to get a boy to turn to the correct page.

John [softly]   Page 88. You're on the wrong page.
Sherman   Oh.

John waits until he turns to the correct page and then moves on. Another boy has his book open to the correct page but appears to be staring out into space. As he passes his desk, John taps on the open book with his right index finger. With a sigh the boy begins to look down at his book. After checking each student, John returns to the front of the room. Beth continues to read. A boy at the back of the room continues to sink lower in his seat until he is able to avoid John's gaze by hiding behind the student in front of him. He places his chin on his open book and stares ahead vacantly.

John   Okay, you can stop there. So when we figure out the volume of something, we find out how much it can hold . . . what its capacity is. Uh . . . what are some things that we'd want to know the volume of? [Pointing at a student whose hand is raised.] Karen?
Karen   A box.
John   Yeah, we might want to know how much a box would hold. Ray?
Ray   What about a swimming pool?
John   Good. We'd want to know how much water it would hold. Anyone else? Yeah, Perry.
Perry   A drum. [Two students giggle.]
John   A drum?
Perry   Yeah, a drum like you'd put oil in.
John   Oh okay. Isn't that usually called a barrel?
Perry   I don't know.
John   Well you're right, we might want to know how much oil a drum would hold. [Continuing.] Any other objects we'd want to know the volume of? [No response.] Actually there are hundreds of objects that we'd want to know the capacity of. How many of you've got a silo at your place? [A few hands go up.] I'm sure your dads know the capacity of them. How many of you have helped your parents move furniture in a rental truck? [Again a few hands go up.] You've got to know how much the truck holds. [Pausing.] Now how do we measure volume? What did Beth just say? Patricia?
Patricia   You measure it in cubes.
John [chuckling]   Not quite. In cubic units. Cubic feet. Cubic inches. [Noticing Ron's hand.] Ron?
Ron   How come they measure engines in cubic inches? It's not a container.
John   Good question, Ron. Who knows the answer?
Alan   It's like how much space it takes up.
John   Exactly. So a 400-cubic-inch engine takes up a lot of space . . . and [chuckling] a lot of gas. [Pausing.] Now what is a cube? [No response.]

A cube is a solid shape with six square sides. The length, width, and height are all equal. And all the angles are what kind?
Several students in unison Right angles.
John Good. They're all right angles. Now, a cubic inch is the space occupied by a cube that is one inch long, one inch wide, and one inch high. So what is a cubic foot? [Several students blurt out the correct answer, but at different tempos.] Wait, wait. Let's just have one answer so we can all get it. Beth?
Beth It's one foot long, one foot wide, and one foot high.
John Okay. Everyone got that? [A few students nod.] Now look on page 90. The picture shows how many cubic inches there would be in a cubic foot. Everyone look. Does everyone see that there'd be 144 cubic inches in each one-inch layer of the cube? [He holds his open book to his left side and points to the illustration.] Then to fill in the cube it'd take 144 times 12, or 1,728 cubic inches. Right? [He looks at his students; a few nod to indicate that they understand.] Now there's an easier way to do this, isn't there? Instead of counting all these little one-inch cubes we could just multiply the length times the width times the height, couldn't we? [Again only a few students nod.]

John goes to the board and writes the formula $V = l \times w \times h$ in large letters. He then draws on the board a rectangular box that is six inches long, three inches wide, and four inches high.

John Now look at this rectangular box. Figure out the volume of the box. How many cubic inches would it be? [He waits for a minute while his students do the calculation.] Okay. What did you get? Helen?
Helen Seventy-two?
John Seventy-two what?
Helen Uh . . . cubic inches.
John How many of you got 72 cubic inches? [About half his students raise their hands.] Good. Just remember the formula, volume equals length times width times height. Okay? [Pausing.] All right. We've got one more formula to learn. The volume of a cylinder. [He goes to the board and draws a cylinder.] Everyone look up here. We've got a cylinder, and we want to find its volume—how much it'll hold. We do just like we did for finding the volume of a cube or a box. We take the area of the base times the height. [Pointing to the base of the cylinder.] What kind of a plane figure is the base? Cecil?
Cecil It's a circle.
John Exactly. So we just take the area of the base, or this circle, times the height. Let's write it as a formula. What would it be? [He slowly writes on the board "$V = r^2h$" and then draws a line under it.] That's all there is to it. [He places the chalk back on the chalk tray and then picks his book up off his desk. He walks around in front of his desk and sits on the edge.] All right, listen up. Here's what I want you to do for

homework. Page 91. One through 20. These are story problems, but if you set them up right, they'll be easy. I'll give you the rest of the period to work on them.

Perry We have to do all of them?

John What did I just say?

Perry I was just asking.

Alan You want us to show our work?

John Yes. I can't tell what you did wrong if you don't. It'll help if you make a little drawing for each one. Try to do that. Oh and remember to give your answer in cubic units. You're figuring out the volume for all of these.

Jim What time is it?

John Sh! Get to work. It's time to work.

Sherman [to Jim] Hey, man, quiet. I'm trying to do my work.

Henry Yeah, you guys shut up.

John All right, let's be quiet.

John notices a girl next to the window with her hand raised. He walks over to her desk to see what she wants.

John Karen, having trouble?

Karen I can't do this one.

John What don't you understand about it?

Karen I don't know what to do.

John Well read the problem. What does it ask for?

Suddenly two boys seated across from one another and about eight feet behind John begin squirming violently trying to contain their laughter. In an attempt to camouflage his laughter, one boy begins coughing loudly. Two other students nearby, a girl and a boy, turn to see what the noise is about. After a quick glance, they return to their seatwork. At this moment John turns and snaps his fingers for silence. The two culprits' clowning lessens somewhat, but neither one makes an attempt to resume work on the assignment.

Karen [reading] The body of a truck is eight feet long, 6 and one-half wide, and four feet deep. What is its capacity?

John What shape is the truck body?

Karen A cube?

John Are all the sides equal?

Karen [hesitating] No.

John Well then it can't be a cube, can it?

Karen [softly] No.

John So what shape is it?

Karen [slowly] I don't know.

John   Look, it's eight feet long, six and one-half feet wide, and four feet deep. What does that describe?

Karen   A rectangle?

John   [becoming frustrated]   No, that's a plane figure. [To the entire class.] Class, in number one, what kind of a solid is the truck body? Jim?

Jim   A rectangular solid . . . like a box.

John   Right. Right. I even drew a picture of one on the board. [He points to the drawing on the board.] That's what the truck body looks like. [To Karen.] Do you see that?

Karen   That's what I said.

John   No, you said it was a rectangle, not a rectangular solid.

Karen   Oh.

John   Now I want you to go back and read page 89 where it talks about how to find the capacity of a rectangular solid. Then see if you can work it.

John turns the page of Karen's book and points to the appropriate section. Then he steps back a couple of paces from Karen's desk and surveys the rest of the class. Apparently satisfied that everyone is working on the assignment, he walks to his desk and sits down. He opens one of his desk drawers, removes some student papers, and thumbs through. After glancing at these papers for a few seconds, he returns them to the drawer and then removes another set of papers from another drawer. After making a slow row-by-row scan of his class, he begins to grade the papers.

Nearly all John's students are working quietly now. A boy leaves his desk at the front of the room and walks back to sharpen his pencil. The two boys who had been laughing uncontrollably a minute ago work on their assignments, occasionally stopping to exchange a whispered comment. A girl in the middle of the row by the window rests her chin on her left palm and stares out the window.

For the remainder of the period, John grades papers at his desk looking up periodically. From time to time students go up to his desk to ask for help. The room is now very quiet and the voice of the world history teacher across the hall occasionally drifts into the room.

After about 15 minutes, a boy sitting near the front finishes his assignment. He matter-of-factly closes his math book and takes out a paperback book, which he begins reading. John notices that the boy is reading a book, but he allows him to continue.

About five minutes before the bell rings, the noise level gradually begins to increase as students disengage from their work. Several pupils start gathering their books and chatting softly with one another. John looks up more frequently now but does nothing to prevent the gradual escalation of noise and activity.

A few minutes later nearly every student is prepared for the bell to ring. Books piled on top of their desks and restlessly drumming their fingers or tapping their feet, they watch the red sweep second hand on the room's clock as third period draws to a close. With about 20 seconds remaining, John gets up and walks around in front of his desk.

John   Remember to finish your homework tonight if you didn't finish it in class today. And also check your work. Check your work. Everyone should get a perfect paper. There's no excuse. [The bell rings. John begins speaking in a loud voice to compete with the noise of students who immediately begin to leave.] Tomorrow we'll check your homework in class, and then we'll learn how to figure out the volume of triangular prisms. [Fading out.] See you tomorrow.

As his students leave the room, John walks back to where Mr. Swenson is seated.

John   Well that was third period.
Mr. Swenson [getting up from the student desk]   Good class.
John   Today was typical . . . some really understood and, then, a few didn't.
Mr. Swenson   Well they seemed to be pretty responsive. Like you said, they're a good group of kids.
John   Yeah, they try.
Mr. Swenson   I was wondering . . . do you have lunch right now?
John   Yes I do.
Mr. Swenson   Well I thought we could go to the faculty lunchroom and talk about what I observed. You did a lot of good things, and I want to go over those. Also I have some questions about the way you handled a few of the interactions with the kids . . . some situations you might have handled differently.
John   Okay.
Mr. Swenson   I'd also like to get more of your reactions to the class . . . what you thought went well and what didn't work out so well.
John   Great. But how do you feel it went overall?

CENTERVILLE SCHOOL DISTRICT
Teaching Observation Form

Teacher's Name: _____ **Date:** _____

Class: _____ **Period:** _____

Observed by: _____

	Poor, needs improvement	Weak	Acceptable	Very good	Excellent
1. Introduction of lesson	1	2	3	4	5
Comment:					
2. Organization of content	1	2	3	4	5
Comment:					
3. Clarity of instructional objective(s)	1	2	3	4	5
Comment:					
4. Pacing of lesson	1	2	3	4	5
Comment:					
5. Variety of activities during lesson	1	2	3	4	5
Comment:					
6. Corrective feedback given to students	1	2	3	4	5
Comment:					

(continued)

	Poor, needs improvement	Weak	Acceptable	Very good	Excellent
7. Praise and/or support given to students	1	2	3	4	5
Comment:					
8. Interaction with entire class	1	2	3	4	5
Comment:					
9. Interaction with small groups	1	2	3	4	5
Comment:					
10. Interaction with individual students	1	2	3	4	5
Comment:					
11. Monitoring of seatwork	1	2	3	4	5
Comment:					
12. Pleasant room atmosphere	1	2	3	4	5
Comment:					
13. Classroom management procedures—roll taking, etc.	1	2	3	4	5
Comment:					
14. Teacher's acceptance of individual differences	1	2	3	4	5
Comment:					
15. Overall effectiveness of lesson	1	2	3	4	5
Comment:					

Additional Comments:

QUESTIONS

1. As John spends the opening minutes of this class period taking attendance, his students for the most part sit and wait for the lesson to begin. How might John have used this time more effectively?
2. For the most part does John try to motivate his students extrinsically or intrinsically? What other motivational techniques might he have used?
3. How effectively does John use praise? What specific suggestions would you have for him?
4. Following the large-group lesson, Karen asks John for help in determining the capacity of a truck body. Critique the interaction John has with Karen. How might he have been more effective in working with Karen?
5. If you were to observe John's teaching using the Teaching Observation Form at the end of the case, how would you rate his performance? What are his overall strengths and weaknesses?
6. If you were to use a systematic observation schedule, such as Flanders' Interaction Analysis, to observe John's interactions with his students, what kind of picture would emerge about his teaching? For example, what is the ratio of pupil talk to teacher talk? What is the ratio of teacher indirect and direct behaviors? How do such interaction patterns relate to student achievement, particularly in ninth grade math? What other systematic observation instruments could be used to observe teacher-pupil interactions?
7. What kinds of classroom questions does John ask? How do his questions relate to the different levels of Bloom's Cognitive Taxonomy?
8. How well does John's teaching style take into consideration the backgrounds and characteristics of his students, especially in terms of socioeconomic status and grade level?
9. What instructional objectives does John seem to be pursuing? Could you state two or three in the form of behavioral objectives? How well do his instructional strategies fit his objectives?
10. How well does John deal with disruptions? In terms of Kounin's theory of classroom management, does John exhibit withitness? Desists? Does John respond appropriately to Paul and Cecil who enter the classroom just after the bell rings? How else might he have handled their tardiness?

CASE 7

INDIVIDUALIZED INSTRUCTION

Eric Brown is 42 years old and has been teaching general mathematics, algebra, and geometry for eight years at Westwood High School in Pleasantville, a city of about 60,000 in a midwestern state. Westwood High, with an enrollment of about 900, is one of four high schools in the city. Most of Westwood's students are either from working-class families or from farm families that live within a 20-mile radius of the city. About 90 percent of the students at Westwood are white, about 8 percent are black, and the remaining 2 percent are Hispanic.

The modern, single-story school building is situated on the northwest edge of the city and covers half a city block. On the south the school is bounded by a new housing development and on the north by a corn field. The grounds of the school are well maintained, and the school's football field and newly surfaced track are the envy of Pleasantville's three other high schools.

Today is teacher records day at Westwood. It is the last day of the first semester, and students have been given the day off. Westwood's 52 teachers are spending the day computing semester grades and planning for the second semester.

Eric is meeting with Hazel Winger and Faye Clark, the school's other two teachers of general mathematics. Hazel is in her late fifties and has been at Westwood for 17 years. Faye is 24 and in her second year at the school. The three of them are seated in a small circle at student desks in the classroom Eric and Hazel share.

Eric Hazel, I'm anxious to hear about what you learned at the district in-service last week. Something about a strategy for increasing the amount that general math students learn?

Hazel This professor from the state university claimed we can increase student learning by at least 20 percent. She really pushed the idea of individualizing instruction for basic level math students.

Faye [enthusiastically] That would be fantastic.

Hazel I've looked at the first semester test results in the three sections of general math that we teach, and I think we need to do something. The kids just aren't learning as much as they should.

Eric [seriously]   I agree. At this rate they're not going to be ready for algebra next year.

Faye   If they don't start learning this year, it's just going to be that much harder for us next year.

Eric [with some urgency]   Go ahead, Hazel, tell us what this approach involves.

Hazel   Well individualization is based on the idea that every student works at his or her own pace. The course content is broken down into separate modules or learning activity packages, and students work through them at their own rate. If each student is working individually on the skills he or she needs to work on, then the teacher is free to work with individual students who really need one-on-one help.

Eric   Does the teacher do any large-group instruction?

Hazel   Actually very little. The content is really presented by the materials not the teacher.

Faye   What does the teacher do then?

Hazel   As I said, the teacher is free to provide individual attention to students who really need it.

Eric   It sounds like the approach has some advantages, but I wonder if our students are mature enough to direct their own learning.

Faye   Yeah, I was wondering about that, too. Did the professor get into that at the in-service?

Hazel   Yes, she did. She says that students respond entirely differently if they know they're in control of their own learning. It really makes a difference if they're able to work on material that's at the right level and if they can work at their own rate.

Eric   I don't know about that . . . I'd have to see it to become convinced.

Hazel   I understand your skepticism, but she was a real believer in the kids' ability to handle it. As a matter of fact, one of the teachers at the in-service really challenged her on it. She invited him, or any of us for that matter, to visit two schools over in River Town that are using an individualized approach in all of their basic level courses.

Eric   Hmm. I've got another question. What about materials? It seems to me that this approach would depend on having the right kind of materials. We couldn't use the textbooks we're using now, could we?

Hazel   No, that would be disastrous.

Eric [continuing]   And for us to rewrite the materials into learning activity packages or modules would take more time and energy than any of us have. We've each got four other classes we need to think about.

Hazel   You're right, it wouldn't make sense for us to develop our own materials. After the in-service I asked her about that, and she said she thought our district had purchased several sets of commercially prepared individualized materials in general math. [She pauses and then continues excitedly.] Well, I did a little checking at the central office and found out that these materials are just sitting over in the bookroom at

Eastside High. They've got enough sets for us to use next semester, and nobody over there's going to use them.

Faye [gleefully] Wow, what luck!

Hazel Not only that—the central office said we could order the computer software that's available now to augment the materials.

Eric I bet John Germaine in the computer lab would help us set it up so we could bring kids in there once a week or so.

Hazel [smiling broadly] I already asked him about that. He said we could.

Eric This is great. It seems as though everything is falling into place. Maybe we ought to give individualized instruction a try.

Faye I think so too.

Hazel I was hoping you'd both feel that way.

Eric [anxiously] We've got a lot to accomplish between now and next Wednesday when the kids return. We've got to get those materials over here and get familiar with them.

Faye Plus we have to decide what kind of diagnostic test we're going to use so we know where each kid should begin.

Hazel You're right. We do have a lot to do, but I think it'll be worth it.

***

It is next Wednesday, and Eric is standing in front of the 26 ninth grade students in his third period general math class.

Eric All right, the bell rang. Everyone should be in their seats. We need to get started. We've got a lot of ground to cover this semester.

The few students who had been out of their seats, visiting with a friend, sharpening a pencil, or looking out the window, scurry to get into their seats. After a moment the room is quiet, each student waiting for the new semester to begin.

Eric [with a broad smile] Welcome back. I hope you're all rested up and ready to work. [A few students grimace in mock pain at the mention of the work that lies ahead.] Jim, you look ill. You're not getting sick on me are you? [Several students laugh.]

Jim [with mock exhaustion] Oh we worked so hard last semester, Mr. Brown, aren't you going to give us a break this semester? I don't think I could take another semester like the last one.

Eric [good naturedly] Well, Jim, this semester I am going to take your energy levels into account. [Directing his remarks to the entire class.] Each of you is going to be able to work at your own pace on the skills you need to master. [A few of the students express their approval with a little pitter of applause and excited squirming in their seats.] I have several sets of these individualized materials on basic math skills. [He puts his left hand on a bright red box on his desk. The box is titled

Foundation Mathematics: An Individualized Mastery Approach.] Also we'll be going down to the computer lab every Friday to use the software that goes with the *Foundations Mathematics* program. [Several students, excited at the prospect of using the computers, clap their hands. Two boys at the back of the room begin giggling and typing hysterically on imaginary computer keyboards.] All right, John and Frank, settle down. [Pausing.] In just a little bit I'll be giving you a diagnostic test to see where each of you should begin working with these materials.

Amy [waving her hand]   Mr. Brown, you mean everybody's going to be doing something different?

Eric   That's right, Amy. There's no sense in your working on adding fractions if you already know how, is there?

Amy [hesitantly]   No, I guess not.

Eric   That's why it's known as individualized instruction. You study only what you need to study, and you work at your own speed. [Noticing Chris at the back of the room.] Chris, what's your question?

Chris   What about grades? How can we get graded if we're all working on different stuff?

Eric [nodding his head]   That's a good question, Chris. Your grades will also be individualized. In other words, half of your grade will be based on how much you learn, the other half on how hard you work. In just a few minutes, we'll take a diagnostic test to see where each of you should begin. Then at the end of the semester, we'll take a final test that will be just like today's diagnostic test. Also halfway through the semester I'll give you my own test just to see how well you're doing. [Eric notices that Martha has a question.] Martha?

Martha   What if we get stuck and can't figure out what to do?

Eric [chuckling]   Don't forget about me. I'm here to help you learn. With this approach I can give each of you the help you need. [Pausing.] Okay we need to get started with the diagnostic test. [He picks up a set of test booklets from his desk.] Please use your own paper for this test. Don't write in the test booklets. The test begins with the material we covered last semester: addition, subtraction, multiplication, and division of whole numbers; fractions; decimals; and percentages. That part of the test should just be a review for most of you. Then the test goes over some areas we haven't covered yet: measures of distance, weight, and time; measures of lines, angles, and perimeters of plane figures; computing areas and volumes; and finally different kinds of graphs. [He moves across the front of the room, standing before each row of students as he counts out the number of booklets needed for the students in that row.] As soon as everyone has a booklet, we'll go over the directions together. You'll have until the end of the period.

***

Four weeks later Eric is seated at his desk checking a mastery quiz Amy has just completed on finding the least common denominator. She stands patiently to his left, gazing down intently as her teacher quickly skims his answer key, occasionally marking an answer incorrect with a large red X. Three other students are lined up in front of Eric's desk, fidgeting restlessly as they wait their turn.

The rest of Eric's students are intently involved in their seatwork. One student, a tall, thin boy who looks older than his classmates, leans over to ask his friend for a sheet of paper. Another student gets up and walks over to a table that holds four boxes of the *Foundation Mathematics*. He removes the lid of the box with a large number three on it, thumbs through the multicolored tabs, and then inserts a booklet titled, "Finding the Area of a Triangle." He replaces the lid and then uncovers box number two and begins thumbing through the booklets.

Eric You did pretty well, Amy. You just made the 80 percent mastery level on finding the least common denominator.

Amy [with a big smile] Oh, good, I finally made it. Which one do I do next?

Eric Well let's take a look at your progress profile for fractions. [He reaches for the thick green three-ring notebook on the corner of his desk. He finds the thumb tab with Amy's name on it and opens the notebook.] Let's see where we are here. [He thumbs through several pages of Amy's progress profile before he finds the correct one.] Okay, first let's give you 80 percent for finding the least common denominator. [He enters Amy's score of 80 percent.] Now according to your progress profile graph, you need to work on multiplying a fraction by a fraction next.

Amy [with a surprised look] I thought I already did that.

Eric No, you did skill practice A and B for multiplying a fraction by a fraction, but you didn't take the mastery quiz for that skill. See. [He turns the notebook so she can see better and points to the initials he recorded for the two skill practices.]

Amy [matter of factly] Oh I see.

Eric Why don't you go ahead then and give the mastery quiz a try. If you don't get 80 percent, then you can work on that skill this Friday in the computer lab.

Amy [with a smile] All right. Thanks, Mr. Brown. [She walks back to her desk.]

Eric [looking up at the three students who have been waiting] Wow, you guys are really stacking up here. I better get with it if I'm going to keep up with you. Let's see, Allen, I guess you're next. What are you working on?

Allen I did the mastery quiz on finding the areas of parallelograms.

Eric That's great. You're really moving right along.

***

It is a Friday afternoon six weeks later and Eric and Hazel are in their classroom. Hazel is seated behind the teacher's desk, and Eric sits in a student desk just across from her.

Eric [sighing]   I was really disappointed in how my general math kids did on my test. The highest score was 78 out of 100. The average was 65.
Hazel   You're right, that's not very good.
Eric   I just have my doubts about this individualized approach we've been using.
Hazel [somewhat defensively]   My kids seem to be doing really well with it.
Eric   Mine *seemed* to be doing well also. If I hadn't given them my own test, I probably still wouldn't know how little they're learning.
Hazel   You don't think they're learning?
Eric   Well things really seemed to start off well. The kids really seemed to like the approach. They were getting individual attention, and they liked the idea of charting their progress. [Pausing.] But the further we got into the program the more I began to doubt what was really going on.
Hazel   What do you mean?
Eric   I actually began to feel as though I wasn't teaching them anything. They were doing all these sets of problems and I was just grading them and recording their progress. It began to get harder to work one-on-one with the kids that needed it. Every time I'd look up from my desk, there'd be a line of kids waiting with stuff for me to score. To keep ahead of all this I started to tell the kids who had questions to try to figure it out themselves or wait until they could work on it in the computer lab.
Hazel [sympathetically]   I know the feeling. Individualization does require a lot of organization.
Eric   It's almost as though it transforms you from a teacher into a manager of materials and a progress monitor. The more involved you get in managing the whole thing, the more out of touch you get with what students are really doing.
Hazel [shaking her head]   But my students do seem to be enjoying the approach.
Eric   It's not that they don't enjoy individualization. I just think they're not grasping the concepts. They can pass the mastery quizzes, but they don't understand the concepts. It's like they're figuring out their own approaches to solving the problems on the practice sheets and the mastery quizzes. Then when they encounter a slightly different application of the concept—like on my test, for example—they can't work the problem.
Hazel   You may be right. That could be happening.
Eric   I even have my doubts about what we're doing in the computer lab. I think the software the kids are using is nothing more than an electronic workbook that presents drill and practice on low level skills.
Hazel   But computers really hold the interest of some of the hard-to-motivate kids, don't you think?
Eric [thoughtfully]   Well I guess for some it does, at least for awhile. I think the novelty of the computer can wear off, and it can become just as boring as a traditional workbook.

Hazel [slowly and with authentic concern] Well you've got a lot of reservations now about the individualized approach, don't you?

Eric [hesitating] I . . . I guess you're right, Hazel. In theory individualization makes sense, but it just doesn't seem to be working right for me and my students. I'm not sure what I should do now.

Hazel What do you think your options are?

Eric Well I think I've really only got two options. One, I could drop the program and maybe start using that other textbook I found in the bookroom. [Slowly.] But that doesn't really appeal to me. I think the materials we're using are basically good, and I might end up throwing out the baby with the bath water. And, two, I could try to change the way I'm individualizing in the classroom. [Pausing.] But I'm not sure how I'd do that. [Sighing.] You don't seem to have the same doubts I do, Hazel. What do you think I ought to do?

Foundation Mathematics: An Individualized Mastery Approach

PROGRESS PROFILE

Student's Name: *Amy Walker*
Skill Area: *Fractions*
Skill Practices and Mastery Quizzes Validated by: *Mr. Brown*

Mastery Skill	Practice A	Practice B	Mastery Quiz
1. Raising fractions to higher terms	E.B.	E.B.	89%
2. Reducing fractions to lower terms	E.B.	E.B.	95%
3. Changing whole numbers to fractions	E.B.	E.B.	100%
4. Finding the least common denominator	E.B.	E.B.	80%
5. Adding fractions	E.B.	E.B.	84%
6. Subtracting fractions	E.B.	E.B.	86%
7. Multiplying fractions			
8. Multiplying fractions by whole numbers	E.B.	E.B.	90%
9. Multiplying whole numbers by fractions	E.B.	E.B.	92%
10. Multiplying whole numbers by mixed numbers	E.B.	E.B.	86%
11. Multiplying a fraction by a fraction	E.B.	E.B.	
12. Multiplying mixed numbers			
13. Dividing fractions			
14. Dividing a fraction by a whole number			
15. Dividing a whole number by a fraction			
16. Dividing a fraction by a fraction			
17. Dividing mixed numbers			
18. Dividing whole numbers by mixed numbers			
19. Dividing a mixed number by a proper fraction			
20. Dividing a proper fraction by a mixed number			
21. Dividing a mixed number by a mixed number			
22. Checking division of fractions			

QUESTIONS

1. Why do you think Eric was not more successful in implementing an individualized approach in his classroom? What might he have done to make the approach more effective?

2. How effectively does Eric introduce the individualized approach to his students? How might he have introduced it even more effectively?

3. What is individualized instruction, and what are its strengths and weaknesses? What are mastery learning, programmed instruction, computer-assisted instruction (CAI), Keller's personalized system of instruction (PSI), individually guided instruction (IGE), and individually prescribed instruction (IPI)? What are the advantages and disadvantages of each?

4. How well is the individualized instruction approach used by the three general math teachers suited to the rural, working-class backgrounds of their students? What are field dependent and field independent learners? How well is individualized instruction suited to these two types of learners? What kinds of students benefit the most and which benefit the least from individualized instruction?

5. What is aptitude by treatment interaction (ATI)? How could this procedure be used to examine the impact of the individualized instruction approach upon different types of students?

6. What is criterion-referenced evaluation, and how is it being used in the individualized instruction approach? What does Eric mean when he tells Chris that half his grade will be "based on how much you learn, the other half on how hard you work"?

7. In terms of Bloom's Cognitive Taxonomy, to what levels of learning do the individualized materials and tests seem to relate? What does Eric mean when he says, "They can pass the mastery quizzes, but they don't understand the concepts"?

8. What does Eric mean when he says, "I actually began to feel as though I wasn't teaching them anything"? What are teaching and learning? How much interaction do students need with their teachers and peers? How can teachers reduce the manager or record-keeper role? What is the most effective role a teacher can play when using individualized instruction? Are there changes that the three teachers can make to improve the individualized instruction approach?

CASE 8

MAKING THE GRADE

Bixby High School is located in a small southern city of approximately 15,000 people. The building is relatively old but well kept and well equipped. BHS serves a 75 percent white and 25 percent black population, and approximately 60 percent of its graduating seniors enter college each year. The dropout rate is only about 25 percent even though Bixby does not have a large or well-developed vocational education program.

Jan Newell is a 21-year-old graduate of a nearby small teachers college who is beginning her first year of teaching. As a social studies teacher, she has been assigned to teach three sections of U.S. history, two sections of world history, and a study hall. It is the Friday before classes are scheduled to begin, and Jan is meeting with Frank Conway, the head of the social studies department, in Frank's classroom. Jan and Frank sit in chairs facing one another in front of Frank's desk.

Frank Well are you all set for Monday, Jan?
Jan [smiling] As ready as I'm going to be, I guess, Frank. I do have a few things I'd like to go over with you though.
Frank Fire away!
Jan Well I'm starting to get together my first exams and quizzes, and I find myself wondering about Bixby's grading policies. I notice that the report card says that 95–100 is an A, 88–94 is a B, 77–87 is a C, and 70–76 is a D. Does everyone follow that system?
Frank [frowning] Well you know, Jan, we place a strong emphasis on preparing our kids for college. There is no official, required grading system, but a teachers' committee did agree on those standards a number of years back. And almost all the teachers use those standards.
Jan [frowning] Does everyone grade on a curve?
Frank I think it's safe to say that practically everyone in the academic areas like English, math, and our own department does.
Jan Testing and grading is one aspect of teaching that really concerns me, Frank. They always taught us in teachers college that learning is what education is all about. And from having been a student myself for so many years I know that the way you evaluate seems to affect learning more than almost any other single thing.

111

Frank I agree that the way you grade makes a big difference. A poor grading system can undo good teaching faster than anything I know. It can make or break your teaching.

Jan [with animation] And grading on a curve especially bothers me. That means you have winners and losers instead of taking each child where he is and moving him along as far as he can go. Once some kids finish at the bottom of the curve a few times, they seem to get struck there and give up.

Frank Fortunately or unfortunately, Jan, that's the American way. Our society and our colleges are based on competition, and that means winners and losers. One of the lessons of life is to learn to deal with failure and to overcome it. They have to learn it sometime.

Jan [frowning] Well could you explain a little of the nitty-gritty in using the grading standard? For example what do you do to take into consideration the fact that some tests turn out to be more difficult than others no matter how hard you try!

Frank [smiling] First off, practically all of us in social studies, especially in history classes, use objective tests—mostly multiple choice, matching, and fill in the blank. That eliminates a lot of arguments with both the students and their parents. And dealing with test difficulty differences is pretty easy. Just curve the grades and feed them back into the standard. Do you know what I mean?

Jan I think so. In other words, if a test is real difficult and the top grade is say, 80, then just add so many points to every grade to change the distribution to the school's standards.

Frank That's it exactly! I think you're going to do just fine, Jan! And I don't want to make the grading system here seem too rigid either. For example there's no reason why you can't experiment a bit. Trying out new ideas is what being a beginning teacher is all about.

Jan Thanks for the advice, Frank. Now there are one or two other things I wanted to ask you about . . .

***

It is the following Monday and Jan meets her second period U.S. history class for the first time. She explains her grading system to the class.

Jan I know that you are wondering what your grades will be based on. I plan to give you a quiz each week, usually 10 items, and a large unit exam at the end of each unit. All these tests will be objective, and the big unit exams will have anywhere from 75 to 100 items on them. Yes, you're Beth, right?

Beth Yes, Miss Newell. Will the quizzes be "pop" quizzes?

Jan No, they'll be announced in advance. I may have them on Fridays. I haven't decided yet. [Pause.] Now besides the tests there will be group projects and individual reports that will be graded. For example, our first unit is on the Age of Discovery. We'll get into the European background that led to the discovery of the New World. Some of you may want to do reports on different explorers, such as Ferdinand Magellan and John Cabot. When I grade your reports I'll be looking to see if you carefully follow the reporting format that I give you. Yes, Jerry?

Jerry What kinds of group projects will we do?

Jan I was just coming to that, Jerry. I'll put you in small groups of five to six people and you'll get to meet in class at least one day each week—probably Friday after the weekly quiz. One group might want to construct a model ship like the one Magellan or Columbus used. Another group might want to get into the food and clothing that people used at that time—or even the medicine and health care. Yes, Beth?

Beth How will you grade the group projects?

Jan [laughing] Very subjectively, I'm afraid! I'll be looking at your originality and how much work you put into it mostly. Also how well you present what you have done to the class. Of course everyone in the group will receive whatever grade the group project earns. Yes, Bill?

Bill How much will these different things count?

Jan I haven't decided that yet. I'll let you know. I guess the exam and quizzes have to count the most. Then I'll probably give more weight to the individual reports than to the group projects. We'll see. Now let's get into the first unit . . .

***

It is three weeks later, and Jan is returning the exams for the first unit test to her second period U.S. history class. The test was very difficult, and Jan had to transform the distribution to fit the school's grading standards by adding 13 points to everyone's score.

Jan Does everyone have his or her paper? [Pause.] Now if you'll look at your score in the upper right-hand corner, you'll notice where I subtracted the number you missed from 100 and then I added 13 points onto the remainder. That's because the highest score was only 87. By adding on the 13 points, I made the scores fit the school's grading standard that's printed on the report cards. We didn't do very well on the unit exam, and I must admit I am somewhat surprised and disappointed. The test may have been a little difficult, but I also have a feeling that some of us didn't study as hard as we might have or else we didn't study the right way. Now that you've had one of my big tests and know what to expect, perhaps we'll do better on the next one. Yes, Bill?

Bill [pointing at the distribution on the blackboard] How come there were only three A's?

Jan As I said, Bill, I converted the scores to the school's grading standard where 95–100 is an A. Therefore a score of 81 would be a 94 when you add on the 13 points and a high B.

Bill [without raising his hand] That doesn't seem fair! This was a hard test, and there were only four scores in the 80's. Why shouldn't all the 80's have been A's? Why do you have to use the school standard all the time? What makes it so sacred?

Beth [with emotion and without raising her hand]   I agree with Bill even though I made one of the A's. Miss Carter, my English teacher, doesn't pay any attention to the school's system. She uses 90–100 for an A, 80–89 for a B—

Jan [interrupting vigorously]   All right, people! Settle down! [Pause.] Now I don't know what other teachers do, but in here we're going to follow the school's standards. Unfortunately, Bill, you have to draw the line somewhere to divide the A's from the B's, and your score happened to fall on the wrong side of the line. I remember watching a championship basketball game on T.V. last season where one team beat the other by one point. Because of that one point one team, Indiana I think, became national champion, and the other team finished second.

Bill [without raising his hand]   That's sports and this is school. I don't think it's the same thing at all! This is the first B I have ever received on a big test, and I studied hard!

Jan   Bill, I'm sure we'll all do better on the next unit exam, and don't forget that you have individual reports and group projects that can get your grade over the A level—especially when you are only one point from an A. [With strong emphasis.] Let me remind all of you that I didn't have to add 13 points onto your papers. I could have let the scores stand as they were, and then the highest grade would have been a B. An 81 [looking at Bill] would have been a C. Let's all learn from this and do better next time. Now let's go over the test items one at a time and answer any questions you might have about them.

***

Two days later Jan is talking to Frank Conway in his room after school.

Frank   Are you having grading problems in all your classes, Jan?

Jan   To some extent, yes. The kids are constantly complaining about their grades, but my second period U.S. history class is the worst by far. There are two students in there, Bill Nelson and Beth Clark, who really get upset if they don't get an A every time.

Frank   I'd say that's partly due to pressure from home. You know who they are, don't you?

Jan   Well not really. I—

Frank   Bill's father is on the school board and Beth's mother is an elementary principal in this school district.

Jan   Boy I didn't realize that. I—

Frank   Jan, can I make a suggestion?

Jan   Why, of course, Frank, that's why—

Frank   Jan, I know that I emphasized following the school's grading policy to you, but don't feel like you have to follow it slavishly. Grading is just a tool, a means of expressing how much students have learned. Please understand that I'm not talking about you individually now, but teachers often hide behind their grading scheme to protect themselves from criticism. The result is the tail begins to wag the dog. Grades become more important than learning. [Pause.] My suggestion to you is that you loosen up a bit with your grading. You can generally follow the school's grading policy, but adapt it in ways that make the most sense in terms of student learning. Be flexible. [Pause.] Also, in terms of what you've told me, perhaps you could make your tests a little less demanding and place a little more weight on your group and individual projects. Any time you see good students like Bill and Beth fall down in their grades even though they are working hard, you need to look hard at your grading system and consider how you might revise it.

Jan [weakly and with a stunned expression] Well okay, Frank. I see what you mean. Learning is certainly more important than grades.

***

It is three weeks later and report card day at Bixby High School. The students receive their report cards in homeroom and carry them to each class. Each teacher collects the cards and puts on the grades during a portion of the class period and then returns the cards to the students before the end of the period. Second period has just ended, and Bill Nelson, Beth Clark, and three other students are standing outside Jan Newell's classroom in the hallway comparing their report cards.

Jack Well, Bill, I see you got all A's again. Must be nice having your old man on the school board.

Bill Yeah, well, that's got nothing to do with it! You just don't know talent when you see it!

Beth I see you got an A in U.S. history too. Practically all the people I talked to got an A or a B.

Bill Yes, old Newell really changed! She started out tough, but then she seemed to get easy. I really like U.S. history now! She makes it interesting! [Beth and Jerry agree in unison.]

Jack U.S. history?! Interesting?!

Bill Yes, my man, interesting! I'd say it's my favorite class now. She's always got something new and different happening in there—a regular zoo!

Beth It isn't real clear what you are supposed to do to get an A, but if you work and pay attention practically everybody gets one. It's like you don't have to worry about grades in there if you work.

Bill Yes, and I really like this thing she added about letting you grade yourself.

Jack Grade yourself?!

Bill Yeah, and then she sits down with you at the end of the grading period and you sort of negotiate the grade you get. Of course as bright and good-looking as I am—[Bell rings to begin next period.] Oh boy! You guys are going to make me late to class!

***

Three days later after her last class Jan enters the office of Mary Smiley, the building principal.

Jan Did you want to see me, Mrs. Smiley?

Mary [smiling and motioning to Jan to take a seat] Yes, Jan, I do. [Short pause.] A problem has come up that I need to talk to you about. Several teachers have come to me about the way that you are grading your students.

Jan [stunned] My grades! Why?

Mary Well, Jan, Frank Conway tells me that he explained to you our school's grading policy. We don't expect teachers to follow it rigidly, but problems do develop when teachers deviate from it too far.

Jan [with surprise] Frank told you I wasn't following the school's grading policy?

Mary No, Jan. Several parents have called certain teachers accusing them of grading too hard. Some of them have even called the guidance counselors asking that their children be transferred to your class. Some of the teachers came to me to complain about your easy grading.

Jan [struggling for control] Mrs. Smiley, you can't believe what I've been through on grading! First I was accused of being too tough of a grader, and now I'm being told I'm too easy! I've tried to work with Frank Conway on this all along—

Mary Yes, Jan, I know that you have. Grades are one of the toughest things that beginning teachers have to learn to deal with. [Smiling.] Let's work this out together, shall we?

Jan Of course, Mrs. Smiley, I'd appreciate any guidance you can give. All I want is to be the best teacher I can be. I just don't know if it can be done!

Mary You mean become a good teacher?

Jan No. I mean develop a grading system that's not too tough or too easy, that motivates my students to learn, and that keeps my fellow teachers happy! I'm not sure it can be done, Mrs. Smiley!

Distribution of Scores in Miss Newell's Second Period U.S. History Class: Unit 1 Exam

(100 Points Possible)

87	(Beth's score)
86	A
85	
81	(Bill's score)
78	
77	B
76	
75	
74	
73	
73	
73	
73	C
65	
65	
65	
65	
65	
64	
63	
62	
62	D
62	
58	
58	
56	
54	E
52	
48	
36	
31	
28	
26	
14	
12	
8	

QUESTIONS

1. In grading group projects, should a teacher give everyone in the group the same grade or assign different grades on the basis of how much each student contributed to the group's effort?
2. Evaluate Bixby High's grading scale. Is it fair? Should it be applied in all subject areas and with all types of students?
3. What is the purpose of grading? How can a teacher make the best educational use of grading in the classroom?
4. Are there any conditions under which students should be allowed to grade themselves? Explain your answer. Are there any conditions under which students might have input in determining their classmates' grades?
5. What is your opinion about contract grading, that is, when students make a contract with the teacher regarding the requirements to be met for a particular grade?
6. Examine the distribution of scores for the unit I exam that Jan gave her students. How would you assign grades to her students?
7. What is norm-referenced evaluation, and what are its strong and weak points compared to criterion-referenced evaluation? What does "grading on a curve" mean? What are standard scores, and how can they be used to grade on a curve? Should a teacher grade on a curve in some classes and not in others?
8. How important is it for students to experience competition and failure? From a developmental standpoint, how much failure should a student face and at what age? If failure is viewed as punishment from an operant conditioning standpoint, what are the possible effects of punishment in the form of grades on student behavior?
9. What are objectivity and subjectivity in scoring? What are the relative merits of objective and essay type tests? How do they differ in terms of their ability to measure learning at the different levels of Bloom's Cognitive Taxonomy?
10. What are the most effective ways to report student progress to parents? How effective are parent conferences? Should parents be involved in both formative and summative evaluation? How frequently should they be involved?
11. How desirable is it to have a school and/or school systemwide grading standards? How much latitude should teachers be given as professionals to set their own individual grading standards? How much commonality needs to exist among teachers?
12. In Jan's case does giving higher grades than other teachers mean she is an easier grader, or do her stimulating teaching procedures result in higher grades? What can a teacher do to keep grades from becom-

ing more important than learning? What are the best ways of dealing with high need achievers like Bill and Beth?

13. From a motivational point of view, what has Jan done to make her class more interesting? If, from an operant conditioning perspective, Jan's grades are viewed as reinforcers, what behavior change has Jan produced and how?

CASE 9

WHAT IF THEY CAN'T READ?

Victor Burns, a 35-year-old social studies teacher, has taught at Gulf Coast High School for seven years. Gulf Coast is located in a small coastal town in a southwestern state. The school has an enrollment of about 900 students, two-thirds of whom are from low-income families. Seventy percent of the students at GCHS are white; 20 percent Hispanic; 7 percent black; and three percent Vietnamese.

The attendance of many GCHS students is irregular due to the fact that about one-third have parents who are migrant farm workers, while another one-fourth have parents who are involved in the Gulf Coast shrimp industry. GCHS administrators and teachers therefore work closely with the state's Department of Health and Rehabilitative Services to ensure that the educational needs of these students are met.

GCHS teachers also face a challenge in the language abilities of their students. About 20 percent have been classified as limited-English–speaking and another five percent as non-English–speaking. To address the special needs of these students, the school has one English as a second language (ESL) teacher who teaches three classes and acts as a resource person for regular classroom teachers.

On an unusually warm October day, Victor and Helen Watkins, another social studies teacher, are sitting in Victor's classroom at the end of the day discussing the reading abilities of their students.

Victor I've been here seven years, and I don't think I've ever seen so many reading problems. I mean usually it's one or two kids per class that have problems with the text. But this year it seems like half my students can't read the book!

Helen [with sympathy] I've noticed the same thing, Vic. It seems to be getting worse.

Victor [with a long sigh] Take my fifth period world history class. That's probably the worst. They're a good bunch of kids. I don't have any discipline problems really. But how can I teach if my kids can't read? [He shrugs his shoulders.] So what I end up doing is lecturing the entire period, telling them what the book says. They're ninth graders, and their reading levels range from the third grade to about the seventh or eighth.

Helen [nodding her head] Hmm. Right.

Victor I have a degree that says I can teach history not reading. [Becoming more emotional.] I had one reading course as an undergraduate. Is that supposed to make me a qualified reading teacher? No. I'd be the first one to admit it.

Helen Well maybe the workshop we're having next month with the reading specialist will give us some ideas.

Victor I hope it does. But I don't know. How much difference can one three-hour workshop make? We really need to have a full-time reading specialist at the school.

Helen Now, Vic, you know the chances of getting a reading specialist assigned to GCHS are about zero.

Victor Maybe so, but I don't see why the district can fund some things and not others. I think it's all politics anyway.

Helen Yes, but—

Victor [interrupting] I'm going to talk to the principal about it. We'll never get a reading specialist unless we ask and put some pressure on.

***

Three days later Victor is visiting with Mr. Henderson, the principal of GCHS. The door to Mr. Henderson's office is closed. Mr. Henderson is seated behind his desk, and Victor sits in a chair in front of the desk.

Victor [with emphasis] How can we teach if the kids can't read? I know I'm speaking for all of the social studies teachers when I say we *desperately* need a reading specialist here.

Mr. Henderson I'm glad that you and the others recognize the importance of reading, Vic. I've always felt that every teacher needs to be a teacher of reading.

Victor But that's just it, Mr. Henderson. We're *not* reading teachers! We teach world history, American history, and geography, not reading.

Mr. Henderson [somewhat testily] I understand that. What I mean is you should stress basic reading skills *while* you teach your content. You stress vocabulary, reading for the main idea, and outlining and skimming, don't you?

Victor Well, yes.

Mr. Henderson Then you *are* teaching reading. Every teacher has to do that.

Victor I agree with you, but the reading problems this year seem to be worse than ever. It's really overwhelming. In my fifth period world history class, for example, at least half the kids can't read the book. We simply need a full-time reading specialist!

Mr. Henderson I understand your frustration, Vic, but the district couldn't even come close to funding a position. We're lucky we've got an ESL teacher.

Victor Something's got to be done though. We've got the state assessment tests coming up in March, and the tests are based on textbooks half our kids can't read. We really need some help!

Mr. Henderson You're forgetting that we have the reading-in-the-content-areas workshop coming up next month. That's one of the topics you teachers voted to have a workshop on.

Victor [solemnly] I know. I just wish we could get more than a one-shot workshop. You don't think there's *any* chance we could get a reading specialist assigned to the school?

Mr. Henderson I'm sorry, Victor. I've seen the district budget through next year, and it's really tight. Maybe the year after that. Until then we'll have to do the best we can.

***

Several weeks later Victor and Helen are in the social studies office enjoying a cup of coffee 20 minutes before the start of first period. The room is small, barely large enough to hold the two desks Victor and Helen are seated at. Beneath the only window in the room is a work table on which sits a ditto machine and a large electric coffee pot. The top three shelves of a large metal bookcase to the left of the door hold the department's collection of social studies textbooks and curriculum guides. The bottom three shelves are filled with ditto paper, cans of ditto fluid, and miscellaneous office supplies.

The door opens and Karen Sanders, another social studies teacher, enters. She puts her books on Helen's desk and then sits on the end of the work table.

Victor Karen, we missed you yesterday at the workshop.

Karen Jamie had a fever of 102, and I had to take him to the doctor. But he was fine this morning. You know how kids that age bounce back. [Pausing.] I hated to miss the workshop. How was it?

Helen Well this presenter from the university gave us a lot of materials.

Victor She spent most of the time showing us how to prepare different kinds of study guides for the kids to use.

Helen I think she had some good ideas.

Victor [tilting his chair back] You're not going to believe this, but I stayed up past midnight last night making study guides for my fifth period world history.

Helen and Karen in unison Wow!

Victor Here, take a look at these. [He removes several pages from a foot-high stack of dittoed papers. Helen scoots her chair close to Victor, while Karen hops down from the work table and walks over to Victor's desk.]

Karen [looking down at the pages Victor holds] You've been busy.

Victor I've got three kinds of study guides for the chapter we're starting on Roman civilization. First I made this overview guide. [He holds up a page with two paragraphs on it.] I summarized the chapter in two paragraphs. We'll read this and discuss it before they actually start to read the chapter.

Karen That sounds like a good idea.

Victor Then I made a vocabulary guide with all the key words. [Holding up a two-page handout and pointing as he continues.] See, I've got the new word, a definition, the page where it first appears, and then a sentence in which the word is used. [He reads several of the vocabulary words on the handout.] Plebeian. Tribune. Republic. Patrician.

Karen I like that too.

Victor This last guide we learned how to make is called a learning-from-text guide. [He shows Helen and Karen his third handout.] Kids fill this out as they read the assignment. See, I've got questions plus the page numbers and paragraphs where the answers can be found.

Helen [with excitement] Maybe these study guides might be the answer we've been looking for!

Victor Well I'm going to start using them today. I'll let you know how they work.

***

Later that same day Victor is teaching his fifth period world history class. He stands in front of a world map on the side wall of his classroom. Twenty-six ninth graders are seated at moveable desks arranged in a large circle.

Victor Okay does everyone have a copy of the overview study guide? [He holds his copy aloft as several students nod their heads.] The overview guide is to give you an idea of what chapter four, "The Rise and Fall of Rome," is all about. This chapter tells us how the city of Rome grew and conquered an empire that stretched from Spain on the west to the Caspian Sea on the east. [He sweeps his right hand across the map to indicate the approximate size of the Roman Empire.] And who knows what happened to the Roman Empire? Where is it today? [Noticing Juan's raised hand.] Juan?

Juan It collapsed—just fell apart.

Victor Exactly. So what we're going to read about is the fantastic story of Rome. Who would like to begin reading from the study guide, just the first short paragraph. [Harold is first to raise his hand.] Harold, would you start?

Harold [slowly and with moderate difficulty] At the start of the fifth . . . uh . . . century, Rome was a small . . . [He stops at the next word.]

Victor [encouragingly] Italian . . . Italian town.

Harold [continuing] Italian town. During the next several centuries, the Roman Empire became even more powerful . . . uh . . . [correcting himself] larger and more powerful than Alexander the Great's empire. The Romans were great . . . What's that?

Victor Sculptors.

Harold Sculptors and . . .

Victor Architects.

Harold And architects and . . .

Victor Philosophers.

Harold And philosophers. The Roman civi . . . [slowly] civilization was known for its system of laws based on the will of the people.

Victor All right. Who'd like to read the next paragraph? [Sheila raises her hand.] Sheila, would you read then?

Sheila [also reading with difficulty] The greatest Roman leader was . . . what's that name?

Victor [slowly] Julius Caesar.

Sheila [haltingly] Julius Caesar. He was commander of all the Roman . . .

Victor Legions. Those were the Roman armies.

Sheila Legions. The Roman sentence . . . uh, senate tried to get . . . What's his name?

Victor Caesar.

Sheila Caesar to give up command of his army. Instead Caesar marched on Rome and a civil war began. Caesar defeated the senate's armies and became the leader of the Roman Empire. He was a wise and just ruler who fought cor . . . [She stops.]

Victor Corruption.

Sheila Corruption and tried to improve life for all Romans. On March 15, 44 B.C., however, he was . . . [She stops again.]

Victor Assassinated. He was murdered.

Sheila He was assassinated.

Victor Okay. Thank you Sheila. That was a very quick overview of what Chapter 4 is about. Now I have another kind of study guide here. [He hands a set of the vocabulary guides to the nearest student.] Here, John, take one and pass the rest on. [He waits while the vocabulary guides are being passed around.] Does everyone have one? [A few students nod their heads.] Now this guide has all the key vocabulary words from Chapter 4 on it. [He holds his copy up and points to the first page.] See, it gives you the new word and a short definition for the word. Then it also gives you the page number in the chapter where the word first appears. And the last thing it gives you is the sentence where the word is used. We've got 32 vocabulary words in Chapter 4. Let's go through the guide and pronounce each one of them. I'll pronounce the word first, and then you repeat it after me. Okay? [A few students nod their heads.] Republic.

Class in unison Republic.

Victor Patrician.

Class Patrician.

Victor Plebeian.
Class Plebeian.

Victor continues pronouncing the words and his students repeat after him. By the time Victor gets to the end of the list, his students are repeating the words with energy.

Victor Okay. Good. Keep this list and use it as you read the chapter. Now I've got one more kind of study guide to help you. [He hands a stack of the learning-from-text guides to a student.] Take one and pass the rest. This study guide has several questions based on Chapter 4. For each question you also have the page and the paragraph number where you can find the correct answer.

Victor waits until all his students have a copy of the study guide before he continues. As the papers are being circulated, he walks to the front of the room and sits on the edge of his desk.

Victor Everyone take a look at the first question. [He reads the question slowly.] It says, "What two groups of people influenced the early Romans?" Then it tells you the answer is on page 57, the first paragraph. So let's look that one up. Who can find it? [Calling on Sharon.] Sharon?
Sharon [reading slowly from her book] The early Romans were influenced by two peoples who had settled in the Italian . . . [She hesitates.]
Victor Peninsula.
Sharon Peninsula—the Greeks and the . . . [She stops this time.]
Victor That's Etruscans.
Sharon [very slowly] Etruscans.
Victor Okay. There's the answer—the Greeks and the Etruscans. Now I want you to begin reading chapter four and filling out the study guide. I want you to fill out the guide as you read the chapter. But be sure to read the chapter. Don't just answer the questions. I'll come around to see how each of you is doing.

***

It is three weeks later, and Victor, Helen, and Karen are having their morning coffee in the social studies office.

Karen So tell us, Vic, how's it been going with the study guides? [Chuckling.] I don't believe I've ever seen anyone run off so many materials on the ditto machine. You're going to burn this thing up! [She gives the ditto machine next to her a tender pat.]
Victor [glumly] I'm about ready to give it up. I've been killing myself writing these study guides! [Pausing.] I'm beginning to think it doesn't make any difference.

Helen Are you sure they're not helping the kids?

Victor Well I gave them a unit test this Monday, and the grades weren't any better than they were before I started writing all these study guides. Oh I think they might be helping a few of the kids, but just a few. Most of the kids have just as much trouble reading the guides as they do the book. I just feel like I'm creating a lot of work for myself. What about you, Helen. Did you try the study guides?

Helen I put together one set that I tried out in my American history classes. [She shakes her head.] Like you, I didn't think they made that much difference. And frankly they take a lot of time to write. If I'm going to spend that much time on something, I want to see a bigger payoff.

Victor Exactly. [With frustration.] I don't know what to do. The only thing I can think of is rewriting the book, but that doesn't make much sense. I don't know. What do you do when the kids can't read the book?

GULF COAST HIGH SCHOOL

Class: Ninth grade world history
Teacher: Victor Burns
Period: Fifth

Name	Eighth Grade Percentile	Reading* Stanine	Reading Comprehension**	Vocabulary Grade Equivalent
1. Andrews, John	33	4	5.7	5.9
2. Arciero, Tony	4	1	3.2	3.3
3. Azar, Juan	15	3	4.7	4.8
4. Baber, Sharon	55	6	7.9	8.1
5. Bailey, Heather	29	4	5.4	5.5
6. Becker, Jill	42	5	5.7	5.7
7. Booth, Jane	5	1	3.4	3.6
8. Bowen, Harold	9	2	4.0	4.1
9. Burrows, Sheila	18	3	4.8	5.0
10. Colton, John	19	3	4.8	5.2
11. Diaz, Ernesto	11	2	4.5	4.6
12. Dill, Scott	30	4	5.1	5.2
13. Espitia, Enrique	27	4	4.9	5.0
14. Fan, Kuo-Chin	49	5	7.7	7.8
15. Fernandez, Carlos	30	4	5.2	5.2
16. Foster, Amy	36	4	5.3	5.7
17. Gilbert, Kim	24	3	4.8	4.9
18. Gutierrez, Jose	29	4	4.9	5.2
19. Kee, Chang	51	5	7.8	7.9
20. Kerr, Brian	28	3	5.2	5.3
21. Lawson, Buck	5	1	3.5	3.6
22. Mercer, Cecil	10	2	4.4	4.8
23. Nguyen, Thuy	39	4	5.9	6.0
24. Platt, Karen	35	4	5.4	5.4
25. Sanchez, Dolores	43	5	6.0	6.0
26. Wilson, Tommy	28	4	5.0	5.1

SOURCE: *Eighth grade *Metropolitan Achievement Test.*
**Decimal scores refer to months, e.g., 7.8 = seventh year, eighth month.

QUESTIONS

1. What special techniques should teachers employ in order to be more effective in working with limited-English–speaking students? With non-English–speaking students?
2. Do you agree with Mr. Henderson that "every teacher needs to be a teacher of reading?" Why or why not?
3. What can a teacher do when students are unable to read the text?
4. What pupil characteristics are related to success in reading?
5. What are the pros and cons of encouraging a student to use his or her special language or dialect? How can this best be done in the school?
6. Should every secondary teacher be a reading teacher as well as a subject-matter specialist? What role could a reading specialist play at Gulf Coast High School that an ESL teacher could not play? Is high school too late to begin working with students like those at GCHS on reading?
7. How could Victor have taken advantage of the cognitive theory of David Ausubel in designing his overview guide? How could he have taken advantage of Robert Gagne's seven types of learning in developing his vocabulary guide and learning-from-text guide?
8. What interpretation can be made of the data presented at the end of the case on the reading abilities of Victor's fifth period class? What are percentiles and stanines? What is a grade equivalent? What are reading comprehension and vocabulary?
9. Should all students be made to learn standard English regardless of their racial or ethnic origin? How can this be done without destroying students' native language competency, their self-image, or their cultural identity? When such students constantly make errors in reading, speaking, and writing English, what are the best procedures for a teacher to use for correcting the errors?

PART IV

GROUP MOTIVATION AND DISCIPLINE CASES

CASE 10

FRACTIONS AND INTERACTIONS

Sherry Anderson is 28 and in her fourth year of teaching mathematics at a junior high school located in a small community in a southwestern state. About half the school's 850 students are from families that are involved in farming or ranching; the other half from families that live in the community of less than 8,000.

It is 3:30 on a Monday afternoon, and Mrs. Anderson has just entered the office to sign out for the day. Arnold Grimes, the school's principal for the last eight years, stands behind the counter, greeting teachers as they sign out. He is handsome and in his late fifties.

Mr. Grimes Hello, Sherry. How'd it go today?
Mrs. Anderson Pretty well, Mr. Grimes. You know how Mondays can be.
Mr. Grimes [sympathetically] Right. [Pausing.] Say, Sherry, do you have a minute? I'd like to set up a time for me to observe one of your classes next week.
Mrs. Anderson [somewhat uneasily] Oh, it's that time already?
Mr. Grimes Well I need to observe everyone at least twice this year, so I better get started next week. [He removes a small appointment book from the inside pocket of his sports coat.] What would be a good time for you?
Mrs. Anderson Hmm. How about fourth period? I've got a seventh grade general math class then.
Mr. Grimes Good. What day would be best?
Mrs. Anderson How about Wednesday?
Mr. Grimes [looking at his appointment book] Wednesday'd be fine. [He writes her name and the time in his appointment book.]
Mrs. Anderson Is there any kind of lesson you'd like to see?
Mr. Grimes [chuckling] No, Sherry, just business as usual. Of course I'll be interested in the interactions between you and your students. I'm using a slightly different observation form this year.
Mrs. Anderson Oh well, they're not hesitant to interact. You'll see a lot of that.
Mr. Grimes Good. I look forward to my visit.

***

It is Wednesday of next week and the bell signaling the end of third period has just rung. As soon as Mrs. Anderson's third period students begin to stream out into the hallway, Mr. Grimes, who had been standing just outside the door, enters and walks to the back of the room. He selects a student desk seat and pulls it into a far corner. After sitting down he removes an observation form from a manila folder and, in pencil, begins to enter information, such as the date, teacher's name, and the subject. When finished he looks up and begins his observation.

Mrs. Anderson is seated at her desk arranging the dittoed handouts she plans to use this period and checking her record book. It is 10:26, two minutes before the bell that marks the start of fourth period will ring. Fourteen students are already in their seats arranging their books and materials. Occasionally some of them turn to look at Mr. Grimes. Two girls stand near the pencil sharpener talking with one another. Two boys pause for a moment in the doorway surveying Mrs. Anderson's classroom before they turn and dart off down the hallway. In spite of the random individual activity and the fairly high noise level in the room, Mrs. Anderson continues to work at her desk. A girl enters the room and stops at Mrs. Anderson's desk before taking her seat.

Girl   What are we going to do today?
Mrs. Anderson [looking up]   We'll get started in just a moment. [This response seems to satisfy the girl, and she walks back to her desk.]

Students continue to file into the room. At 10:28 the bell rings. Mrs. Anderson looks up and surveys her class. Twenty students are in their seats. Several of them are just sitting looking around the room. Two students are lined up at the pencil sharpener. Another three students are walking toward their desks. A boy suddenly leaps up and runs to the pencil sharpener.

Boy [to the other two students at the pencil sharpener]   Come on, hurry up! [The girl at the pencil sharpener turns and gives the boy a sneer.]
Girl [angrily]   Just wait your turn! [She casts a quick glance at Mr. Grimes.]
Mrs. Anderson [noticing the students at the pencil sharpener]   Hurry up back there. We need to get started.

This warning seems to have little effect on the students who continue to talk. Mrs. Anderson turns to a girl seated just in front of her desk.

Mrs. Anderson   Pam, would you give each person one of these worksheets? [She holds out the set of papers.]
Pam   Okay, Mrs. Anderson. [She gets up and takes the worksheets.]

Mrs. Anderson continues to work in her record book, looking up every 15 seconds or so to see how many of her students are present and in their seats. The two boys who appeared momentarily in the doorway minutes earlier now reenter the room and, as if to acknowledge their lateness, begin to tiptoe to their desks. When they see Mr. Grimes, however, they stop tiptoeing and quickly take their seats. Pam continues to move up and down the five rows of desks passing out worksheets and pausing every now and then to say something to a fellow student.

At 10:31 Mrs. Anderson opens her record book to the page with her fourth period roster. Pointing at the names with a ballpoint pen held in her right hand, she scans the list.

Mrs. Anderson   Amy? Does anyone know anything about Amy?
Alice   She's still out. I think she's got the flu.
Mrs. Anderson   Okay. [Continuing to scan the roster.] What about Ralph? He was out yesterday, wasn't he?
David [from the back]   Yeah, he ain't here.
Mrs. Anderson   All right. [Continuing.] Harold not here?
Harold [from the pencil sharpener]   Hey, I'm over here! I ain't absent.
Mrs. Anderson   Well that's what happens when you're not in your seat. [She takes a book from the top of her desk and holds it aloft.] Did anyone leave this book in here? I found it after class yesterday.
Dick [calling out]   What's the name of it?
Mrs. Anderson   Let's see. *The Red Badge of Courage.* It's from the library. [Opening the cover.] It's overdue. Due November tenth. [No one claims the book, so Mrs. Anderson places it back on her desk.]

At 10:33 Mrs. Anderson gets up and walks over to the door and closes it. She then walks back to her desk and stands in front of it.

Mrs. Anderson   Okay. Let's get started, class. I've given each of you a worksheet on adding fractions. You've got 25 addition problems. I've checked your papers from yesterday, and I wasn't too pleased.
Several students in unison   Ohhh. Nooo.
Mrs. Anderson   It seems like we don't understand fractions. But maybe we'll do better today.
Billy [calling out]   Are we gonna get our papers back?
Mrs. Anderson   I'll return them later. [Pausing.] Open your books to page 39, and let's go over some of this again. [She takes her book from her desk and opens it to page 39.] Look at the sample problem at the top of the page: $\frac{1}{2} + \frac{1}{2}$. Why is that equal to $\frac{2}{2}$ and not $\frac{2}{4}$? A lot of you made that mistake yesterday. [Noticing Beverly's hand.] Beverly?
Beverly   Cause when the numbers on the bottom are the same, that's what you put on the bottom of your answer.
Mrs. Anderson   Okay. But what do we call the number on the bottom? Who remembers? Stanley?

Stanley   The denominator.
Mrs. Anderson   And the number on the top?
Five students in unison   The numerator.
Mrs. Anderson   Good. Okay what do we call it when we have two denominators that are the same? [Three students raise their hands.] Look back on page 38. [Turning the page in her book.] What is the third key term it defines there in red type?
Eight students reading in unison   Lowest common denominator.

It is 10:37, and Billy walks back to the pencil sharpener and begins slowly sharpening his pencil. Mrs. Anderson notices him but does not say anything.

Mrs. Anderson   Right. Lowest common denominator. Once we have that, we can add or subtract. So whenever we have fractions with unlike denominators the first thing we need to do is what?
Carol [blurting out]   Find the lowest common denominator.
Mrs. Anderson   Right. Now let's look at exercise one on page 39, finding the lowest common denominator. Let's just do this out loud real fast. There are only 10 of them. Number one—$\frac{1}{4}$ and $\frac{1}{8}$.
Several students in unison $\frac{1}{8}$!
Mrs. Anderson   Good. Now $\frac{1}{3}$ and $\frac{1}{6}$.
Several students in unison   It's $\frac{1}{6}$!
Mrs. Anderson   Good. What about $\frac{1}{5}$ and $\frac{1}{10}$.
Several students in unison   That's $\frac{1}{10}$!
Mrs. Anderson   And $\frac{1}{5}$ and $\frac{1}{25}$.
Several students in unison [after a slight pause]   It's $\frac{1}{25}$.
Mrs. Anderson   Good. Number five—$\frac{1}{7}$ and $\frac{1}{3}$.
Wanda [in a loud voice]   It's $\frac{1}{7}$.
Mrs. Anderson   No. Who knows?
Pam   It's $\frac{1}{21}$.
Mrs. Anderson   Good, Pam. How'd you get that?
Pam   I multiplied.
Mrs. Anderson   Multiplied what?
Pam   The denominators.
Mrs. Anderson   Okay. Number six—
Dick [calling out]   Why didn't she divide three into seven?
Mrs. Anderson   That's a good question, Dick. That's how we test to see if we have the lowest common denominator. We ask if we can divide one denominator evenly by the other. So will three go into seven an even number of times?
Dick [tentatively]   No.
Mrs. Anderson   Right. So we need to find the smallest number that can be evenly divided by *both* of the denominators. And to get that we multiply three times seven. That gives us what?
Dick   Twenty one.

Mrs. Anderson Right. And both 7 and 3 will go into 21 an even number of times. Right?

Dick Right.

Mrs. Anderson Look at number six. This one's tricky—$\frac{1}{3}$ and $\frac{3}{27}$. [Noticing Heather's raised hand.] Heather?

Heather Eighty-one.

Mrs. Anderson Is that the lowest common denominator?

Heather [slowly] No. I guess not.

Mrs. Anderson What is it?

Heather I don't know.

Mrs. Anderson Does anyone know? Who can help Heather?

Eric [calling out] Ninths.

Mrs. Anderson Good, Eric. Nine is the lowest common denominator. Let's look at number seven. [Noticing Heather's raised hand.]Heather, you have a question?

Heather How'd he get nine?

Mrs. Anderson Eric, you want to answer that?

Eric First you change $\frac{1}{3}$ to $\frac{9}{27}$. But then you can divide everything by three to get ninths.

Mrs. Anderson Good. Does everyone see that?

Hank But why didn't he just multiply the denominators and get 81 like we did on the others?

Mrs. Anderson You can do that, but what you get is a common denominator of 81. It doesn't give you the *lowest* common denominator. [She then moves to the blackboard and quickly writes "$\frac{1}{3}$ and $\frac{3}{27} = \frac{27}{81}$, and $\frac{9}{81} = \frac{3}{9}$ and $\frac{1}{9}$."]

Mrs. Anderson Does everyone see that? [No response.] Okay. Let's take a look at the next one—$\frac{1}{81}$ and $\frac{1}{9}$. What's the lowest common denominator there?

Eric and Pam in unison Nine.

Mrs. Anderson Okay. Number eight—$\frac{1}{8}$ and $\frac{1}{5}$. What's that one? Let's see. Cecil?

Cecil Thirteen?

Mrs. Anderson No. You added the denominators. You multiply them. What do you get then?

Cecil Forty.

Mrs. Anderson Right. [Pausing.] Number nine—$\frac{1}{2}$ and $\frac{1}{7}$.

Pam Fourteen.

Mrs. Anderson Good. And the last one—$\frac{1}{3}$ and $\frac{1}{9}$.

Pam [quickly] Twenty-seven.

Mrs. Anderson All right. Now when we add or subtract fractions, our first step is to see what the lowest common denominator is. Once we have that, the problem is half solved. Right? [Mrs. Anderson then walks up to the blackboard, picks up a piece of chalk, and turns to face her students. It is 10:41.]

Mrs. Anderson Now let's try a few addition problems.

She turns and quickly writes the following problems on the board:

$$\frac{1}{4} + \frac{1}{8} = \qquad \frac{1}{5} + \frac{1}{4} = \qquad \frac{1}{18} + \frac{1}{6} =$$

$$\frac{3}{4} + \frac{1}{2} + \frac{1}{3} = \qquad \frac{1}{5} + \frac{1}{10} + \frac{7}{20} =$$

As Mrs. Anderson is writing on the board, a chubby boy on the window side of the room casts a quick glance at Mr. Grimes and, seeing that he is looking in another direction, throws a paper wad at a boy seated two desks in front of him. The missile, right on target, hits the boy in the back of the head and falls to the floor. The victim bends over, picks the paper off the floor, and shakes his fist good naturedly at his grinning assailant.

Mrs. Anderson [now facing her students.]   Look at the first one. [She points to the first problem.] Everyone look up here please. What is the lowest common denominator? Ricky?
Ricky   Four. No, no, eight. Eight.
Mrs. Anderson   Okay. It's eight. So $\frac{1}{4}$ becomes how many eighths? Ricky?
Ricky   Ah, two. [Mrs. Anderson rewrites the problem as $\frac{2}{8} + \frac{1}{8}$.]
Mrs. Anderson   So now we have $\frac{2}{8}$ plus $\frac{1}{8}$. What's that?
Ricky   It's $\frac{3}{8}$.
Mrs. Anderson   Good. [She writes the answer on the board.] Let's take a look at the next one—$\frac{1}{5}$ plus $\frac{1}{4}$. The lowest common denominator, what is it? [Several students' hands go up.] Pam?
Pam   Twenty.
Mrs. Anderson   Right. So $\frac{1}{5}$ would give us how many twentieths? Randy?
Randy   Two.
Pam [spontaneously]   That's wrong. Should be four.
Mrs. Anderson   Right, Pam—$\frac{4}{20}$. Then how many twentieths would $\frac{1}{4}$ give us, Randy?
Randy [softly]   I don't know.
Mrs. Anderson [slightly impatiently]   Well how many times will 4 go into 20?
Randy [slowly]   Five.
Mrs. Anderson   Okay. So you'd have $\frac{5}{20}$, right? [Continuing.] And $\frac{4}{20}$ and $\frac{5}{20}$ is how many twentieths? All right, Billy?
Billy   Nine.
Mrs. Anderson [writing Billy's response on the board]   Right. Now let's look at the next one [pointing to the next problem.]—$\frac{1}{18}$ plus $\frac{1}{6}$. What's the lowest common denominator here? [Five or six students who have been participating most raise their hands.] Come on, what about the rest of you? Randy, can you tell us? [Randy doesn't respond.] Can someone help Randy? Pam?

Pam Eighteen.

Mrs. Anderson Okay. And what do we do next?

Pam Change $\frac{1}{6}$ to eighteenths.

Mrs. Anderson [beginning to write on the board] So we get $\frac{1}{18}$ plus how many eighteenths?

Pam Three.

Mrs. Anderson Plus $\frac{3}{8}$. That gives us $\frac{4}{18}$. [She writes $\frac{4}{18}$ on the board.] Can we reduce this any further? Billy?

Billy Yeah. It's the same as $\frac{2}{9}$.

Mrs. Anderson Good, Billy. [She writes $\frac{2}{9}$ on the board.] Now let's look at the next one. Here we've got three fractions, but it's really just the same as the other problems, isn't it? [A few students nod their heads.] We have $\frac{3}{4}$ plus $\frac{1}{2}$ plus $\frac{1}{3}$. The lowest common denominator is what? [She stands with chalk in hand, poised to write.]

Pam [calling out] Twelfths.

Mrs. Anderson So that would give us how many twelfths here? [She points to $\frac{3}{4}$.]

Eric Nine.

Mrs. Anderson [writing on the board] So $\frac{9}{12}$ here. And here?

Eric Six.

Mrs. Anderson Yes, $\frac{6}{12}$ here. And for the last one?

Pam It's $\frac{4}{12}$.

Mrs. Anderson [writing Pam's response on the board] Okay. So all we have to do now is add the three numerators. Nine plus six plus four are what?

Eric Are 19.

Mrs. Anderson Okay. [She writes $\frac{19}{12}$ on the board.] And what can we reduce $\frac{19}{12}$ to?

Dick It's $1\frac{7}{12}$.

Mrs. Anderson [writing Dick's response on the board] All right, $1\frac{7}{12}$ [Turning to the class.] Does everyone see that? [A few students nod their heads.] Okay. We've got one more up here [pointing to the last problem] —$\frac{1}{5}$ plus $\frac{1}{10}$ plus $\frac{7}{20}$. [Slowly and with emphasis.] First of all, what do we look for? Cecil?

Cecil [softly and with difficulty] You reduce.

Mrs. Anderson No that might come later. What do you do. What's the first step? [No response from Cecil.] Well what have we been doing with all these problems? [She points to the work on the board.] What have we been talking about?

Cecil [shrugs his shoulders] Numerators and denominators?

During Mrs. Anderson's exchange with Cecil, a boy at the end of the row on the window side of the room begins a long yawn, his outstretched arms reaching toward the ceiling. Suddenly his yawn becomes noticeably audible, a change which causes him to stop yawning and start giggling. Two students turn and look in his direction. He smiles at them and then glances at the clock on the wall to his right. It is 10:50.

Mrs. Anderson   Yes but we've been working on finding the *lowest common . . .*

Cecil   Denominator?

Mrs. Anderson   Right! The lowest common denominator. [Sighing.] So what's the lowest common denominator here? [She points to the three denominators in the problem on the board.]

Cecil   Uh, 20?

Mrs. Anderson   Good! So we have 20 as our denominator in all three fractions. [She rewrites the three fractions, converting each to twentieths.] That would give us $\frac{4}{20}$ plus $\frac{2}{20}$ plus $\frac{7}{20}$, right? [She looks at Cecil who nods his head. She then points to the three numerators.] And four plus two plus seven is how much? Cecil?

Cecil   [after a long pause]   Thirteen.

Mrs. Anderson   All right. That gives us $\frac{3}{20}$. [She writes this fraction on the board.] Now is everyone clear about how we got that? Does everyone understand? [About seven or eight students respond by nodding their heads; the rest sit woodenly staring at their teacher.] Okay. [She glances at the clock, which reads 10:54.] We've got about 20 minutes left. That will give you a good start on tonight's homework. [A few students moan.] I want you to do the 25 problems on the worksheet Pam handed out. If you work fast, you might be able to finish before the period is over. [Noticing David's raised hand.] David?

David   Is this the right worksheet, Mrs. Anderson? These problems aren't like the ones we just did.

Mrs. Anderson goes over to Pam's desk and glances down at her worksheet. Three students get up and walk over to the pencil sharpener. Once there they begin talking in low tones as one of them slowly sharpens her pencil.

Mrs. Anderson   [chuckling to herself]   Oh I see what I did. I gave you the worksheet with mixed numbers to add. [Speaking to the entire class.] Class you've got the wrong worksheet. It's one on mixed numbers. We'll go over that tomorrow, so just hold on to it. [She walks over to her desk and picks up a set of papers.] Here's the one I want you to do for tomorrow. [Walking back to Pam's desk.] Pam would you pass these out?

Pam   [taking the papers from Mrs. Anderson]   Okay.

Mrs. Anderson   Please take your time as you work these problems. I think a lot of your mistakes are the result of carelessness. Take your time. Check your work. Everyone should be able to get a perfect paper.

As Pam goes up and down the rows passing out the correct worksheet, the room is filled with the sounds of students moving papers and books, snapping three-ring folders, sharpening pencils, and talking softly with one another. Mrs. Anderson takes a seat at her desk where she begins to enter homework grades in her record book.

Two boys in the middle of the room sit sideways in their seats and lean toward one another, engrossed in animated talk. One of them punches the other in the shoulder playfully and starts giggling. When Pam comes by and places a worksheet on their desks, they try to strike up a conversation with her. Pam, however, continues to move down the row. The boys then turn around in their seats and begin to examine the worksheet.

At 10:59 Mrs. Anderson looks up and surveys her class. Her students are working quietly now.

Mrs. Anderson If you have any questions, be sure to come up and ask me. [A few students look up from their work.]

Mrs. Anderson closes her record book and takes a set of papers which she begins to grade. Moments later Billy gets up and walks to her desk.

Billy [softly] Can I go to the washroom?
Mrs. Anderson [looking at the clock, which says 11:01] Can you wait? The bell's going to ring in about 15 minutes.
Billy [frowning] Oh all right. [He turns and walks back toward his desk. As he passes Carol, he grabs a pencil out of her hand and then flips it back on her desk.]
Carol [in a loud whisper] Stop that, you creep!

Billy continues sauntering toward the back of the room. When he arrives at his desk, he makes two complete turns on his heels before dropping into his seat. He then emits a loud yawn, which causes two nearby students to look in his direction. Billy looks at his worksheet and then decides to put his head on his desk.

Three minutes later two boys walk up to Mrs. Anderson's desk for help. Mrs. Anderson talks to them in low tones, using her red pen to point out the errors on their worksheets. As she speaks to them, a girl, also needing help, arrives at her desk. She stands in line behind the two boys.

While Mrs. Anderson is working with the students at the front of the room, David takes this opportunity to turn around in his seat and begin copying the paper of the girl behind him. As he copies the work, the girl follows Mrs. Anderson's moves closely. The girl also checks on Mr. Grimes and sees that he, too, is also watching Mrs. Anderson.

When Mrs. Anderson is finished helping the students at her desk, she stands up and begins to arrange the papers on top of her desk. Moments later she begins to walk up and down the aisles checking on her students' progress. Those students who previously had been daydreaming or visiting now begin to work.

Mrs. Anderson [continuing to walk]   I notice that several of you didn't get too far. [Two boys behind her giggle at her observation.] That means you'll have homework tonight.

Mrs. Anderson spends the next few minutes walking around the room stopping occasionally to answer a student's question. With the period drawing to a close, the noise level gradually increases as students prepare to leave.

At 11:17 the room is quiet. Twenty-five students sit with their books on top of their desks waiting for the bell to ring. Mrs. Anderson stands in front of her class. Most eyes are on the clock watching the sweep second hand as it moves. With seconds remaining in the period, two boys who apparently know exactly where the second hand is when the bell rings begin counting backwards from ten.

Boys in unison   Four, three, two, one!

At the appointed instant the bell rings and, amidst much chatter and the harsh sounds of moving desks and chairs, most of Mrs. Anderson's students dash out of the room. The two boys and three girls who are left behind gather up their books and follow their classmates at a much more leisurely pace.

As soon as the room is empty, Mrs. Anderson walks back to the corner where Mr. Grimes is seated. He stops sorting through the papers on his desk and motions to her to pull a nearby chair up next to his desk.

Mr. Grimes [smiling]   They're an energetic bunch, aren't they?
Mrs. Anderson [sighing]   You're right about that.
Mr. Grimes   You have a lunch period now, don't you?
Mrs. Anderson   Yes, I do.
Mr. Grimes   Well I won't hold you up. I'll just leave a copy of this completed observation form with you and you can look it over between now and our postobservation conference. Okay?
Mrs. Anderson   That sounds good. [She takes the observation form from Mr. Grimes and glances at it.] This may tell me more about my teaching than I want to know. [She chuckles nervously.] Could you . . . could you just give me your reactions? How do you think it went? Did I have good interactions with my students?

QUESTIONS

1. Review the opening minutes of Mrs. Anderson's class period. How might she have begun class more effectively?

2. Should a teacher respond to *every* instance of misbehavior during a class period? What criteria should a teacher use in deciding whether or not to respond to a student's misbehavior?

3. Research has shown that teacher expectations have a significant influence on student achievement. What expectations does Mrs. Anderson convey to her students, and what effects do these expectations appear to have on students?

4. If you were to use a systematic observation instrument, such as Flanders' Interaction Analysis, to record the interactions between Sherry and her seventh graders, what kind of picture would emerge? For example what is the ratio of teacher talk to pupil talk? What is the ratio of teacher indirect and direct behaviors? How do such interaction patterns relate to student achievement? What other systematic observation instruments could be used to observe teacher pupil interactions?

5. How effective is Sherry in the area of classroom management? From the standpoint of Kounin's classroom management theory, how well does Sherry deal with disruptions like those involving the pencil sharpener, paper wad throwing, and shoulder punching? To what extent does she demonstrate withitness?

6. From the viewpoint of motivational theory, how well has Sherry taken her students' needs into consideration? Is some student boredom and yawning inevitable? Is there anything Sherry could do to make the material more interesting?

7. What are Sherry's instructional objectives. State two or three in the form of behavioral objectives. What levels of Bloom's Cognitive Taxonomy do Sherry's objectives seem to involve? Do her instructional strategies fit her objectives?

8. What kinds of classroom questions does Sherry ask? What levels of Bloom's Cognitive Taxonomy do Sherry's questions seem to involve?

9. How would you evaluate Sherry's performance as a teacher? What do you base your judgment on? Could Mr. Grimes have collected other data on Sherry's teaching besides his observation of classroom interactions?

CASE 11

MEETING INDIVIDUAL NEEDS

Sam Goodman is 29 years old and in his second year of teaching junior high school mathematics. He teaches in the small (3,000 population) rural town of Parsons, a primarily agricultural community with approximately a 35 percent low-income population. Parsons High School typically graduates 30 seniors, and Parsons Junior High School, which has a physical plant constructed in 1939, has an all white student body.

It is the first full day of classes as Sam begins a new school year. The bell has rung, and the students finally become quiet and wait for Sam to begin class. Sam smiles as he looks at the mixture of 32 faces in his third period eighth grade math class.

Sam   Welcome to Math 8! I hope that we're all resigned to the fact that summer vacation is over and it's time to get back to work. [Several students moan and groan while others laugh.] There now you got the last of it out of your systems. [Smiles.] If you open your books to the table of contents, you'll notice that we're going to cover a lot of important material in this class—math concepts that should be valuable to you no matter what you do in life. We'll get into ratios, proportions, percents, decimals, dividing and multiplying fractions, working with positive and negative numbers, and taking square roots. You'll notice that we begin tomorrow with equations. [Pause.] I know that some of this is old hat for a few of you, but others have just broken out into a cold sweat. [Several students laugh.] Don't worry though. We're going to take it slow and have fun as we do it. [Sees a hand raised.] Yes, what's your name?
Shawnna   Shawnna Crowder. How will we be graded, Mr. Goodman?
Sam   I was just coming to that, Shawnna. Our work in here will follow a pattern. On Monday of each week I'll introduce and explain the math concepts that we'll be working on. As I said before, we'll start with equations this week: equations and the proportions of whole numbers. It will be real important for you to pay attention to the explanations and examples I give if you want to have the following Friday off to have fun! [Sees another hand.] Yes, Bill?
Bill [excitedly]   Does that mean you're going to let us do that lab thing if we do our homework?!
Sam [smiling]   You guessed it, Bill! Maybe it would be more accurate

to say that your sister, Vickie, told you about it. [Bill nods his head affirmatively.] Yes, it worked so well last year that I'm going to try it again this year. [Several hands go up.] Okay, let me explain, and maybe it will answer a lot of your questions. [Brief pause.] You see, to get a good grade in here it's important that you do the weekly assignments that I give you on Monday as I begin a new unit. These are due not later than Friday. If you turn them in on Friday, you get to spend your class time in my enrichment lab. [Smiles and speaks teasingly.] You're going to love the enrichment lab! It's full of math games, math puzzles, interesting filmstrips, records, and computers. If there isn't something there that you'd like to do—maybe a hobby or something—I'll try to make it available if it doesn't cost too much. [Points to a hand that is raised.] You're Jimmy Bob, aren't you?

Jimmy Bob   What happens if we can't finish the assignments?

Sam [tauntingly]   Don't even think that way, Jimmy Bob. It's a fate worse than death! [Opens his eyes wide and speaks slowly for emphasis.] You have to work on your assignments while the other students have fun in the enrichment lab. [Everybody laughs.] And you have to do something else worse than death: You have to sit down and write your parents a letter explaining to them why you didn't finish your math assignments. [Several moans.] It gets worse. If I don't get the letter back on Monday signed by your parents, then I'll call them to see what happened. [Pause.] Any questions? [Pause, total silence.] I really can't emphasize enough how important it is for you to keep up each week and do your assignments. [Brief pause.] Now let's all open our books to page one.

***

Two months have passed. Sam is sitting in the classroom of Joe Turpin after school. Joe is the oldest and most experienced math teacher at Parsons High School. Sam is seeking Joe's advice on the suggestion of Si Busby, Sam's principal.

Sam   Joe, I really appreciate your seeing me like this on such short notice! Mr. Busby said you are the best math teacher in the county and could give me good advice if anybody could.

Joe [smiling]   I'm happy to help any way I can, Sam. What's the difficulty?

Sam   Well as you probably already know, this is my second year of teaching, and I find that things that worked really well for me last year are not working for me this year—at least not in my third period math 8 class.

Joe   How is your third period class different?

Sam   I don't really know! I use the same procedures of making assignments on Monday that are due Friday and letting them have enrichment time on Friday if they turn them in. If they don't turn them in, I make them write a letter of explanation to their parents to be signed and brought back on Monday. It's just that it doesn't seem to work with the third period students.

Joe Sounds like a good approach to me. You mean it doesn't work with any of the third period kids?

Sam Well, actually, now that I think about it, there are four students, three boys and a girl, that I'm having the most trouble with.

Joe Tell me about them.

Sam First there's Jimmy Bob Billings, Bobby Joe Stone, and their leader, David Bowling. They began by not bringing pencils, paper, books, and other materials to class. Then they stopped turning in their assignments on Fridays. They have become a sort of gang, with David as their leader. They spend Fridays together writing letters to their parents and working on the assignments they never turn in.

Joe I assume you've tried to talk to them about why they're not doing their work.

Sam Oh yes! Nothing but excuses! The dog eats their assignments, the bus driver throws them away, or some other child they don't really know tears the assignment up. [Pause.] I think Jimmy Bob has the biggest problem in some ways.

Joe How's that?

Sam He doesn't believe he can do the work. Says his parents weren't good at math either and that it wouldn't do any good even if he turned his assignments in. Of course I'll never know since I never see them!

Joe What does the ringleader, David, say?

Sam Nothing but lies! Nothing is ever his fault. He's always the victim and blames everything on someone else. He even told his mother that I've been absent most Fridays so he couldn't turn his assignments in! When I confronted him about this, he said that he had to tell his mother something or he'd be in big trouble—that the whole thing was his mother's fault for being too hard on him and working him so hard around the house! Then when I told his mother what he told me, David tells his mother that I scared him and put pressure on him, so he had to tell *me* something! The whole thing, of course, was my fault for being so hard on him!

Joe Oh boy! And what about this Bobby Joe?

Sam Bobby Joe is somewhat different from Jimmy Bob and David even though he hangs around with them in class. He's generally quieter than the others and isn't much of a discipline problem. Basically he's a potential dropout. He wants to become a mechanic like his 19-year-old brother. [Pause.] And I really don't think his parents would care.

Joe Speaking of parents, I gather you've talked with them.

Sam I think it's fair to say that I've really tried, but I've gotten no response from Jimmy Bob or Bobby Joe's parents. They don't return my calls or letters and don't have time for conferences. They generally sign the letters the boys bring home but they don't write notes or communicate in any way. [Pause.] Now in David's case I've talked to his mother as I told you. But she's not going to do anything to help. She keeps asking me what *I'm* going to do about the situation. Apparently the father travels or something. Whatever he does, she always says he's too busy to help.

Joe Well sounds like you've got a fine kettle of fish there, Sam! And you say there's a girl who's a problem too?

Sam Yes, Shawnna Crowder.

Joe Is she part of this gang?

Sam No, she's from an entirely different background.

Joe What do you mean?

Sam Shawnna is from a middle-class home in which both parents work and push her to do well in an overprotective way.

Joe What's she doing in your class?

Sam Very little. Her parents say that she doesn't like school, especially math. When I point out to them that she doesn't do her weekly assignments, they tell me about Shawnna's busy schedule with swimming, dancing, piano lessons four times a week, and so forth. They say these activities are as important to her future growth as her schoolwork. The problem is that the schoolwork is just too demanding, especially math. They are in the process of getting her tested and want to have a conference when the results are in.

Joe It sounds like this third period class is quite a challenge!

Sam To say the least! Certainly for a beginner like me. Any advice?

Joe Don't put yourself down, Sam. It would be a challenge for most teachers. [Pause.] As for the three boys, have you tried to move them apart and separate them?

Sam Yes, but it didn't help.

Joe I think your instincts are good. I'd continue trying to have conferences with the kids individually and keep trying to talk to the parents.

Sam Yeah, but Joe, I find myself spending a lot of time figuring out how to motivate those four! I can't keep spending all that time on them. I have other students in the class too, and I'm beginning to think I'm neglecting them.

Joe Somehow I really doubt that you are, Sam. I think your approach is sound and that you need to keep at it. Let me know how things are going in a month or so.

Sam I'll sure do that, Joe! Thanks for listening.

***

Two weeks later Shawnna's parents call Sam and ask for a conference after school. Mason Crowder, an electrical engineer, and his wife Melinda, a nurse in a nearby hospital, sit in chairs next to Sam's desk.

Mr. Crowder Well, Mr. Goodman, as we told you on the phone, we had Shawnna tested. We wanted to share the results with you. [Hands Sam test results.]

Sam   Thanks. Mr. Sayres, Shawnna's counselor, has already gone over them with me. Shawnna has high potential as a student.

Mr. Crowder   Yes and it really worries us that she doesn't like school. She should be bringing home straight A's. We know that she has a busy schedule with her piano lessons and all—but that's all that seems to keep her going. She says that life is more than homework, and I somewhat agree with her.

Sam   Have you seen any of the weekly math assignments that I have them do? I put them in the form of games, puzzles, and everyday life as much as possible. For example, the one I assigned last week on fractions was deliberately built with Shawnna in mind. [Holds up lesson with picture of piano at top.]

Mrs. Crowder   Yes I did see that one! I wondered about that!

Sam   And yet Shawnna didn't complete that one either.

Mr. Crowder   [frowning and serious]   I hear what you're saying, Mr. Goodman, but Shawnna's life is very full of activities and pressures now, things that are just as important to Shawnna's future as academics. I can see that you have tried to make math as interesting as possible, but Melinda and I have come to the conclusion that this school's academic demands are just too much. We don't want Shawnna to become totally turned off to school.

Sam   Well what are you going to do, Mr. Crowder?

Mr. Crowder   I'm afraid that we're seriously considering having her transferred to another school. If nothing else, to a good private school, although heaven knows we really can't afford it.

Sam   [sighs]   Well I guess you know what's best for your daughter. All I know is she mostly doesn't pay attention when I go over things in class, and she doesn't do the weekly assignments no matter how interesting I try to make them.

Mr. Crowder   Don't think we're blaming you, Mr. Goodman. It's just the school—the system. Shawnna is just turned off and we have to do what we think is best for her.

Sam [standing up]   I understand. Please let me know if I can help in any way.

***

Two days later Sam sits at his desk 15 minutes after the end of the last period. In walks Bobby Joe Stone with a frown on his face.

Bobby Joe   You said you wanted to talk to me after school, Mr. Goodman.

Sam   Yes, Bobby Joe. [Pointing to a chair.] Have a seat.

Bobby Joe   [sitting down]   Did I do something wrong?

Sam   No, I just want to talk to you to try to understand why you aren't doing your work in my class.

Bobby Joe [sighs]   Mr. Goodman, to be honest with you, I'm just waitin' to get to be 16 so that I can drop out of school and work with my brother. He's a mechanic and can get me a job in the shop he works in. Nothin' against you, Mr. Goodman, but I'm just bored, real bored, and the only thing that makes school interestin' is cottonin' up with my friends.

Sam   But, Bobby Joe, even as a mechanic you'll need to know basic math skills. You're going to have to know how to calibrate measurements, calculate percentages, and understand decimals. Even something as simple as selecting the right wrench can involve understanding fractions or how to convert measurements to the metric system.

Bobby Joe   If I have any problems, I'll get my brother to help me figure them out. He's pretty bright about stuff like that, and he dropped out of school when he was 16.

Sam   Well, Bobby Joe, I just hope that your brother is always around to help you when you have a problem.

Bobby Joe   Well, we're pretty close, and he's only 19. He'll be around a while. [Pause.] If it's all right, I need to go, Mr. Goodman, you see I've. . . .

Sam   Okay, Bobby Joe, I guess we're finished anyhow! Please let me know if I can help in any way.

Bobby Joe [standing up]   Yeah, thanks a lot, Mr. Goodman. See you later.

***

It is Friday of the following week. All the students except David, Bobby Joe, and Jimmy Bob are involved with enrichment activities. Sam talks with the three boys as they sit at the front of his desk. There is a considerable amount of noise and movement from the other students in the classroom.

Sam   Guys, it's the same old story. What's your excuse this time, Jimmy Bob?

Jimmy Bob   Mr. Goodman, you know I can't do this stuff! It's hard! My mother said she couldn't do it when she was in school either.

Sam   You've told me that before! One thing is sure. You can't do anything if you don't try! [Pause.] What's your excuse, David?

David   I had it all done, but it must have fallen out of my notebook.

Sam   I wondered what you were going to say happened to it this time.

David [smiling sheepishly]   It's true, Mr. Goodman! I can't help it if the darn paper clip didn't hold.

Sam   Fine. Then I don't guess you'll have any problem doing it again. All three of you spread out and get busy writing your letters and working on the assignment.

David [smirking]   I can't, Mr. Goodman. I don't have a book or anything to write with.

Jimmy Bob   Neither do I.

Sam [sarcastically]   How convenient for all three of you! [Pause.] I've had it with all three of you. I think that it's time you went to Mr. Busby's office and told him your hard luck story!

***

Sam meets again with Joe Turpin in Joe's classroom after school the following Tuesday.

Sam Thanks, Joe, for seeing me again. I've got some decisions to make and I need your input.

Joe I assume that we're talking about the same four kids.

Sam That's right.

Joe Well, let's start with the girl. What was her name?

Sam Shawnna. Shawnna Crowder.

Joe Yeah, that's it. Whatever happened with her?

Sam Her parents got her tested and decided that the school isn't helping her reach her potential. First they were thinking about transferring her to a private school, but now they want an interdistrict transfer to another school in the county where they think she can make A's in her subjects. Since Si Busby has to agree to such a transfer, he wants my recommendation. I know she'd be better off if she stayed at Parsons and got down to work. But Shawnna has her parents tied around her little finger. All she has to do is whine and cry a little bit, and she can get out of anything she wants to. So with that being the way things are, I feel like I may as well go along. But that makes me feel guilty, like I'm copping out. Do I give in to all the Shawnnas that I have from now on?

Joe Good question. I definitely know where you're coming from. [Pause.] And the three musketeers?

Sam They've become mild discipline problems. You know, smart answers, entering class late, constantly being mildly disruptive, and other things like that. Of course they hardly ever do their assignments or bring their work material to class. I tried to have a conference with them the other day and ended up sending them to Si Busby's office when I got fed up.

Joe What did Si do?

Sam He questioned them and dressed them down good. Later he asked me what I thought he should do with them. They're goofing off in all their classes, and their parents won't help. Si wonders if he shouldn't expel them and see if that helps straighten them out.

Joe What do you think?

Sam I don't know, Joe. It's like Shawnna. I really don't think expulsion is the answer, but I really haven't been able to get any work out of them when they're in class. Expelling them seems like the easy way out again. [Pause.] So tell me, what would you do if you were in my place? Is there any way to reach these kids if I do keep them? Is there anything I can try that I haven't already tried?

Information Compiled by Mr. Goodman from School Cumulative Records

Student	Parents' Occupations	Parents' Education	Number of Siblings
Shawnna	Electrical engineer (F) Nurse (M)	College Nursing school	2
David	Traveling salesman (F) Sales clerk (M)	High school High school	1
Bobby J.	Construction worker (F) Housewife (M)	Tenth grade High school	5
Jimmy B.	Foreman, steel mill (F) Housewife (M)	High school High school	4

ACHIEVEMENT TEST SCORES
(Metropolitan Advanced, in Stanines)

Student	Math	Basics Total	Complete Total
Shawnna	6	7	7
David	4	5	5
Bobby J.	2	3	3
Jimmy B.	5	4	4

QUESTIONS

1. What might account for the fact that Sam's mathematics assignments worked for him last year but not this year?
2. Imagine that you are Joe Turpin. What advice would you give Sam?
3. Should Sam have sent David, Bobby Joe, and Jimmy Bob to Mr. Busby's office for not being prepared to work on their assignments? Explain your answer.
4. In addition to expelling them, what other options does Sam have in working with his four resistant students? Which option would you recommend?
5. From the perspective of motivation theory, what different types of needs seem to be dominant in the cases of Shawnna, David, Bobby Joe, and Jimmy Bob? Is there anything that Sam can do to change his curriculum or teaching methods to take the different needs into consideration?
6. What is attribution (or locus of control) theory? Are Jimmy Bob's attributions internal or external? Is Jimmy Bob an example of "learned helplessness?" How effective are attribution training programs in cases like Jimmy Bob's?
7. Sam employs a number of behavior management techniques in his class. See if you can identify examples of the Premack Principle, response cost, and contingency contracting. Why do these techniques seem to be not working in the cases of Shawnna and the "Three Musketeers?"
8. What are the defense mechanisms of projection and rationalization in psychoanalytic theory? How well do they explain David's behavior? What can be done?
9. What does research identify as home and parent variables that correlate with student success in school? How might the home environment help explain Bobby Joe's intention to drop out as well as David and Jimmy Bob's behavior? How is the overprotectiveness of Shawnna's parents affecting her behavior? What are the most effective programs that have been developed to get the home and school working together on behalf of the child?

CASE 12

AND IF THEY DON'T ALL WANT TO LEARN?

Waterford Junior High School is located in a poor, high-crime section of a major metropolitan area in a midwestern state. Two decades ago the surrounding neighborhood was made up of small, well-kept homes belonging to middle-income families. Today the neighborhood reveals the ugly scars of creeping urban blight. A few neat, well-maintained homes remain, but they are outnumbered by those that have fallen into disrepair. Unkept yards, wrecked cars in driveways and on the streets, and spray-painted graffiti on fences are testaments to the decline that has swept over the area.

The school, a three-story warehouse-like structure built at the end of World War II, also shows signs of deterioration and abuse. For years the building's yellow brick walls have been the target of graffiti artists. Nearly a dozen street-level windows are boarded over, an admission by the school's maintenance crew that it can no longer keep up with the destruction of rock-wielding vandals.

Nearly one-quarter of the students who attend Waterford are from families where English is not the primary language, and more than half are from families on some form of public assistance. Rightly or wrongly, Waterford students have a reputation throughout the city for below-average achievement, absenteeism, and chronic misbehavior.

It is 7:45 A.M. on the fourth day of school, and five teachers are seated around a table in the lunchroom having coffee. Sue Adams, a first year social studies teacher and a recent graduate of a private liberal arts college in another state, walks up to the table. William Hanover, a mathematics teacher in his fifth year at Waterford, is the first to notice Sue.

William Morning. [Standing up and extending his hand to Sue.] You must be the new social studies teacher. William Hanover, mathematics.
Sue [shaking his hand] I'm Sue Adams. You're right, it is social studies. I'm replacing Mrs. Watkins.
William Right, she retired. A great lady. [Pointing to the others in the group who, one by one, stand and shake hands with Sue.] This is Betty Franklin, English. Mildred Hawkins, English. Frank Burns, mathemat-

ics. And this fellow on my right is David Sharp [with exaggerated respect] science teacher *extraordinaire.* [Everyone in the group laughs.]
Sue [to all]   I'm very pleased to meet you. [She sits down.]
Frank   So how'd you end up at Waterford?
Betty [slapping Frank on the shoulder]   That's a terrible way to put it!
Frank [playfully]   Come on now. Everyone knows Waterford's reputation.
Sue   Well I just graduated last year and, believe it or not, I wanted to teach in an urban school.
Mildred   I guess you know that Waterford's had its share of problems?
Sue   Well not really. Is there something I should know?
Mildred   It's just that the school's gotten a lot of bad press in the past.
Betty   Some teachers feel the kids are really hard to handle, but I haven't found them to be that bad. [Pausing.] I mean, look at the homes a lot of our kids come from. Some of them have gone through things that we couldn't even imagine: parents involved in drugs, child abuse, unemployment—
Frank [interrupting]   Right. You name the social problem, you'll find it well represented at Waterford.
Sue [uneasily]   Well just how bad is it? You can teach the kids, can't you?
Betty [laughing]   What a terrible introduction! We've got you all worried. It's not really that bad. A lot of the kids really want to learn.
Frank [in a serious tone]   Betty's right. Plus it's hard to generalize. Some teachers have problems, others don't have many at all. It's hard to say. Some people just seem to adjust better than others.
David   You should remember one thing, Sue. If you ever want to talk to someone, we're always here. We may not have any answers, but we're always willing to listen.

***

Four weeks later Sue is standing at an overhead projector in front of 27 eighth graders in her sixth period social studies class. Her students, 12 girls and 15 boys, are seated in five parallel rows. Projected on the screen behind her is a multicolored outline map of the world.

The students seated near the front of the room appear to be involved in the lesson. They are either looking directly at Sue or writing in the names of countries on the outline map of the world Sue has just passed out. Many of the students seated in the back half of the room, however, squirm restlessly and exhibit a variety of off-task behaviors. A black girl matter-of-factly braids the hair of the girl who sits in front of her. A red-headed boy seated to the right of her yawns and then places his head on his desk. Two boys look out the window at four youths who are seated on the steps leading into a run-down apartment building across the street. An overweight girl leaves her desk without permission and walks across the room to deliver a note to a friend.

Sue   Okay, class, look at this transparency of the world. [She steps back a few steps and points to the screen.] Sheila, sit down right now! I didn't say you could get up. [Waiting until Sheila takes her seat.] Now how many people are living right now on the earth? [Noticing Carla's raised hand.]

Carla   One hundred million.

Harold [blurting out]   That's crazy! There's a whole lot more people than that!

Sue [sternly]   All right, Harold! That's enough. If you want to say something raise your hand.

Harold [continuing to speak out]   Aw, she's way off!

Wanda [turns in her chair and looks menacingly at Harold]   How many do you think, big head? At least she's got an idea. [Wanda turns back and smiles at Carla who is giggling.]

Sue   Okay, Wanda. Settle down.

Harold [intimidated by Wanda]   I don't know. But there's a lot more than 100 million.

Freddie [yelling out from the back of the room]   Hey, Miss, what's this tape on the floor? [He points to a circle on the floor made out of masking tape. The circle has a diameter of about eight feet.]

Sue   That's for an exercise we're going to do a bit later. Don't worry about it. [Pausing.] Now Harold is right. There *are* a lot more than 100 million. In fact there are more than five billion people in the world. That's five thousand millions.

Juan [with hostility]   How do they know that? You can't count everybody in the world!

Rick   Yeah! Besides there's people born every day.

Sue [with frustration]   Let's calm down! I said there are more than five billion. We don't know how many more, but the number's *about* five billion. [She looks directly at Juan and Rick, both of whom have contemptuous looks on their faces.] Here's another piece of information you probably didn't know. How long will it take for the population of the world to double? [Calling on Dave whose hand is raised.]

Dave   A thousand years?

Sue   Good guess, Dave. Actually it's much shorter than that. Thirty-eight years. Every 38 years the population of the world doubles.

Rick [with disbelief]   Every 38 years?

Sue   That's right. By the time you're about 50, there will be about ten billion people in the world. [She pauses as though deciding what to do next.] Let's imagine that we were all the people on the earth right now, just the 28 people in this room. And let's imagine that the earth was no larger than this room.

Harold [spontaneously]   Oh, no, I couldn't get away from that! [He points to Wanda.]

Wanda [angrily]   You shut your mouth, boy!

Sue [Moving toward Harold]   Hey, watch it you two! [Harold stares straight ahead.] So in 38 years we'd have about 56 people in this room. In another 38 years, we'd have about 112 people. After another 38 we'd have about 224, and so on. So what's going to happen eventually?

Willie Peoples be fallin' off the earth! [He laughs heartily. Several other students begin to laugh as well.]

Sue [smiling weakly] I don't think they'd start falling off of the earth, but it would get pretty crowded, wouldn't it? [A few students nod their heads.]

Sue walks back over to the overhead projector and points to the outline map of the world with her pen. The silhouette of her pen and hand is projected on the screen.

Sue I hope you've labeled the countries. [Looking at the back of the room.] Some of you in the back there haven't done a thing all period. [The red-haired boy raises his head from his desk, looks at Sue, and then puts it back.] Now what are the four countries with the largest populations? [Nobody volunteers an answer.] All right. Look at this transparency. [She puts another transparency on the projector. It displays the outlines of four countries.] Here are the four countries with the largest populations. Do you recognize them? [She points to one outlined in purple.] What's this one?

Several students in unison The United States!

Sue Right.

Heather What's that on top of the United States?

Frank That's Alaska, dummy.

Sue [looking sternly at Frank] Frank! [Pausing and then pointing to the outline of Alaska.] This is Alaska and I don't know if you can see them, but what are these tiny dots?

Carol [loudly from the back of the room] Hawaii.

Sue Right, the Hawaiian Islands. [Pointing to the outlines of the other countries.] So what are these other countries? [No response.] All right. This is India. [She points to the outline of India.] This is China. And this is Russia. These are the four countries that have the greatest populations. I want you to remember that, because we'll be having a quiz tomorrow. [Several students groan. Sue notices Randy's raised hand.] Randy?

Randy I ain't doin' no quiz! You didn't grade the last one right!

Shawnda Yeah, Miss Adams, you be givin' us too much work!

Sue [with frustration] All right, just quiet down!

Sammy Yeah, and why'd you tell the counselor I was going to fail social studies?

Sue [to Sammy] You don't do your work in class.

Sammy I do my work at home.

Sue Then why do I have all those zeros in my grade book?

Sammy I already know this stuff. We had it in elementary school.

Ronald [yelling out]   We don't need to learn this stuff! Let's do something interesting.
Several students in unison   Yeah, let's do something else.
Sue [trying to keep her composure]   Now everyone, settle down! This is social studies, and we will learn social studies. You need it to get into high school.

Sue then walks over to her desk and picks up a set of dittoed handouts.

Sue   Since some of you seem to have a problem paying attention today, we'll just spend the rest of the period working on these worksheets. [Several students groan.] I'm sorry, you don't give me any other choice. We can't talk about what's in the book, so you're going to answer some questions about it.
Freddie [calling out]   What about the exercise with the circle?
Sue [curtly]   I'm sorry. I've had enough of this foolishness!

Sue then proceeds to give the students at the front of each row enough handouts for the students in that row.

Sue [as she moves from row to row]   Take one and pass the rest back.
Freddie   Oooohhh, she be angry.
Sue   I want all the questions answered on this worksheet by the end of the period. [She points to the clock on the wall.] You'd better get started. You've only got 20 minutes. I don't think anyone can afford another failing grade.

***

The following morning Sue enters the lunchroom for her usual early morning cup of coffee and chat with fellow teachers. She wears a haggard expression that her friends are quick to notice.

Frank   Sue, you look beat, and it's not even first period. Are you having a rough time?

Sue tosses her books and papers on the table and drops into a chair.

Sue [she sighs]   It's really getting to me. I don't know if I can go on like this.
Betty   Did anything happen? Do you want to talk about it?
Sue   Oh I don't know. It just seems to be such a struggle all the time.
Mildred   What's that saying: Nobody ever said teaching was going to be easy?
Sue [continuing]   Mainly it's my sixth period class. I can deal with the

other classes; they're not so bad. But sixth period, they're so hostile. They resist everything!

Frank You have a bad class yesterday?

Sue I'll say! I had this great lesson all planned on world population, and they never even let me really get to it. I ended up giving them a worksheet to do, just to get them to shut up.

David Sometimes you have to do that. We've all done it. If you don't have order, you can't teach. So you do whatever restores peace. Besides, some classes are just like that.

Sue I know, but I don't like doing it. I want to teach the kids, but half of them won't let me. [Pausing.] I don't know . . . Am I doing something wrong?

William Come on, Sue, we've all had classes like that. Don't be so hard on yourself. This is the inner city, and the kids just behave differently. You'll get used to it. Just go with the flow. Do what you can.

David What was your lesson about yesterday?

Sue Like I said, it was on world population. I had this little exercise all planned. To show the kids that the world's population doubles every 38 years, I made a big circle with masking tape on the floor. I was going to start off by having five kids stand in the circle—you know, for the five billion people on earth right now. Then in 38 seconds I'd have another five enter the circle. And every 38 seconds I'd double the number of kids in the circle. In no time flat, of course, the circle would be full.

William Sounds like a great way to get them to understand the concept.

Sue [with disappointment] But they were so terrible yesterday! I didn't even start the exercise. I realized they were acting so badly I'd better skip it. Otherwise I'd have ended up with a riot on my hands!

Frank It's frustrating to make those plans and then not be able to follow through.

Sue I also had this neat little lecture all ready on the effects that population growth has on all kinds of things: food, energy, pollution, housing, jobs, all that stuff. But they didn't want to hear it. It's like they either don't want to learn, or they're daring me to try to teach them.

David [comfortingly] Well maybe they'll be more receptive today.

Sue That's just it. They act like that *all the time!* [Weakly.] I just don't know how to cope with it. How do you put up with that day after day?

Lesson Plan

Teacher: Sue Adams   **Course:** Social Studies 8
Period: Sixth   **Date:** September 28

Goal: At the end of this lesson, students will understand how people are distributed around the world and some of the implications of continued rapid growth in the world's population.

SPECIFIC OBJECTIVES

Students will be able to:

1. Explain why most of the earth's population (two-thirds) lives on only a fraction (eight percent) of the available land.
2. Identify the four countries that make up half the world's population (China, India, the Soviet Union, and the United States).
3. Identify the natural conditions necessary to support large populations.

MATERIALS

1. Transparencies of world, China, India, the Soviet Union, and the United States
2. Masking tape circle on floor, approximately eight feet in diameter
3. Text (chapter 3)
4. Dittoed worksheets for evaluation
5. Chalkboard, overhead projector

PROCEDURE

1. Introduce lesson by determining population of our city and discussing why population is centered here and not in other parts of the state.
2. Explain conditions necessary to support large numbers of people and why the earth's population is distributed as it is.
3. Identify and locate four countries that account for half the world's population. (Use transparencies and dittoed outline maps.)
4. Conduct "circle" exercise to demonstrate how world's population is increasing. Discuss activity and effects of increasing world population.
5. Complete population map of the United States.
6. Complete worksheet on chapter 3 (seatwork).

QUESTIONS

1. Why do several of Sue's students express hostility in the classroom with no apparent provocation? How should a teacher deal with such hostility?
2. Do you agree with Sue's decision to make her students complete worksheets because they have difficulty paying attention? What are the pros and cons of her action?
3. Is Sue's colleague William correct when he says, "This is the inner city, and the kids just behave differently"? Do motivation to learn and behave in a self-disciplined way differ according to socioeconomic class? Explain your answer.
4. Did Sue make the right decision in deciding not to go ahead with her exercise designed to demonstrate how the world population doubles every 38 years? What do you think would have happened if Sue had gone ahead with her exercise? How could she have handled the exercise so she wouldn't have ended up with a "riot" on her hands?
5. Why do you suppose some students appear as though they do not want to learn? Do they *really* not want to learn?
6. What are some coping strategies that Sue could develop so that her sixth period class would not be such a negative experience.
7. In terms of motivational theory, what student needs seem to be operating in Sue's class? How can Sue assess her students' needs and take advantage of them in her instructional planning?
8. From an observational learning perspective, what students are serving as models of disinhibition in Sue's class? What vicarious reinforcers are operating? How can Sue change this pattern of behavior?
9. How do the home environments of Sue's students influence student interests and behavior in Sue's classroom? Is there any way that Sue can involve the home and parents of the students to increase student motivation and learning?
10. How effective are Sue's classroom discipline procedures from the viewpoint of Kounin's model of classroom management? What does she need to work on?
11. What is stress in teaching, and what are the stressors in Sue's situation? What stress management techniques are available to Sue to help her deal with stress? What are the characteristics of teachers who are unable to adjust to difficult school situations like that at Waterford JHS?

CASE 13

TWO DIFFERENT WORLDS

It is 7:50 A.M. on an already warm September day in a suburban area of the Midwest. Lynn Dorsett, an attractive 28-year-old beginning art teacher with long blonde hair, is approaching the entrance of Hawthorne Middle School. Only yesterday she received a call from the superintendent's office offering her a teaching position. In the mornings she would teach at Hawthorne Middle School, in the afternoons at Kennedy Junior High School.

As Lynn follows the curved walkway lined with shrubs, she takes note of her surroundings. The one-story red brick building, not more than a few years old, sits on a well-manicured lawn. The homes immediately across from the school are large and fashionable. Two parents, one driving an expensive luxury car and the other a fancy minivan, pull up into the curved driveway and drop their children off.

At the entrance Lynn pulls open one of the double doors and allows the two children to enter first. Once inside she walks to the main office where she is met by a tall, middle-aged woman standing behind the counter.

Lynn Good morning. I'm Lynn Dorsett, the new art teacher, and I'm looking for Mrs. Thomas, the principal.
Mrs. Thomas Well I'm Mrs. Thomas. I'm so glad to see you, Lynn. [She extends her hand with a warm smile.] We've really been looking forward to your arrival.
Lynn [shaking Mrs. Thomas' hand] I'm very glad to be here. It seems as though you've really got a nice school here.
Mrs. Thomas [with enthusiasm] We just think Hawthorne is the best place in the world! [Pausing.] Let me take you to your room so you can begin to get settled in. You won't meet with any students until Monday, so that'll give you a couple of days to get things organized. [She walks around from behind the counter.] We didn't want to send kids to the art room until we were assigned an art teacher. [She shows Lynn through the door of the main office and out into the hallway.]

On a bulletin board across from the office is a red, white, and blue banner that reads, "Welcome Back Hawthorne Lions." The hallway is crowded with students who stop at their lockers to pick up books and supplies before their first period class. The students go about their business matter-of-factly, and there is a minimum amount of pushing, yelling, or horseplay.

Lynn [as they walk briskly] I'm surprised. The children seem to be really well behaved and polite.

Mrs. Thomas Oh we're proud of our students. They're really motivated. It's their families. We've got a lot of parental support. I don't know if you noticed when you drove up to the school, but we're in a pretty well-to-do area. Our kids are from homes where they tend to put a lot of emphasis on education. They expect their children to learn and [chuckling] they expect us to teach.

Lynn Sounds like we couldn't ask for a better situation.

Mrs. Thomas Well everything's not perfect. But Hawthorne's probably one of the better schools in the district. It's certainly light years away from some other ones around here. By the way, did you tell me what school you'll be at in the afternoon?

Lynn No I didn't. I'll be at Kennedy Junior High.

Mrs. Thomas Oh dear.

Lynn [with concern] What do you mean?

Mrs. Thomas Oh nothing really. I think you'll find Kennedy different from Hawthorne though. [Slowing her pace.] We're almost there.

Lynn I'm really looking forward to teaching. I spent several years doing free-lance art work, and I didn't find that satisfying. I've always wanted to teach.

Mrs. Thomas Oh I see. [Stopping suddenly.] Here we are. [She opens the door to the art room and allows Lynn to enter first.]

The room has six large work tables with six stools around each. A teacher's desk, covered with rulers, construction paper, scissors, a few small jars of paint, and other assorted items, is in a corner. Along the walls are open shelves which hold a wide variety of art supplies. Around the room are different examples of student-made art: sculptures, macrame, oil and water color paintings, pencil drawings, string art, African masks, and model cars and airplanes. Numerous posters and pictures related to art cover the walls.

Mrs. Thomas [surveying the room] Well here it is. Looks like it might need to be straightened up a bit. At least I think you'll have enough supplies. If you don't, just let me know.

Lynn Thanks, Mrs. Thomas. I really appreciate your support.

Mrs. Thomas [turning to leave] I'll send Chad Elliot, our assistant principal, by with your rosters, grade book, and all the paperwork you'll need to get started. Then I'll try to stop by tomorrow just to see how you're settling in.

***

Shortly before 1:00 that same day, Lynn is crossing the faculty parking lot at Kennedy Junior High School. The school is in the southeast corner of the district, an area of run-down multiple-family dwellings and small businesses. More than half of Kennedy's students are from families on some form of public assistance. The school has an enrollment of 650 students, 90 percent of whom are black, with the remaining 10 percent about evenly divided between Puerto Ricans and whites.

As Lynn nears the school she picks up her pace, trying to ignore the stares of several students hanging around the outside of the building. One of them, a tall, thin black boy, calls out to her as she passes.

Boy Hey, beautiful, is you gonna teach here? If you be my teacher, I won't miss no classes! [His buddies break into hearty, unrestrained laughter.]

Lynn gives the boys a stern look and keeps walking. A few moments later she enters the building through the main entrance. The interior of the two-story building, built over 40 years ago, is gloomy and institutional. The hallways are barren. The bulletin board across from the main office, an ideal spot for a display welcoming students back for the new year, is empty. It is hot and musty, and the air has a peculiar, gasoline-like smell to it.

Lynn enters the main office and speaks to the clerical worker closest to the door.

Lynn Hello, I'm Lynn Dorsett, the new art teacher.
Clerk [brusquely] What do you want?
Lynn I was told to report here by 1:10. Is the principal here?
Clerk Mr. Deavers?
Lynn [hopefully] Yes, he's the one I spoke to.
Clerk Well he's not here.
Lynn [becoming irritated] Well could someone tell me where my classroom is? I'd like to get organized.
Clerk Yeah, I guess Mrs. Carter could take you down there. She's in the teachers' lunchroom. Know where that is?
Lynn I just got here. I don't know where anything is.
Clerk [pointing] Well you go all the way to the end of this hall and then take a left. You can't miss it.
Lynn What does she look like?
Clerk She's a black lady, kinda heavyset.
Lynn Is she an assistant principal?

Clerk Yeah.
Lynn [turning to leave] Thank you.

Just as Lynn steps out into the hallway, the passing bell rings. Almost immediately students pour out of their classrooms. A steady crescendo of noise begins to build. Within a minute the hallway is filled with noisy, boisterous students. A small boy races past, bumping Lynn as he tries to elude his pursuer, another boy about six feet tall. The larger boy shouts an obscenity as he brushes past Lynn.

To her right Lynn sees a boy punch the right shoulder of a fat girl who has just closed her locker. She emits a piercing scream and then begins pummeling the boy with her loaded book bag, cursing him with each blow.

Lynn is swept along with the surging flow of students until she sees a room marked "Teachers' Lunchroom" on the opposite side of the hallway. She presses her way over to the room and is about to open the door when another teacher, a tall black male, arrives and opens it for her.

Charles Hi. It's kinda wild out here, isn't it? [Pausing until they are both through the doorway.] I'm Charles Parker. Are you subbing here?
Lynn No I'm not. I'm Lynn Dorsett, the new art teacher.
Charles Well welcome to Kennedy Junior High School. [He extends his hand.] If you ever need any help, just give me a holler. Some of these kids get a little excited every now and then, and they need someone to knock some sense into them. You know what I mean?
Lynn [with uncertainty] I guess so. [Pausing.] Is Mrs. Carter in here? I'm supposed to see her.
Charles [pointing] She's right over there at that last table. She's wearing a green dress.
Lynn Thanks.

***

It is three months later, and Lynn has just completed her last morning class at Hawthorne. She is putting her papers inside her attaché case when Mrs. Thomas enters.

Mrs. Thomas Hi. How's it going? I was in the area, so I thought I'd stop by.
Lynn Hello, Mrs. Thomas. It's really going well.
Mrs. Thomas Good. I'm glad to hear that.
Lynn [excitedly] The kids are just great. Most of them really want to learn. Every once in awhile I get some resistance, but not really that much.
Mrs. Thomas [smiling] Well that's part of teaching . . . motivating those who'd rather be doing something else.

Lynn   The group that was just in here . . . we've been working on papier-mâché masks. I'm really proud of them. Here look at these. [She leads Mrs. Thomas to a counter at the back of the room. Spread out on the counter, drying, are about two dozen papier-mâché masks the students have just painted.]

Mrs. Thomas   These really look good. [Laughing.] I think I'd be embarrassed to be in your class. I have zero artistic ability!

Lynn [placing her right hand on Mrs. Thomas's left shoulder]   Oh everybody's got some. [Glances at her watch.]

Mrs. Thomas   I know you've got to get over to Kennedy. [She begins to walk slowly toward the door.] Tell me, Lynn, how is it going over there?

Lynn [with a long sigh]   I wish I could say it was going half as well as it is here. I don't know. I don't seem to be able to relate to the kids. They're so hostile and aggressive.

Mrs. Thomas   Yes, kids over in the southeast come from different backgrounds from our kids.

Lynn   Sometimes I almost feel like I have a split personality. My mornings and afternoons are so different.

Mrs. Thomas   I imagine so.

Lynn   At first I tried to use the same lessons there that I was using here. Boy was that a disaster! It seemed like the kids had never used scissors, pasted, or painted, or any of the things I thought kids that age would have done in art. And the worst thing is the kids *cannot* listen and follow directions. Even the simplest thing! It's amazing!

Mrs. Thomas   I know what you mean. I taught for three years at an inner-city school. It's a challenge.

Lynn   And discipline . . . it's a constant battle. With at least half my students there, I have to watch them every minute of every period. They . . . they can be so rude, too. I don't believe I've ever heard so much profanity.

Mrs. Thomas   Well I wish I could tell you how to handle it. I don't know . . . some people seem to be able to adjust to that kind of stress and others can't.

Lynn   Well I know one thing. If I didn't spend at least half my time at a school like Hawthorne, I wouldn't last.

***

It is three weeks later, and Lynn is teaching her last class of the day at Kennedy. Seated on stools at four large work tables in her room are 24 eighth grade students. Three of them are Puerto Rican, the rest are black.

The room shows signs of hard use. The blackboard at the front has two top-to-bottom cracks in it. The wooden work tables are covered with countless carvings and assorted messages in pencil and ink. The metal storage cabinets lining a wall are also covered with scrawls made by black felt-tip markers. Several windowpanes have been replaced with plexiglass. A few of the lower panes have black-and-yellow smudges, the work of vandals who wished to determine how resistant plexiglass would be to matches or cigarette lighters.

Most of Lynn's students seem intent either on conversing with their neighbors, munching on potato chips or sunflower seeds, or sprawling out on the tables to take a nap. One boy near the front, to the great delight of his neighbor, tosses sunflower seeds up in the air and tries to catch them in his open mouth. Another girl has dumped the contents of her purse on the table and feverishly hunts through the pile of rubble for an object of importance. A girl at the back has a glazed look on her face as she stares straight ahead, smacking a huge wad of gum that she periodically manipulates so that it erupts with a surprisingly loud crack.

Lynn [loudly and firmly]   All right, class, I want everyone's attention. We're not going to start until everyone is sitting up and looking up here. And put all that food away, right now! I've told you a dozen times not to bring food in here!

Willie [with contempt]   Lady, I don't want to do nothin'. Just leave me alone. I gots to get my beauty rest. [He puts his head down on the table and pretends to begin to take a nap. Several students begin to laugh.]

Lynn [angrily]   Willie, you sit up right now, or you're going to be out of here for the rest of the year! [All attention is on Willie.]

Willie [pulling himself up with greatly exaggerated effort]   Sweetheart, why you always hasslin' me? You have a fight with your boyfriend last night or something?

Lynn [turning red with anger and yelling]   Willie! I want you to go out into the hall! We're going to have a talk! [She points toward the door.]

Several students in unison   Oooooh! She be mad now!

Willie [knocking over his stool as he gets up]   I'm leavin' now, but I ain't waitin' on you, you cross-eyed bitch! [He stalks over to the door, opens it and, pausing for a moment, casts a contemptuous glance back at Lynn. Then he slams the door shut.]

Lynn [trembling]   All right, class. Let's get down to business. Don't worry about him. Cassandra, stop smacking that gum, please.

Cassandra [whining]   Ah, Miss Dorsett. I be quiet.

Lynn   Okay, today we're going to begin our watercolor still lifes. [Taking a deep breath.] I've arranged three compositions up here on the counter. [She gestures toward the counter to her left where she has arranged the three studies: several pieces of fruit in a straw basket, four hardcover books and two bookends, and a blue vase with white carnations in it.] I want each of you to select one and do a sketch of it and then a water color.

Herb [from the back]   You gonna let him back in class?

Lynn   What?

Herb   Willie. You gonna let him back in class?

Lynn   That's between me and him. Don't worry about it. [Firmly.] Now I want you to get to work.

Herb   Ah, I don't wanna do this. It's *boring*.

Several others in unison   Yeah, it's boring!

Lynn [with her hands on hips]   You *will* finish this assignment, or you will not pass art! It's up to you.

Shirley   We don't care.

Michael   You can't fail us if we come.

Darrell [from the back]   Come on, you guys. Shut up and give the lady a chance. [A few students nod in affirmation of Darrell's request, but most ignore him.]

Julius   I don't want to do this crap.

Shirley   She can't make us do it if we don't want to.

Lynn's students seem to sense that their teacher might be weakening, and they begin to escalate their resistance. Cassandra starts snapping her gum again. The boy with the sunflower seeds continues tossing them into the air, missing at least twice as many as he catches. On the floor near his stool, dozens of seeds are scattered. A girl right next to Lynn openly and provocatively begins to tend to her hair with a huge purple hair pick. A solid, well-muscled boy emits a loud moan of disgust as he pushes his art supplies out to the center of the table and puts his head down. Two boys in the back begin tapping out a wild staccato beat using their water color brushes.

Several of Lynn's students sit with amused, nonchalant expressions as they watch the confrontation unfold between their teacher and their more aggressive classmates. About four students, however, work on their sketches, as though oblivious to the surrounding drama.

Lynn [with great difficulty]   I will fail everyone for this marking period who does not begin right now! [She walks over to her desk and picks up her green record book. Amid various grumblings and a few barely audible curses, most students begin to go through the motions of starting on their sketches.]

Carlos   Why you gotta be so hard, Miss? [He starts to position his paper to begin his sketch.] We just don't wanna do this drawin' and stuff.

Lynn   This is one of the projects you have to do to get credit. [With resolution.] Everyone has to do it.

She begins to walk around the tables, stopping here and there to give a student directions. As Lynn paces about the room, her students continue to make noise though at a somewhat reduced level. With uncanny sensitivity most students comply with her demands and yet continue to misbehave almost as brazenly as they did earlier. Resigned to the shaky, limited truce she has been able to negotiate with her students and emotionally depleted from her previous angry outbursts, Lynn makes no further attempts to discipline her class as a whole.

***

The following afternoon Lynn enters Charles's empty classroom several minutes before the start of her first class at Kennedy. Charles is seated at his desk grading papers.

Charles [looking up]   Hi, Lynn. [With concern.] You look troubled. Is anything the matter?

Lynn [sitting in a student desk]   My last period yesterday. It was just terrible. [With emotion.] I don't think I can go on.

Charles   What happened?

Lynn   My kids were just awful. It seems like I can't relate to them. Every day it's the same thing . . . a huge battle to get control. My other classes here are a bit better but not much. [Hesitating.] I . . . I don't think it's a racial thing. I'm not prejudiced. But I really feel they hate me.

Charles   It takes a while to develop rapport with some of our kids.

Lynn   I know that. But some of the kids seem so malicious. [Pausing.] I wonder if there's something I'm doing. It's almost like they gang up on me to see how much I can take.

Charles [slowly]   This is hard for me to ask, Lynn, but how do you feel about the kids? How do you really feel about them?

Lynn   Well I . . . I want to teach them.

Charles [gently]   But how do you *feel* about them?

Lynn [slowly]   Well I think I like most of them. [With a trembling voice.] Some of them I'm afraid of. I really don't understand them . . . the way they speak, the way they dress.

Charles [nodding]   Hmm, hmm.

Lynn [hesitating]   And some of the boys make these comments about me and a boyfriend that I don't even have. Things like that, you know. Am I worried about getting AIDS? Would I date a black man? Would I marry one?

Charles [sighing]   They know how to get to us. [Pausing.] Tell me, how's it going in the mornings over at Hawthorne?

Lynn [with a long, deep sigh]   Oh it's a lot better. I get along well with the kids, I think. Every once in awhile I have to discipline them, but nothing out of the ordinary. They're learning. I really like it there.

Charles   Have you seen Mr. Deavers about your classes here?

Lynn [with frustration]   I caught up with him finally. He just made me feel like it was my fault. If I just did a better job of motivating the kids, then I wouldn't have any problems.

Charles   That sounds like Deavers.

Lynn [beginning to cry]   I . . . I've always wanted to teach, but I can't go on like this. I don't know what to do! Charles, how do I relate to kids like these!

Family Background Data on Students in Lynn Dorsett's Eighth Grade Art Class

Name	Eligible for Free Or Reduced Lunch	Parent(s)/ Guardian Present in Household	Mother's Education	Mother's Occupation	Father's Education	Father's Occupation
1. Anderson, Willie	Yes	Mother	8th	Homemaker	6th	Unemployed
2. Bond, Julius	No	Mother, father	10th	Nurse's aide	10th	Painter
3. Cross, Harriett	Yes	Guardian (aunt)	8th	Homemaker	unknown	Unknown
4. Dixon, Shirley	No	Mother	12th	Teacher's aide	10th	Truck driver
5. Fidalgo, Carlos	Yes	Guardian (grandmother)	7th	Homemaker	5th	Laborer
6. Garrett, Harold	No	Mother, father	8th	Maid	8th	Construction
7. Hall, Greg	Yes	Mother, father	9th	Homemaker	9th	Cook
8. Johnson, Michael	No	Mother, father	8th	Homemaker	8th	Bartender
9. Kerr, James	Yes	Mother	10th	Homemaker	9th	Unemployed
10. Lawrence, Fred	Yes	Mother	12th	Waitress	7th	Unemployed
11. Mack, Theresa	Yes	Mother	9th	Beautician	8th	Janitor
12. Mitchell, Audry	No	Mother	12th	Restaurant owner	10th	Musician

(continued)

Name	Eligible for Free Or Reduced Lunch	Parent(s)/ Guardian Present in Household	Mother's Education	Mother's Occupation	Father's Education	Father's Occupation
13. Northcutt, William	No	Mother, father	1yr. college	Bank teller	1 yr. college	Real estate sales
14. Odom, Carol	Yes	Mother	10th	Clerical	10th	Butcher
15. Payne, Dorothy	Yes	Guardian (grandmother)	9th	Homemaker	9th	Unemployed
16. Pitts, Donna	No	Mother	10th	Supermarket manager	9th	Unemployed
17. Ramos, Victor	Yes	Guardian (grandmother)	8th	Homemaker	7th	Unemployed
18. Reyes, Herb	No	Mother, father	10th	Homemaker	10th	Pawn shop owner
19. Reynolds, Cathy	Yes	Mother	9th	Homemaker	7th	Unemployed
20. Sanford, Darrell	No	Mother, father	8th	Waitress	9th	Landscaper
21. Walker, Andrew	No	Mother, father	2 yrs. college	Beauty shop owner	12th	TV repair
22. Washington, Cassandra	Yes	Mother	10th	Homemaker	9th	Unemployed
23. Webb, Bill	No	Mother, father	11th	Clerical	10th	Auto repair
24. Wild, Jerry	No	Mother, father	1 yr. college	Cook	12th	Appliance salesman

QUESTIONS

1. How do the "climates" at Hawthorne Middle School and Kennedy Junior High School differ? What factors determine a school's climate? What can teachers and administrators do to improve a school's climate?

2. Could Lynn have avoided the confrontation she had with Willie? How? Did she make the right decision in telling him to step out into the hall so they could talk? Should she allow Willie back into class? How should she respond to him if he returns?

3. What should a teacher do when confronted with large-scale student resistance such as Lynn faces at the end of the period? How effective is her threat to fail those students who do not begin to work? Is a teacher ever justified in using such threats?

4. How do the intrinsic and extrinsic views of motivation differ? Which view is Mr. Thomas taking when she says, "Well, that's part of teaching . . . motivating those who'd rather be doing something else"? How do the needs of the students at Kennedy differ from those at Hawthorne? What can Lynn do to take these differences into consideration?

5. What social class, racial, and home environmental differences exist between the students at Kennedy and those at Hawthorne? What teaching and classroom management procedures are most effective with these two groups?

6. What teaching objectives does Lynn seem to have developed for teaching art at the two schools? State two or three. How appropriate are her instructional strategies for these objectives?

7. Would the classroom management models of Thomas Gordon (Teacher Effectiveness Training) or William Glasser work at both Kennedy and Hawthorne? How should Lynn handle the discipline problems at Kennedy?

8. Given the family background data at the end of the case and Mrs. Thomas' comment, "It's their families . . . we've got a lot of parental support," what differences exist between the socioeconomic backgrounds and home environments of the Kennedy and Hawthorne students? What kinds of programs and procedures have been developed to get the parents involved in the school? How can a teacher develop rapport with culturally different students?

9. Considering the work of Robert Rosenthal and others on the self-fulfilling prophecy, especially in terms of teacher expectations, what kinds of perceptions and expectations has Lynn developed regarding the students at the two schools? What kinds of perceptions have the students developed in return? What can be done to change such perceptions and expectations?

CASE 14

TWO CLASSES IN ONE

Canyon High School is located in a city of about 100,000 in a western state. The school is situated on a four-acre site surrounded by modest ranch-style homes. Built in the mid 1960s, the school serves students who are, for the most part, from middle-class families. During the last three years, the school experienced a steady increase in enrollment when large numbers of families from economically depressed cities in the Midwest and Northeast began to move into the city. Currently the school's enrollment is just over 1,000. Eighty-five percent of the students are white, with the remaining 15 percent about evenly divided among black, Hispanic, and Oriental students.

When the doors to Canyon High were first opened, it was billed as one of the state's most innovative schools. The school featured six open-concept "pods," which were devoted to the following areas of the curriculum:

Pod A—English and foreign languages
Pod B—Mathematics
Pod C—Sciences
Pod D—Social studies
Pod E—Health, physical education, music, and art
Pod F—Industrial arts and vocational education

Within a year after Canyon High opened, however, teachers had begun to use portable room dividers, bookcases, and storage cabinets to divide the pods into self-contained areas. A group of teachers who felt strongly that the open concept was not an appropriate design for a high school also began to pressure the superintendent to authorize the permanent partitioning of the pods into separate classrooms. After six years of effort that involved petitions, appearances before the school board, studies by architects, engineers, and contractors, the teachers finally succeeded in getting the pods divided into individual rooms.

On a cool, pleasant October morning, Roy Folsome, a black English teacher who first came to Canyon High five years ago, pulls his red sports car into the faculty parking lot. He smiles and chuckles to himself when he sees that he is lucky enough to get a parking spot right next to his classroom in the English pod. In his trunk is a heavy bundle of newspapers for students in his third period junior level remedial skills class, and he is especially pleased that he will not have to carry the papers very far.

As Roy is about to remove the newspapers from his trunk, Vera Waters, chairperson of the English department and the only Canyon High teacher who has been at the school since it first opened, pulls up and parks in the spot next to Roy. For the moment Roy puts off lifting the papers from his trunk and, instead, walks over to greet Vera.

Roy [opening Vera's car door with great ceremony] Morning, Vera. Looks like the gods must be smiling on us. Two parking places like this right next to the English pod.

Vera [chuckling] Oh, I know what you mean. This is the closest I've ever been able to get. [Stepping out of her car.] How are you this morning, Roy?

Roy Good. [He walks back over to his trunk.] I've got these newspapers here I'm going to use in my remedial skills class. [He surveys the bundle of newspapers for a moment, deciding on the best way to lift them out of his trunk.]

Vera [noticing Roy's briefcase standing on the pavement next to his car] Here, let me take your briefcase.

Roy Thanks, that'll help. [Roy leans over and grasps the twine that binds the newspapers together. In a smooth, powerful motion, he removes them from his trunk. Vera closes his trunk.]

Vera [as they walk the 20 yards to the English pod] I think it's a great idea to use newspapers in our remedial skills classes.

Roy Well, I think it'll help. I've really had trouble with my skills class this year. It seems like the class is almost split 50-50 between students who really are remedial level, or even learning disabled, and those who might be able to function in a regular class.

Vera Oh it's hard when you've got a class with kids at both ends of the spectrum.

Roy Right. When you meet the needs of one group, you're probably short-changing the other group and vice versa. [Pausing while Vera opens the door to the English pod.] I guess grouping kids by ability is all right when the placements are accurate. But I just don't know with my third period class. [He enters the pod and then begins walking briskly toward his room.]

Vera How's the discipline in there?

Roy [his voice beginning to show the strain of carrying the newspapers] That's probably my biggest problem. When I gear my teaching for the slower kids, the others get bored and restless. When I aim for the faster kids, then the slower ones get frustrated and give up. [He comes to his room and puts the newspapers on the floor in order to fish his keys out of his pocket.] Whew! That gets heavy after awhile. [Taking his briefcase from Vera.] Thanks. I'm really glad you came along.

Vera Any time, Roy. [Turning toward her classroom, which is right next to Roy's.] Let me know how the newspapers work. I might give them a try in my remedial skills class.
Roy Sure thing.

***

Later that morning Roy is standing in front of his 15 remedial skills students. Each student has an open newspaper on his or her desk.

Roy Okay. Turn to page 8C; we're going to read an article about a man who won the lottery. [Students begin turning pages.] It's the third column, right underneath his picture.
Ben [calling out] Hey, I ain't got no page 8.
Alex It's 8C, dummy. Why don't you just look at the pictures, you can't read anyway.
Ben Buzz off!
Roy [moving toward Ben] All right, you two. It's 8C. That's page 8 of the third section. Does everyone have it now?
Students in unison Yes.
Roy Before we start reading, let me ask a question. How do you think your life would change if you won a million dollars?
Raymond [blurting out] I'd quit my job!
Roy [firmly] Raise your hand, Raymond. [Noticing Anne with her hand raised.] Anne?
Anne You'd start getting bothered by all these people who wanted money. [Students laugh.] You'd probably have to change your telephone number.
Roy That could happen. In fact there might be some real drawbacks to winning a million dollars. That's what the man in this article found out.
Julius [spontaneously] Hey, no way a million bucks would be a problem. It's a problem when I ain't got it. [Several students laugh.]
Roy [smiling good naturedly] Maybe so, Julius, But let's find out what happened to this man in the article. I think you might be surprised. [Scanning his students before he selects a student to read.] Lisa, would you begin reading?
Lisa [in a strong, confident voice] "When Norman Swanson decided six months ago to buy one lottery ticket each payday, little did he realize the profound impact that one decision would eventually have on his life. . ."

As Lisa reads it is obvious that several students are not paying attention. One boy at the back of the room is reading from a history book that he has placed on top of his open newspaper. Another boy has his head down on his desk. Suddenly two girls begin to whisper loudly about a rock music magazine they have been passing back and forth. Lisa stops reading. All students turn toward the back of the room.

Roy [walking toward the girls]   All right, ladies, put the magazine away. [Speaking to one of the girls, a very attractive, physically mature brunette whom several boys in the class stare at almost constantly.] Gloria, why weren't you paying attention?
Gloria   Newspapers are just so boring.
Roy   Well it would help if you followed along. [Pointing to the newspaper on her desk.] Now let's pay attention. [Turning to the other girl.] Martha, you too.
Gloria   Well what about David? [She points to the boy who had been reading his history book.]
David [angrily]   Hey, mind your own business. I know where we're at.
Julius [pointing at David and referring to him by the nickname his classmates have bestowed upon him]   Yeah, "School" is cool. He can read two books at the same time . . . one with each eye. [He laughs heartily.]
David [to Julius]   At least I can read! [Several students burst out with comments about how studious David is. Others take advantage of the sudden noise and confusion to begin talking among themselves. Within seconds the class is close to becoming out of control.]
Roy [gesturing for silence with both hands raised and yelling as loudly as he can]   All right, class! Let's calm down! [Startled at the potency of their teacher's response, the class becomes quiet almost immediately. All eyes turn toward Roy.]
Roy [continuing in a normal voice]   I can see that some of us are apparently not mature enough to read and to discuss the news. So I want each of you to write an essay of at least 200 words on "What I Would Do If I Won a Million Dollars."

About half Roy's students immediately proceed to get out paper and pencil or pen in order to write their essays. Within moments they are busily writing. The remaining students, however, sit there, either staring off into space, casually turning pages of the newspaper, or doodling on their sheets of notebook paper.

Roy [to those students who have not begun to write]   Come on now, I want a paper from everyone.
Ben [defiantly]   I ain't never gonna get a million dollars, so why should I do it?
Roy [firmly]   Because if you don't do it you won't pass this course.

At Roy's comment Ben starts to write his name slowly on a sheet of paper. Once he finishes his name though, he begins to twirl his pencil.

Ben   This is too hard. I'll start it tomorrow. [A boy and a girl sitting next to Ben nod their heads in agreement.]

Roy   It's not going to be any easier tomorrow. Besides it's due today at the end of the period. [Pointing to the clock on the wall.] You've got 15 minutes.

Harold [turning in his seat so he can see Ben and the boy and girl] Man, this isn't hard. All you guys gotta do is write about what you'd do with a million bucks. What's the big deal?

Frank [from the front]   Yeah, all you gotta do is start writing.

Roy   All right. Don't worry about what other people are doing. Just take care of your own business.

Alice [as though she didn't hear her teacher's command]   All you guys ever do is complain about how hard the work is. If you'd just shut up and do it—

Ben   Maybe we don't wanna do it.

Mary   Yeah, maybe we think it's dumb.

Roy   Hey. Hey! Just a minute here.

Gloria [becoming quite angry]   Well you guys never want to do what we wanna do.

Martha   Yeah.

Frank   Well like all you guys ever want to do is those dumb word-search puzzles or look up words in the dictionary.

To counter the rising tension and hostility between the two groups of students, Roy decides to try to refocus their attention. He walks purposefully to the front of the room. Once there he turns dramatically and, hands on his hips, begins to address his students.

Roy [trying to contain his anger]   Now, everyone, listen real carefully. I will *not* have you at each other's throats like this, do you understand? The next person that talks out of turn gets a zero on this assignment. Furthermore, anyone who does not turn in an essay at the end of the period . . . your parents can expect a telephone call tonight.

Several students in unison   Oooooh. No.

Roy [seriously]   I mean it. I won't put up with it. [Pointing again to the clock.] You've got less than 15 minutes.

Within moments, all Roy's students are busily writing. He begins to walk up and down the rows, monitoring their progress.

***

Later that day after Canyon High students have been dismissed, Roy is in the office of the principal, Bruce Wilkins.

Roy   So out of the 15 students I've got in that remedial skills class, I'd say about half of them don't really belong there. I really think they ought to be in a learning disabilities class.

Mr. Wilkins Students are assigned to the skills classes on the basis of their scores on the state's assessment test. They wouldn't be in there unless they had a problem on the test.

Roy [placing a paper on Mr. Wilkins' desk] But look. Here's a list of my students and their reading comprehension and vocabulary grade equivalent scores. You can see that about half of the kids are one to two grade levels higher than the others. [Sliding the paper across Mr. Wilkins' desk.] Their grades for English last year are also on there.

Mr. Wilkins [glancing quickly at the paper and then returning it to Roy] I understand what you're driving at, Roy, but the learning disabilities class is running at full capacity. That teacher couldn't handle another kid. [Clearing his throat.] Besides by the time you had any of your kids evaluated by the school psychologist and assigned to the learning disabilities class, the year'd be over.

Roy [frowning] That's what I was afraid of. [Pausing.] What I've got in there really are two classes in one.

Mr. Wilkins Well remember, any class is always going to have students at different levels.

Roy I know that. But with this group of kids, it's almost like they've taken sides, the faster ones versus the slower ones. When I aim things at the faster ones, the slower ones get frustrated and start acting up. When I try to satisfy the slower ones, then the others get bored and restless.

Mr. Wilkins Um, um.

Roy I've tried putting them into two separate learning groups, but remedial level kids just can't handle being on their own in a small group. They need to have constant direct supervision, or else they go wild. But when I put the whole group together, it's like trying to mix oil and water. [Looking directly at Mr. Wilkins.] How do you teach a class like that? How can I give the faster kids what they need and not lose the slower ones or vice versa?

CANYON HIGH SCHOOL

Class: Eleventh grade remedial skills English
Teacher: Roy Folsome
Period: Third

Name	Reading Comprehension*	Vocabulary Grade Equivalent*	Tenth Grade English
1. Adams, Ben	7.2	7.7	D
2. Arnold, Alex	8.3	8.9	D
3. Barns, Lisa	9.2	9.4	C
4. Cestero, Gloria	6.5	6.6	C
5. Driscoll, Martha	6.4	6.7	D
6. Fox, Raymond	7.8	8.1	D
7. Garcia, Anne	8.9	9.1	C
8. Jefferson, Julius	6.7	7.0	D
9. Kennedy, David	8.3	9.0	C
10. March, Harold	9.1	9.7	D
11. Nelson, Frank	9.2	9.5	C
12. Schroeder, Alice	8.4	8.6	C
13. Skinner, Mary	6.0	6.1	D
14. Thompson, Robert	5.7	6.2	C
15. Washington, Lula Mae	9.1	9.3	D

*Decimal scores refer to months; e.g. 9.1 = ninth year, first month.

QUESTIONS

1. Why do you suppose Roy had difficulties when trying to gear his teaching to either group? How realistic would it be for Roy to gear his teaching to the individual needs of his 15 students?

2. Are all the students in Roy's class at the remedial level? If not, why were they assigned to a remedial class?

3. If students are to be grouped according to ability, what criteria should be followed in making the assignments? Achievement test scores? Teacher recommendations? Grades? Motivation? Other criteria?

4. From a motivational perspective, how do the needs of the two groups differ? What is frustration and how does it help explain the behavior of the low-ability group? How do you explain the bored and restless behavior of the regular-ability group in motivational terms? Do the two groups share any common needs and interests that Roy can capitalize upon?

5. Examine Roy's discipline procedures from the standpoint of Kounin's classroom management theory. To what extent does he display withitness?

6. What does low ability mean in the context of this case? Is it the same thing as slow learner, or underachiever, mentally retarded, specific learning disability, or culturally disadvantaged? What teaching methods work best with such students?

7. From the viewpoint of Rosenthal's self-fulfilling prophesy theory, what expectations has Roy developed regarding the students in the two ability groups? What expectations have the students in the two groups developed regarding one another? How does this relate to the research in social psychology on labeling, stereotyping and pigeon holing? How much similarity is there between this class and a mainstreamed class in special education, and what does research say about the effects of mainstreaming upon the attitudes of the teacher, the regular students, and the mainstreamed students?

8. What teaching strategies have been found to be most effective in working with classes divided along ability lines? How effective are cooperative versus competitive versus independent study teaching procedures?

9. What is the best interpretation of the reading comprehension and vocabulary data presented at the end of the case? Do these data indicate that the low-ability students are candidates for a specific learning disability class as Roy contends?

PART V

PUPIL ADJUSTMENT CASES

CASE 15

SHY SALLY

Brooks Elementary School serves a primarily white (75 percent) K–6 student population in a rural area of a populous western state. The building was constructed in the 1950s but is well maintained and well equipped. Mary Powell is a veteran teacher of 21 years' experience and is currently teaching 24 sixth graders. It is early in the school year (November), and Mary is moving from student to student as they work on math problems. Mary moves to the desk of Sally Gorman who is staring at a blank sheet of paper.

Mary [frowning]   Are you having trouble, Sally?

Sally [startled, whispers]   No. I just don't know how to do it.

Mary [bending down next to Sally's desk and pointing to a problem on her paper]   Don't you remember when we went over these yesterday?

Sally [staring at the paper]   Yes but I forgot.

Mary   Don't you remember I called on you and you got the answer right?

Sally   Yes but I really can't do them!

Mary [raising her voice slightly]   Can't or won't, Sally? Weren't you daydreaming just now?

Sally [bearly audible]   I guess so.

Mary   You're a very smart girl, Sally, but you have to pay attention and do your work.

Sally   But I can't do these! I don't know how!

Mary   Go ahead and try, Sally, and I'll be back in a little while to check on your work.

***

After school is over and Mary has finished supervising the loading of her students onto school buses, Mary goes back into the building to the office of Emma Buell, the school's guidance counselor.

Emma   Why, Mary, hello! Have you come to visit me?

Mary [smiling]   Hi, Emma. I wish I could say this is a social visit, but I'm afraid that I've really come to find out what you can tell me about one of my kids—Sally Gorman.

Emma [searches in a file cabinet and pulls out Sally's folder]   Well I can tell you several things about Sally. Are you having trouble with her?
Mary   Well she's very shy and is content to sit and do nothing. She doesn't contribute to class discussion and, when I try to draw her out, she speaks in a very low voice—almost a whisper—so I have a hard time understanding her. When I try to talk to her one on one, she keeps telling me that she doesn't understand and can't do the work, even though I know she can and does on occasion. It's very frustrating, Emma! Sally doesn't pay attention and seems to spend most of her time daydreaming.
Emma [opening Sally's folder]   I think you're right about her being able to do the work. Her I.Q. was 111 last time she was tested—a definite underachiever. I think that a lot of Sally's problem is her mother.
Mary   I've never met Mrs. Gorman. She didn't come to the open house in October.
Emma   That's an experience you can do without, believe me!
Mary   What do you mean?
Emma   She's a noisy, aggressive, thoroughly obnoxious woman! The most negative parent I've ever been around! It's no wonder that Sally's shy. I'm sure that her mother beats her down all the time!
Mary   What about Mary's husband?
Emma   They're divorced, of course. Poor man probably couldn't take it!
Mary   Then, Mrs. Gorman works?
Emma   Yes, she works on the assembly line at Central Electric. I'll bet she can cuss with the best of them too! [Pause.] Yes, I'd say that Sally's problem stems from home.
Mary   Any suggestions?
Emma   It's hard to try to compensate for that kind of a home disadvantage. You might begin by trying to get some kind of a self-concept measure on Sally and then try to use it to draw her out. Perhaps you could use that sentence completion inventory that you used a couple of years ago.
Mary   Good idea, Emma. I'll have all the kids do it along with that projective thing of having them draw a picture and tell a story about their home. Then Sally won't feel singled out. Great idea!

***

It is two days later, and Mary is conducting a science discussion on animals as a precursor to an upcoming field trip to the zoo. She deliberately stands in front of Sally so Sally cannot daydream during the discussion.

Mary   And now, boys and girls, let's talk about what the book has to say about the cat family. What is the biggest cat? [All the students except Sally raise their hands.] Yes, Roger?
Roger   The lion.

Mary [smiling] Ah, ha! I fooled you! You all thought it was the lion, didn't you?

Becky [without raising her hand] I didn't!

Mary [with a twinkle in her eye] You didn't, Becky? What is the right answer?

Becky The tiger.

Mary That's right! Now how many of you knew that? [All hands but Sally's go up.] Oh I don't think so! I think that some of you are trying to fool me! [Several children titter.] Now let's all look at the picture of the members of the cat family on page 43. As you look at the picture, which cat is the largest? Sally?

Sally [points to the tiger.]

Mary That's right, Sally! What do we call that cat?

Sally [barely audible] Tiger.

Mary That's right! Say it louder, Sally, so we can hear you.

Sally [whispers] Tiger.

Mary That's better. Now class, let me ask you a very difficult question. What is the largest cat in the Western Hemisphere? [Pause—no hands are raised.] I'll give you a hint. It has spots, but it's not a leopard. Anyone know? Becky?

Becky Is it the puma?

Mary No. This cat has spots. [Sally very tentatively raises her hand and then takes it down.] Sally?

Sally [shakes her head.]

Mary I told you this was a tough one. Jerome?

Jerome A bear. A black bear.

Mary No, Jerome. The bear is neither a cat nor does it have spots. Okay, Becky, you want to try again?

Becky A jaguar?

Mary Right, Becky! You know the answer! [Looks at Sally.] Did you know the answer too, Sally?

Sally [shakes her head "yes" but says nothing.]

Jerome [without raising his hand] Yeah, I'll bet! If she knew the answer, I knew it too! [Sally lowers her head and looks down at the floor.]

Mary That's enough, Jerome! We can't read other peoples' minds, can we? I know Sally is a person who tells the truth, and I think she did know! [Pause.] Now let's talk about some of the smaller cats. [Sally continues to stare at the floor.]

***

It is the next afternoon after school. Mary has asked Sally to stay after class and sits in front of her desk talking to her.

Mary Don't worry, Sally, I'll get you to your bus on time. I just wanted to talk to you a minute. [Sally stares down at the floor.] I was so pleased yesterday when you knew about the jaguar. [No response.] You studied

that lesson, didn't you? [Sally nods her head "yes" but continues to stare at the floor.] Sally, I'm so pleased for you because I've been a little worried about your work. You haven't been doing your work and participating in class.
Sally [whispers] I can't.
Mary Sally, you're a very smart girl. I know you can if you try.
Sally [whisper] I try, but it's too hard.
Mary [very gently] Sally, why don't you talk more in class?
Sally [whispers] I don't know.
Mary I noticed that you don't play with the other kids at recess. Why not?
Sally [whispers and looks at the floor] They don't like me.
Mary Do you mean the other children?
Sally [nods her head "yes."]
Mary Well, Sally, I like you and want you to do well. Maybe I should talk to your mother to see if she can help. Would that be okay?
Sally [looking up at Mary for the first time with fear in her eyes.] I guess so. [Pause.] It doesn't matter.
Mary [sighs] Okay, Sally. Run along and catch your bus.

***

It is one week later, and Mary has arranged a conference with Sally's mother in her room after school. Mrs. Gorman is in her middle thirties and is overweight and somewhat disheveled in appearance. Her face seems lined in a permanent scowl.

Mary [nervously] Thanks so much for coming, Mrs. Gorman! I know you're very busy, and I wouldn't have asked to see you if I wasn't so concerned about Sally.
Mrs. Gorman [frowning] What's the matter with Sally? I knew her grades weren't too good, but that's because she's lazy. [Raising her voice.] If you'd give her a good whack or two she'd straighten up and get to work.
Mary [hesitantly] Well, Mrs. Gorman, Sally doesn't seem to believe in herself and doesn't try. She thinks she can't do the work when she's really a very bright little girl.
Mrs. Gorman [with a glint in her eye] I think she's got your number! I'm telling you, all you've got to do is give her a kick in the pants. I'll tell you, she sure doesn't pull that stuff at home! I'll guarantee you she does her work around the house! I just don't put up with any crap! [Pause.] Look, Mrs. Powell, I'm very busy and I really don't have any more time for this! I expect teachers to do their jobs just like I do mine! I would appreciate it if you would not bother me about Sally unless it's really important! I've got another, uh, appointment that I've got to go to. Goodbye.

***

It is two days later, and Mary is speaking to her class as she passes out papers.

Mary Students, I think you're going to find what we're going to do now is a lot of fun! Now first look at the sheet of paper that says "Sentence Completion" at the top. We're not doing English when we fill it out. You get to make up your own answers to complete each sentence. There is no right answer—just tell how you really feel. This will help me get to know each of you better and do a better job of teaching. [Short pause.] When you're through completing the sentences and turning your paper in, I want you to draw me a picture and write me a story about it. Take two blank sheets of paper from this pile [pointing] and first draw me a picture of your home. Then write me a story about what it's like to live at your house. Yes, Kevin?

Kevin Are we supposed to color our picture?

Mary You may if you like. It would be nice if you did, but do what you feel. [Pause.] Okay, let's begin. [Mary stands next to Sally's desk to make sure she participates.]

***

It is Monday of the following week, and Mary meets with Emma Buell, the guidance counselor, in Emma's office after school.

Emma How did your conference with Mrs. Gorman go?

Mary Just like you predicted. An aggressive, almost masculine, woman.

Emma [laughing] One thing's sure—she's certainly no gentleman!

Mary [smiling] Yes, I'll bet she more than holds her own with the other workers. [Short pause.] It helped me understand poor Sally better. [Short pause.] What did you think of Sally's response on the sentence completion inventory and the picture and story she wrote.

Emma Well I'm certainly no expert on projective techniques, but I didn't think the picture and story revealed much. They almost seemed to be more of an academic exercise than a revelation of Sally's view of her world. But the sentence completion responses were certainly interesting!

Mary I thought so too. What do they tell you?

Emma They reveal a girl who is very depressed and who has very little confidence in herself. I could call Sally in and give her a self-concept inventory, but I think we both know what it would tell us.

Mary [sighing] Yes, it would tell us that Sally has a very negative self-concept. [Pause.] Emma, what am I going to do? How do you help a child like Sally?!

Sentence Completion

Interest Inventory   **Name:** Sally Gorman

1. My father likes me best _Don't know. Don't see him. (Hardly ever)_

2. My mother likes me best _When I do what she tells me. (If she's in a good mood.)_

3. I feel Proudest _Nothing. I can't think of anything. When I do right._

4. When I finish school I want to be _Don't know. Maybe work at Central._

5. My favorite hobby is _Reading and watching T.V._

6. When I go home after school I like to _Have free time so I can do what I want to._

7. My worst fear is _Doing bad. Making my mother mad._

8. People are happiest _When they get to do what they want. When they are left alone._

9. My friends _I like to be alone. Friends can get you in trouble and tell lies._

10. My favorite school subject is _I like reading stories like fairy tales best of all._

11. School is *Good when they let you do what you like to do. Bad when they make you talk in front of others.*

12. Home is *Working hard and doing what you are told.*

QUESTIONS

1. Evaluate the exchange between Sally and Mary at the beginning of this case. How would you have felt if you were Sally? What might have been a more effective way for Mary to have responded to Sally?
2. How might Sally's shyness be explained in terms of Erikson's stages of personality development? How can such shyness be dealt with?
3. What can a teacher do when he or she encounters a parent who, like Mrs. Gorman, displays some evidence of being a psychologically, perhaps even physically, abusive parent?
4. Some people believe that sentence completion inventories and other projective techniques, such as drawing pictures, represent an invasion of a student's privacy. What is your opinion? What alternative methods could a teacher use to gather data that might shed light on a student's behavior?
5. What is the self-concept and how is it formed? What is the difference between self-concept and self-esteem? How does Sally see herself and her world? How does the self-concept change? What steps could Mary take to increase Sally's self-esteem?
6. How can self-concept be measured? What is the best interpretation of Sally's responses on the sentence completion inventory at the end of the case?
7. What is an underachiever? How does underachievement relate to self-concept? To reinforcement and punishment?
8. What role does Sally's mother seem to have played in the formation of Sally's self-concept and behavior in school? What does Emma mean when she says that Sally has a "home disadvantage?" What can the school do to help compensate for such a disadvantage?
9. From an operant conditioning framework, what relationships exist between punishment and avoidance behavior? How might this help explain Sally's shyness and whispering? What are the sources of punishment in Sally's life?
10. At what levels of Maslow's need hierarchy does Sally seem to be experiencing deficiencies? What about Sally's mother and Mary?

CASE 16

TOUGH JEROME

Bronson Junior High School is located in a large southeastern city. Its student body is divided racially, 55 percent white and 45 percent black. It is the first day of classes as Tara Collins, a white, 29-year-old woman from a middle-class background, sits at her desk waiting for the students in her first period eighth grade English class to file in and take their seats. Tara has taught for seven years, but this is her first year of public school teaching and her first year at Bronson. She had heard that some tough students attend Bronson and had made her mind up not to be "run over" by such students. She tries to appear very businesslike and authoritative. Tara's classroom is in a portable building separated from the main building.

Suddenly Jerome, a six-foot–one-inch black student who is 15 years old, appears at the door. He enters the classroom with a frown and a look of surprise.

Jerome [growling] Whatchoo doin' here? Mr. Dreyfus s'pose to be my English teacher!
Tara [businesslike and authoritatively] Take a seat, please. May I see your schedule? [Jerome, still frowning, walks up to her desk and hands her his schedule.]
Tara Yes, you're in the right place. Mr. Dreyfus has been transferred to another school. I am Mrs. Collins, your English teacher.

Tara hands Jerome's schedule back to him and walks to the doorway to greet other students. She is somewhat shaken by her exchange with Jerome as she thinks to herself, "Who's this rude student? Is he one of the tough black kids they warned me about?" She admits to herself that she dislikes him.

***

It is the end of the first day of classes. Tara walks down to the guidance office and walks into the office of one of the counselors, Melody Coffey.

Melody Hi! Tara isn't it?

Tara Yes. Tara Collins, Melody.

Melody My friends call me Mel. Sit down and tell me how your first day of classes went. I seem to remember from our preschool meetings that this is your first year of public school teaching.

Tara You've got a good memory. My classes are sure different from the ones I had when I taught parochial school. It seems like discipline is going to be a much bigger problem here. Which brings me to one reason why I came to see you. Can I see Jerome Jackson's cum record?

Melody You sure can.

***

Melody goes to a file cabinet, locates and pulls out Jerome's cumulative folder, and pulls her chair next to Tara's so they can look at the cumulative folder together.

Tara [looking at the folder] No wonder Jerome is bigger than the other students—he's 15. I see he had to repeat the fifth grade. His home life may be different, too. His father's stationed overseas and gone a lot.

Melody Yes, you may have a problem on your hands there in Jerome. I suspect that if anyone can handle him, though, you can.

Tara [smiling] I hope you're right. I've heard a lot about some of the tough kids here, and I think maybe Jerome's one of them.

Melody Maybe so. I don't really know him even though he's one of my assignees. Give him the benefit of the doubt though. Appearances can be deceiving.

Tara [standing to leave] I hope you're right! Thanks so much for your help, Mel. I'm sure I'll be back to see you again.

Melody You're certainly welcome any time.

***

Several weeks have passed. Jerome enters the first period English class ten minutes late. Tara and the students stop their discussion and look at Jerome as he laughs defiantly and takes his seat.

Tara [calmly] I see you're late again, Jerome, and didn't bring your book, paper, or pencil to class with you again.

Jerome [smiling] Guess so!

Tara [sternly] I need to talk to you at the end of the period!

Jerome Okay. Got to sharpen my pencil.

***

While Tara and the students watch, Jerome gets up from his desk, walks over to another student's desk and helps himself to a pencil on the top of the desk. When the student reaches for the pencil, Jerome slaps his hand aside, laughs aloud, and quickly moves toward the pencil sharpener. As he moves past the next-to-last student, a white boy, between him and the sharpener, Jerome thumps the student on the back of his head. When the boy puts his hands on the spot where he was thumped and loudly complains, Jerome reaches down and knocks all the student's books, notebooks, and papers on the floor. Jerome then quickly moves to the pencil sharpener as he laughs out loud and says, "S'cuse me."

Tara [angrily]   Jerome, please sit down now! [Jerome walks to his seat smiling. When Tara turns her back he pokes a boy with his pencil and then takes his seat. The student rubs the spot with his hand and says, "Ouch" to himself. Jerome sits at his seat fidgeting and smiling.]

***

As class ends Jerome starts toward the door, but Tara is too quick for him.

Tara   Jerome! I need to talk to you a minute! [Jerome stops, walks back to Tara's desk and suddenly sits down in a chair.]
Jerome   Goin' to be late to class!
Tara [firmly]   Don't worry about that. I'll give you a note. This is more important. Jerome, I'm worried about your attitude. You always seem to come to class late, you never bring books, paper, or pencil, and you seem to have fun poking and hitting other students, knocking their books off on the floor, and knocking chairs over.
Jerome [frowning]   Don't do it on purpose! Just accidents!
Tara   Accidents or not, your behavior is going to have to improve or you're going to be spending a lot of time in the dean's office.
Jerome   Don't do nothin' wrong. Jes' accidents. Don't know why you always pickin' at me! Teachers are always pickin' at me!
Tara [pleadingly]   Jerome, I want you to do well in class. All you have to do is try to be considerate.
Jerome   Goin' to be late to class.
Tara [exasperatedly]   Wish you worried about that in my class. [Pause.] Oh, all right, go ahead! I'll give you a note if you need it.

***

It is several weeks later. As Jerome walks into the room approximately 15 minutes late, several of the students emit audible groans upon seeing him.

Jerome [looking at a white boy and frowning]   What you lookin' at? Don't roll your eyes at me!
Tara [angrily]   Jerome! That's enough! Go to the dean's office right now!
Jerome [innocently]   What did I do? Why are you pickin' at me?

Tara [firmly]   Now, Jerome! Go! [Jerome smiles, shrugs his shoulders, and leaves.]
Tara [firmly]   Now lets all get back to work reading the assignment!

Tara walks back to her desk, sits down in her chair, and emits a sigh. One white student, Bill, nods to four others, and all five of them walk up to Tara's desk.

Bill [in a hushed tone]   Mrs. Collins, can we talk to you for a minute?
Tara   Yes. Go on.
Bill   Mrs. Collins, we've all talked to our parents and want to complain to you about Jerome. He makes it so that we don't want to come to this class; he's always taking things without permission and bugging us.
Marsha   Yes, Mrs. Collins, he's gross. He smells! He never washes his hair, I don't think, and I hate to have to sit so close to him!
Mary Ann   Yes, I almost hate to come to first period anymore! Can't somebody do something, Mrs. Collins?
Tara   Please believe me. It's as difficult for me as it is for you! I've tried just about everything. Nothing seems to make any difference. But I'm still working on it and trying to get help from other people in the school.
Tom [assuming an exaggerated, swaggering manner]   I'm sorry, Mrs. Collins, but I've had about enough from him! Just about the next time he thumps me on the back of my head, I'm going to clean his plow!
Tara [firmly]   Tom, you'll do no such thing! Now I thank you all for letting me know how you feel. However, handling Jerome is my responsibility. Let's all take our seats and get back to work.

***

The same afternoon Tara drops by the office of the dean of boys, Clyde Williams, right after her last class. Clyde is writing at his desk and looks up when Tara enters his office.

Clyde [looking up]   Hi, Tara. Have a seat. Let me just finish marking this sheet, and I'll be right with you.
Tara [sitting down]   That's all right, Clyde. Take your time.
Clyde [after short pause]   Sorry about that, Tara, but I was afraid I'd forget to enter the numbers in the right place on the attendance report. [Smiling.] Now how can I help you? I'll bet you came in to talk about Jerome.
Tara   You're right. I was sorry to have to inflict him on you again, Clyde, but I really didn't know what else to do with him this morning! He always comes to class late and he's constantly disrupting everything that is going on. My first period English class has really deteriorated since the beginning of the year thanks to him! Class morale couldn't be lower. Both the students and I hate to see Jerome show up for class every

morning. And now a running battle seems to have developed between Jerome and Tom.

Clyde [frowning]   Tom Johnson?

Tara   Yes. I've never seen such a change in a boy. At the beginning of the year, Tom seemed almost wimpy, and Jerome used to pick on him all the time. Now Tom has begun to wear camouflage pants to class, and his writing and conversation are all filled with weapons and violence. Bill tells me that Tom's been taking karate lessons. He and Jerome have almost come to blows several times. [Sighing.] Clyde, I'm almost at my wits end!

Clyde   Tara, I'm really glad that you came in today! I didn't know that things had gotten that bad!

Tara   The worst part of it, Clyde, is what it's done to the class. Now that Tom and Jerome are at one another's throats all the time, we're just not getting much work done. The kids are starting to take sides, and racial tensions are surfacing.

Clyde   Tara, let me work on this. Jerome is one of Melody Coffey's counselees. I want to get her and some other people, including parents, involved in this before things get out of hand.

Tara [relieved]   Thanks, Clyde. You don't know how much it helps to have someone support you in a situation like this! Like I said, I'm at my wits end!

Clyde   That's what we're here for, Tara—to help dedicated teachers like you do your jobs. Please go see Melody in a day or two after I've started to put some things in motion.

Tara   Thanks again, Clyde!

***

One week later Tara is sitting in Melody Coffey's office.

Melody   Even before you spoke to Clyde, I'd been calling Jerome in for counseling. I'd say that I've probably talked to him eight times since then.

Tara   Did you talk to him yesterday?

Melody   Yes I did, first thing in the morning before your class. How did you know?

Tara   When Jerome came to class he said, "I guess I should just kill myself; then everyone would be happy!" out loud so that the whole class could hear him. The students all began to applaud. After I quieted them down, I began to think about how serious Jerome's problems are.

Melody [with a serious look]   Yes, they are serious.

Tara   What do you think we should do, Mel?

Melody   We've got to get Jerome's parents involved. Maybe they would agree to professional counseling for him. Maybe we should also explore the possibility of placing Jerome in an emotionally handicapped program.

Tara How can I help?
Melody I'll let you know when I've set up a meeting with Jerome's mother. His father is usually out of the country, you know.
Tara Yes, I remember.
Melody If you agree that he should be placed in an emotionally handicapped program, you'll need to fill out the appropriate forms.
Tara I'd be happy to.

***

The next day Tara is sitting at her desk grading papers. Her last period class has been over about 15 minutes. Melody walks in the door and over to Tara's desk.

Tara Well, hi, Mel! I wasn't expecting to see you again so soon!
Melody [sitting down in a chair] I just finished talking to Jerome's mother on the phone a few minutes ago to try to set up a meeting with her. Naturally she wanted to know what we wanted to talk to her about so I had to tell her.
Tara What did you say?
Melody She resisted the idea of either professional counseling for Jerome or placing him in an emotionally handicapped program. She said that Jerome was just a bad boy and that those things wouldn't help. She admitted that he drives her crazy at home and that she can't control his behavior. She copes with him by letting him do what he wants, since he's too old to tell what to do.
Tara Oh boy!
Melody That isn't all! She also said that Jerome's father is the disciplinarian in the family and that Jerome's behavior had steadily gotten worse since his father had taken his overseas assignment. Jerome's mother sounds indecisive and weak and said that his father would have to decide what to do about him. She did agree to let Mr. Jackson know about the situation as soon as possible though.
Tara This is worse than some soap opera on T.V.!
Melody [laughing] Nobody could dream up a plot like this one!

***

One week later Tara is again sitting at her desk alone grading papers after school. Clyde Williams, the dean of boys, walks in.

Clyde Hi, Tara. Every time I see you you're working hard.
Tara [smiling] Either that or crying on your shoulder about Jerome Jackson.
Clyde [smiling] Yes, well, I think both of us are a bit fed up with Jerome's behavior. [Pause.] Anyway that's why I wanted to catch you before you left: You're going to have a visitor first period tomorrow morning.

Tara Who?

Clyde Mr. Jackson. Jerome's mother talked to him about Jerome's behavior, and he's flown back from overseas to straighten things out. He says that he wants to come to your first period class to observe Jerome's behavior in person.

Tara He must know that Jerome's behavior won't be typical with his father there!

Clyde I'm sure he does. I think that he really just wants to talk to you. He's really a nice, mild-mannered person. He often checks in with me when he's in town. You won't have any problem recognizing him.

Tara What do you mean?

Clyde He's an awesome looking guy—must be almost seven-foot tall.

Tara You're sure he's gentle now?

Clyde [smiling] Guarantee it. He's just a big ex-jock who reminds you of a big teddy bear. You won't have any problem.

Tara If you say so!

* * *

Tara sits at her desk after her last class, which has just ended. Mr. Jackson did not show up first period nor did Jerome. Tara was both disappointed and relieved at that turn of events. However, right after the last student leaves the room, a well-dressed towering black man around six feet, seven inches in height enters the room and walks over to Tara's desk. Jerome trails behind him like a puppy dog and looks very sheepish.

Mr. Jackson Mrs. Collins? I'm James Jackson, Jerome's father.

Tara [shaking Mr. Jackson's hand] I'm pleased to meet you, Mr. Jackson. Won't you sit down.

Mr. Jackson [turning to Jerome] Jerome, would you please wait down the hall by that water fountain. I want to talk to Mrs. Collins alone.

Jerome [quietly] Yes, sir. [Leaves the room.]

Mr. Jackson [meekly] Mrs. Collins, I want to apologize to you for Jerome's acting up. As I've told Jerome's other teachers, I've just about had it with the boy. He's ruining our family life. He just about drives everyone crazy. Sometimes I wish I could dump him in a juvenile home or something. It's bad enough having to work overseas so that we can have a few of the financial benefits in life. Jerome not only doesn't help, he keeps getting in trouble. My wife just doesn't know what to do with him. She can't handle him when I'm away.

Tara Mr. Jackson, has anyone talked to you about the possibility of placing Jerome in one of our special programs for emotionally handicapped students?

Mr. Jackson Why no! Does the school have a program like that? How does it work?

Tara Yes we do. And it's supposed to be excellent. Mrs. Coffey,

Jerome's counselor, would be the best one to explain it to you. However, Mrs. Coffey and I both think that Jerome might be better off in the program right now.

Mr. Jackson   I'd like to know more about it, but I agree. How do we get him in it?

Tara   You just have to fill out some forms in Mrs. Coffey's office to start the process, and she takes it from there.

Mr. Jackson   Well I have to go back overseas right away, but if Mrs. Coffey will send the forms to my wife, she'll sign them.

Tara   It would be better if you talked to Mrs. Coffey yourself so she can tell you all about the program, but I'll be happy to tell her what you said.

Mr. Jackson [standing up and extending his hand]   Well all right then, Mrs. Collins. I'm very pleased to meet you, and I'm very sorry that Jerome has caused so much trouble.

Tara [shaking Mr. Jackson's hand]   Well I'm pleased to have met you too, Mr. Jackson, and I'll tell Mrs. Coffey what you said.

***

Two weeks later Tara is sitting in Melody Coffey's office after school.

Melody   I've tried to contact Mrs. Jackson every day for two weeks, Tara! I've written two letters and still no response.

Tara   I know! I asked Jerome why no one ever answers the phone, and he just says that his mother's never home. My guess is she's changed her mind and just doesn't want to cooperate.

***

Three weeks later Tara is leading a discussion in first period English, and Jerome bursts into class 20 minutes late.

Tara   Jerome, you're late again! You can just go straight to the dean's office and get a tardy slip. [Jerome retreats just outside the door.]

Jerome [becoming enraged and beginning to scream from the doorway]   That's not fair! You just hate me! You don't make the other students go!

Tara [moving to the doorway]   Jerome, you leave right now before you get into worse trouble!

Jerome [screaming]   No!

Tara closes the door on Jerome. Jerome opens the door and begins cursing. Tara then locks the door, becoming frightened. She sends a student out another door to the office to get help. Jerome then leaves the building, goes outside Tara's classroom, sticks his head through the window and shouts obscenities and accusations. The student that Tara had sent to the office returns, but no one else comes from the office. After five minutes, Tom finally jumps up, goes over to the window and pushes

Jerome's head out. Tom then jumps out the window in spite of Tara's yelling at him and chases Jerome toward some woods. At this point some of the black and white students in the class begin to yell at both Jerome and Tom as well as at one another. At that moment a male teacher in the room next door sticks his head in the door.

Tara Ron! Oh thank god you're here!

Ron My god, Tara! What's going on in here! Hey, you guys over there! Quit yelling at one another and sit down!

***

After class the same day, Tara is seated in Melody's office discussing the day's wild events.

Tara Thank god Ron came in when he did! I don't know what I would have done if he hadn't been there.

Melody Yes, I guess the only person in the office was the secretary, and she couldn't get ahold of anyone.

Tara You should have seen the look on Jerome's face, Mel! I'll never forget it! His eyes had a wild look in them, and his lips quivered in a desperate sort of way!

Melody Well thank god everything's under control now!

Tara What happened to Jerome?

Melody He ran home. Clyde tells me that they'll suspend him for 10 days.

Tara What happens after the 10-day suspension?

Melody His mother refuses to sign the papers to put him in a special program, so he'll have to go back to his regular classes like before.

Tara [exasperated] You mean he'll be back in my first period English class again after all that's happened!

Melody [matter-of-factly] I'm afraid so.

Tara [sternly] Just tell me one thing, Mel. What am I going to do with him when he comes back?

BRONSON JUNIOR HIGH SCHOOL
Cumulative Record

Name: Jackson, Jerome Lee
Address: 4118 Grant St.
Father: James V. Jackson   **Occupation:** Off-shore oil rig driller
Mother: Rose M. Jackson   **Occupation:** Housewife
Siblings: Pearl E., age 12
　　　　　Hattie A., age 9
Former Schools: Wilmot Elementary   **Handicaps:** None
Date Entered Bronson: 8/30/87   **Date of Birth:** 4/13/75
General Health: Good   **Age:** 15

TEST RECORD
Intelligence Tests

	Form	I.Q.	Date	Grade
Otis-Lennon Mental	Elementary 1	81	4/81	3
Ability	Elementary 2	73	4/87	6

ACADEMIC RECORD
Grades 1–6 (Year Averages)

	1	2	3	4	5	5*	6
Citizenship	C	C	C	D	F	D	D
Language arts	C	C	D	D	F	D	D
Reading	C	C	D	D	F	D	D
English			D	D	F	D	D
Spelling	D	D	D	D	F	D	D
Writing	C	C	C	D	F	D	D
Social studies			D	D	F	D	D
Arithmetic	D	D	D	D	F	D	D
Music	C	C	C	C	D	C	C

*Repeated fifth grade

Grade 7 (Year Averages)

English	D
Geography	D
Arithmetic	D
Phys. ed.	C
Science	D

QUESTIONS

1. What kind of expectations did Tara convey to Jerome when she first met him? To what extent do you suppose her expectations of Jerome acted as a self-fulfilling prophecy?
2. How would you explain Jerome's hostile, aggressive behavior? What theories are useful in interpreting his behavior?
3. How should Tara prepare for Jerome's return to class following his 10-day suspension?
4. What values does Jerome seem to hold about physical violence and aggression, obscene language, personal hygiene, emotional control, the value of education, and racial prejudice? What values does Tara seem to hold?
5. How does Jerome's home environment relate to his behavior in school? What are some of the effective programs and procedures that schools can employ to involve parents in their childrens' education?
6. At what level of Maslow's need hierarchy does Jerome seem to be operating? Tom? Tara? Jerome's parents?
7. From an operant conditioning perspective, what reinforcers seem to be maintaining Jerome's disruptive behavior? Why do Tara's attempts at punishment not decrease his disruptive behavior? How do Jerome's peers influence his behavior?
8. From an observational learning viewpoint, what models of disruptive behavior might Jerome be imitating? What are symbolic models and vicarious reinforcement and how might they be available in Jerome's environment?
9. From a humanistic frame of reference, how does Jerome perceive the school and himself (self-concept)? How does he perceive his home situation, especially his mother and father? How does the self-concept form, and under what conditions does it change?
10. What is an emotionally handicapped child? Does Jerome qualify? What programs are available for working with such students?

CASE 17

THE CLOWN

Westside Senior High School is one of two high schools in a predominantly middle-class city of 45,000 in a midwestern state. The school, built in the mid-1970s, sits on a barren level field just off an interstate highway. In the center of the one-story brick building is an outdoor courtyard occasionally used by classes on pleasant fall or spring days. At the north end of the school is a blacktop parking lot with room for several hundred students' cars. On most school days, the lot is filled to capacity.

Mary Harvell has been teaching ninth and tenth grade English at Westside since she graduated five years ago with a master's degree in education from the state's largest teachers college. It is a cool November morning, and Mary is making some end-of-class announcements to the 27 ninth graders in her second period class. As she speaks her students gather their books and papers together in anticipation of the dismissal bell.

Mary [loudly] I want you to be sure to finish reading the story by tomorrow. We'll have a short quiz on it at the end of the period tomorrow. [Noticing Kevin's raised hand.] Kevin?
Kevin What kind?
Mary What do you mean, "What kind?"
Kevin [with a touch of impatience] What kind of quiz?
Mary Oh. [To the entire class.] The quiz will be short answer. If you've read the story, I don't think you'll have any problem. [Responding to Heather's upraised hand.] Heather?
Heather How many questions?
Mary You'll have 20 questions, and each one will be worth five points. It'll be just like the quiz we had last week. Any other questions?

At this moment the dismissal bell rings, and the room is immediately filled with the sounds of chairs being moved and students talking loudly and animatedly with one another.

Mary [almost yelling] Okay. See you tomorrow. Be sure you're ready for the quiz!

Her students quickly and anxiously stream out the door, and, within seconds the room is empty and quiet. Once alone Mary sighs and then smiles to herself as she reflects on the boundless energy of ninth graders. She then takes a seat at her desk and begins to organize materials for her next period class, tenth grade English.

***

Later that same day Mary is in the teachers' lounge grading compositions and enjoying a soft drink. Two other teachers, Faye Evans from the mathematics department and Rod Nelson from the science department, are also in the lounge. Mary is working at a large table in the center of the room. Faye and Rod are seated at opposite ends of an old couch donated years ago by a Westside teacher. Faye is grading an exam she gave the previous period, and Rod is reading a science textbook. Suddenly Mary begins laughing.

Mary [to herself]   I can't believe this!

Faye and Rod [in unison]   What's that?

Mary [looking up]   Oh I've got this kid in my second period class, Kevin Walker. I had them write a composition on why getting an education is important and Kevin, who is one of my class clowns, wrote this: "If you want to be somebody, you got to get an education. You got to listen to your teachers and do what they say. They are very important people, just like the President or the Pope." [Pausing.] This is a kid who almost *never* listens to what I say.

Rod [sarcastically]   Tell me about him. Kevin's in my seventh period general science. He's a character all right. I don't think he's a bad kid though.

Mary   No, he's not really bad. Actually I kind of like him. But he seems to need *so* much attention lately, he can be a pain.

Faye   It's funny how kids like that can be such hypocrites, writing about how important teachers are and how they should be listened to. Like they say, it's hard to practice what we preach.

Rod   And when he compared us to the president or the pope, we're in *big* trouble if that's all the respect they can get. [Mimicking Kevin's voice.] Mr. President, my name is Kevin Walker, and I don't think you know what you're doing. [All three laugh at the image of Kevin addressing the president.]

Mary   I just hope he's not getting worse. He started off the year really fine. You know, he was just kind of an average kid. He did his work, usually got C's. But now he's started questioning everything we do. [Sighing.] I'm really beginning to get tired of his lip.

Faye   I think the kids call it back-talking.

Rod   I've noticed the same thing in my class.

Mary [with determination.]   Well if it gets any worse, I'm going to have a parent conference.

***

It is three weeks later, and Mary is conducting an English grammar lesson with her second period class. She stands in front of her 27 students who are seated in five neat, parallel rows. On the wall to her left is a bulletin board featuring an array of randomly arranged book jackets. At the top of the bulletin board is a large gold key on which is printed the message, "Reading: The Key to the Unknown." Near the back of the room is a filmstrip projector which Mary has previously loaded with a filmstrip on the eight parts of speech.

Mary   All right, class. Today we're going to begin our review of the parts of speech. You've had this material before, so if the review goes well, we can go on to something else in a day or two.
Kevin [blurting out]   I wanna go on to lunch. [Several students laugh. A few others though look in Kevin's direction, their scowling faces indicating that they find his comment more annoying than humorous.]
Mary [matter-of-factly]   That's enough of your wise-cracks, Kevin. Okay. Now who remembers how many parts of speech there are? [At least half Mary's students raise their hands.] Annie?
Annie   Eight.
Mary   Good. Now let's see if we can list them on the board here.

She walks over to the blackboard on the side of the room and picks up a piece of chalk. Her students turn in their seats to face the board. Mary numbers from one through eight and then turns toward her students, several of whom have their hands in the air.

Mary   Allen, can you name them?
Allen [beginning rapidly]   Noun, pronoun, adjective, adverb . . . uh . . . verb—[As soon as he begins to falter, Kevin interrupts.]
Kevin   Declarative, interrogative—
Mary   Just a minute, Kevin, you're naming something else.
Kevin [continuing with his list as though he did not hear his teacher]   Introduction, body, conclusion—
Mary   All right, Kevin, stop it! You're just getting too wild here. You can't say just whatever comes into your mind. [At Mary's scolding Kevin breaks into a broad grin and then begins laughing.]
Kevin   Ha, ha, ha, ha! [All eyes turn toward Kevin.]
Mary [angrily]   Kevin, if you don't quiet down this moment, I'm sending you down to the dean's office!

With this threat Kevin stops laughing. His entire body, however, begins to jerk convulsively as he struggles to contain his laughter. Finally he puts his head on his desk in an attempt to control himself. Within a few moments he calms down, and Mary continues her lesson.

Mary Okay. We've got five of the eight parts of speech listed. [Reading from the board.] Noun, pronoun, adjective, adverb, verb. Three more. What are they? Janice?
Janice Conjunction and . . . uh . . . preposition.
Mary [smiling at Janice] Good. That's two more. [She turns to write the terms on the board. When finished, she turns back to her students.] One more. [With drama in her voice.] Who can get it?
Billy Object?
Mary [shaking her head] No, that's one way that nouns can work in a sentence though.

At this moment Kevin, his head still on his desk, begins making strange incoherent noises.

Kevin [in a muffled tone] Ahhhh . . . hmmmmmm . . . ahhhh . . .
Mary Kevin, stop that! Sit up! What are you doing? Are you all right?
Kevin [springing upright in his seat with a broad grin] Who me? I'm fine. [He pulls out the top of his shirt and peers down at his stomach.] Yep, looks all right to me. [Three students giggle at Kevin's response.]
Mary I want you to be quiet! I don't want to hear another peep out of you this period.
Kevin [with a silly look on his face] Chirp.
Mary [with frustration] I said be quiet!
Kevin But I chirped, I didn't peep. [Again a few students giggle.]
Mary Kevin!
Kevin All right, Miss Harvell, I'll be cool. [He draws his right thumb and index finger across his lips as though zipping his mouth shut. He then stares straight ahead with a bemused look on his face.]
Mary Now let's see if we can get back on track. All right, we need one more part of speech. Anyone? [She scans her class looking for a student who might know the answer.] Okay, what do you say if you cut yourself with a knife?
Karen [spontaneously] Ouch!
Mary That's right. That's an example of the eighth part of speech.
Herb [blurting out] Oh, I know what it is!
Mary Go ahead, Herb. What is it?
Herb An interjection!
Mary Very good! We've got them all. [She writes the last term on the board.] Now I want us to watch this short filmstrip on the eight parts of speech. [She walks to the back of the room and turns on the filmstrip projector. Mary aims the bright stream of light at the screen she had previously pulled down.] Would someone please turn off the lights?
Leo I'll get 'em, Miss Harvell.

After Leo flips the light switch, considerable daylight continues to enter the room through three uncovered windows. At best the light in the room has been cut in half.

Leo [responding to a knock at the door] Hey, Miss Harvell, there's a teacher out here who wants to see you.
Mary [beginning to walk toward the door] Excuse me. I'll be right back.

Mary walks to the door and for a moment stands in the open doorway conversing with the other teacher. She then turns to her students.

Mary I have to go across the hall for just a minute. I'll be right back. [As she leaves she closes the door behind her.]

Within a few seconds of Mary's departure, Kevin leaves his desk and begins dancing up and down the center aisle of the room, bathed in the light of the filmstrip projector. Several students begin clapping and encouraging him on in his wild dance.

Willie Go, Kevin, go.
Allen There he is, ladies and gentlemen, the one and only Kevin!

Egged on by a few of his classmates, Kevin suddenly leaps up on Mary's desk and, squinting into the bright light of the projector, begins speaking into an imaginary microphone.

Kevin Ladies and gentlemen, I'd like to thank you for coming to my first live concert. For my first number, I'd like to do a song I wrote myself, "Why Don't You Love Me?"

A few students clap their hands at Kevin's announcement. After pretending to adjust his guitar, Kevin beings singing.

Kevin [obviously making up each line] Baby, why don't you love me? You said you'd always be true. But lately you can be so cruel. So baby, why don't you love me? Whenever I call you—[Kevin's singing is cut short by Mary's return to the room.]
Mary [loudly and with a great deal of anger as she enters the room] Kevin Walker! Get down off that desk immediately!

She walks briskly over to the desk as though intent upon bodily removing Kevin. Kevin, however, has darted back to his seat by the time Mary gets to the desk. He has a contrite look on his face, as though genuinely worried that he might have carried his clowning a bit too far this time.

Mary [very sternly]   Don't let me *ever* catch you pulling a dumb stunt like that again!

Mary mechanically stacks and then restacks some papers on her desk in an attempt to contain her anger and to give herself a moment to decide how to handle Kevin's disobedience.

Mary [in a firm, controlled voice]   I want to see you after class. [She looks directly at Kevin who nods his head slightly to indicate that he understands.]

***

Later that period after the other students have left, Kevin is sitting in a chair next to Mary's desk. Mary, who has just finished putting away the filmstrip projector, walks back to her desk and sits down.

Mary   What in the world got into you today, Kevin?
Kevin [fidgeting and looking down at the floor]   I don't know.
Mary   I've never seen you act like this.
Kevin [softly]   I was just fooling around.
Mary [firmly]   Well I will not put up with it in my classroom. Do you understand? [Kevin nods his head.] I'm really disappointed in your attitude. You began well in here, but then you started to clown around. [Pausing.] Did you finish today's assignment? [She points to the papers she has just collected.]
Kevin [continuing to squirm]   I did all the ones I could get, Miss Harvell.
Mary   Well you got a C in here the first marking period, and the way you've been slipping you're going to be lucky if you get a D this marking period.

Kevin nods his head weakly at this information. The two then sit for a moment in silence.

Mary   Well what I'm going to do about today is send your name down to the office for after-school detention for the rest of the week.
Kevin [suddenly showing more animation]   Ah, Miss Harvell, I promise I won't do it again.
Mary   No, it's too late. I've given you enough warnings. And if I don't see some immediate improvement in your attitude, I'll have to have your parents come in. Do I make myself clear?
Kevin [lethargically]   Yes, Miss Harvell.

***

Two weeks later Mary enters the teachers' lounge with a distraught look on her face. She drops her books on the table and slumps into a chair. Faye Evans and Rod Nelson, both of whom are seated in their usual spots on the couch, look up from their work.

Rod Having a rough day?

Mary [with a long sigh]   Look what I just took from Kevin Walker. [She takes a short rubber knife out of her purse and tosses it to Rod.]

Rod [watching the blade bend as he stabs the palm of his left hand with it]   Up to his old tricks, I see.

Mary I can't begin to tell you how freaked out I was when I first saw that knife. I thought it was real! Kevin and this other kid were fooling around in the hall right before the bell rang. Then all of a sudden Kevin pretends like he's getting real mad, and he pulls out this knife. I just about died! I think I'm still shaking.

Faye This is the kid you were having trouble with before, isn't it?

Mary He's the one. I can't figure it out. We really started off the year well. He's not a mean kid like some others. He's just a clown, and I can't get him to stop. [Pausing.] There's been such a change in him.

Rod I've noticed the same thing in my science class. He started off okay, but lately he's been trying to see how many laughs he can get. You don't think . . . I wonder if he might be getting involved with drugs. I'm sure that some kids sit out in their cars during lunch and take whatever.

Faye [with disgust]   I wish they'd keep the kids on campus for lunch. There's no reason we have to have an open campus.

Mary I really doubt that's the case with Kevin. It seems like it's mainly the older kids or at least a different type of kid that gets involved in that stuff. [With a sigh.] I just wish I knew what to do with him.

Cumulative Record

Name:	Kevin L. Walker
Address:	123 Elm Street
Father:	John Walker
Mother:	Dorothy Walker
Siblings:	Annie, 12 Jane, 16
	Sara, 15 Jim, 17
	David, 16

Home Phone:	333-5678
Occupation:	Painter
Occupation:	Homemaker

Former School:	Maple Elementary
General Health:	Excellent
Handicaps:	None
Date of Birth:	8/20/74

TEST RECORD
INTELLIGENCE TESTS

	Form	I.Q.	Date	Grade
Otis-Lennon School Ability Tests	Elementary I	106	10/10/82	3
	Intermediate	98	10/13/86	7
	Advanced	99	10/15/88	9

ACADEMIC RECORD

Grades 1–6 (Year Averages)

	1	2	3	4	5	6
Reading	C	C	D	C	D	D
Mathematics	B	C	B	B	C	C
Science/Health			C	C	C	C
Social studies				C	C	C
Language	C	C	D	C	D	C
Spelling	B	C	C	C	C	C
Music/Art	C	C	C	C	C	C
Citizenship	C	C	C	C	C	C

Grades 7–8 (Year Averages)

Grade 7		Grade 8	
Eng.	C	Eng.	C
Geog.	D	U.S. hist	C
Math.	C	Math.	C
Science	C	Earth sci.	C
P.E.	B	P.E.	C

Personal Development (Grades 1–6)

	1	2	3	4	5	6	
Conduct	C	C	C	D	C	C	C
Effort	C	C	D	D	C	C	C
Follows directions	C	C	C	D	C	C	C
Initiative	C	C	B	B	B	C	C
Attitude	C	C	C	C	C	C	C
Work habits	C	C	C	D	D	D	
Participation	C	C	C	C	C	C	

QUESTIONS

1. From a classroom management standpoint, does Mary contribute in any way to Kevin's behavior? For example, should she have given her students a specific task to work on when she left the room?
2. What is the most effective way for a teacher to handle a class clown? In regard to Mary's situation, what should she do?
3. What role do Kevin's peers play in regard to his classroom behavior? Could Mary use their influence in some way to lessen Kevin's clownish behavior? How?
4. How appropriate would it be for Mary to use a "classroom meeting" approach (based on the work of William Glasser) for dealing with Kevin's behavior? What might the results of such a classroom meeting be?
5. From an operant conditioning viewpoint, what reinforcers seem to be maintaining Kevin's behavior? Why don't Mary's attempts to punish and decrease Kevin's clowning behavior seem to work? What reconditioning procedures could Mary use to try to change Kevin's behavior?
6. In terms of Maslow's need hierarchy, what need level dominates Kevin's behavior? How can Mary take advantage of this knowledge?
7. According to the social psychology research on class clowns, what are the characteristics and antecedents of class clowns?
8. From the perspective of humanistic and self-concept theory, how does Kevin perceive himself and the classroom situation? Does Kevin evidence insecurities that help explain his clowning behavior? How can a teacher help a student change his perceptual field?
9. What does the portion of Kevin's cumulative record presented at the end of the case tell you about Kevin? What is the best interpretation of Kevin's test record and academic record? Does this information relate to Kevin's clowning behavior?

CASE 18

TROUBLED AMY

It is the first full day of classes at the beginning of a new school year at Springfield High School. SHS draws its overwhelmingly white student body from an even mixture of low-income and middle-class families located in a New England city of approximately 50,000 people.

The bell rings to announce the beginning of third period, and the last few stragglers quickly run into room 111, Sue Suthard's classroom. Sue is 27 and in her third year of teaching in the business education department. She faces the class, smiles, and then begins to speak.

Sue [confidently] All right people. Let's settle down. [Pointing.] And will you two please sit down. [Pausing for five seconds until all are quiet and attentive.] This is general business and I'm Miss Suthard. Everyone in the right room? [No response.] Well according to my records all 38 of you are sophomores. I'll bet you're all glad that you're finished with your freshman year. [Several chuckles.]
Student You can say that again!
Sue [smiling] I'll let you in on a little secret. I think that general business is my favorite course. How many of you think you are going to learn something important to you in general business this year? [All hands but one, Amy Martin's, go up.]
Sue I know several of you from my homeroom last year. Sarah, what do you hope to learn in general business this year?
Sarah Well I guess the most important things are to learn how to budget my money and how to make out my income tax. [Smiling.] At least that's what my dad wants me to learn. [Several students chuckle.]
Sue I would have to agree that those are important things for anybody to learn. We'll not only learn about budgeting and tax preparation but also about a number of other practical things like how to go about getting a job and opportunities for investing and increasing your money once you earn some. We'll have some interesting speakers this year, and we'll see some excellent films.
Student [after raising his hand and being recognized] Will we be taking any field trips?
Sue Yes, Bill, we will. Once I find out what your vocational interests are, I'll be lining those up. So I think we're going to have a fun year.

[Pause.] Right now, though, I guess I'd better call the roll and see if everyone's here. Please raise your hand as I call your name so I can begin to put together your names and faces. [Sue begins to call the names in alphabetical order from her grade book and to mark absences.]

Sue [after calling many names]   Amy Martin? [No response.] Is Amy absent?

Student   No she's right over there. [Pointing.] Amy! Are you with us? [Several class members laugh loudly.]

Amy [with a glazed look in her eyes and responding slowly in a surprised manner.]   What? Yeah, I'm here.

Sue [frowning]   Let's all pay attention now as I call your names!

***

The next day Sue drops by the office of Nancy Rowley, the school nurse, during her planning period.

Nancy [smiling] · Hi, Sue. How's everything going?

Sue   I've got a great load! My favorite courses and only two preparations!

Nancy   That's great! Got a good bunch of kids?

Sue   Generally yes. Very bright and eager. However, I dropped by to talk to you about one of them—Amy Martin.

Nancy   Oh yes. Amy. [Nods her head knowingly.]

Sue   Well Amy wasn't one of my homeroom kids, but I did have her mother in a night class that I taught last year. Her mother was a fine student, although she did miss class more than I liked. But yesterday in class I could have sworn that Amy was high on something.

Nancy   Stoned more than likely. I'm quite acquainted with Amy's situation. She doesn't talk to me anymore because I contacted her parents about her problems with pot and alcohol. I guess she doesn't trust me anymore.

Sue   She has a drug and alcohol problem?

Nancy [emotionally]   Oh yes! I'd say for the last couple of years. In all fairness I'd say that her home situation is a difficult one for a 15-year-old to cope with. They live over in the poorest section of the east side in a very small apartment. Her stepfather has beat Amy's mother several times in the past. Both the stepfather and mother are usually unemployed and on welfare. No wonder Amy has these problems and her attendance record is so poor. The kid has a bad situation.

Sue [listening intently]   Oh, oh! There's the bell, Nancy. I've got to go to my next class. Listen, thanks for the information. We'll talk again.

***

One week later and five minutes into her third period general business class, Sue is passing out a class assignment when Amy walks in smelling strongly of alcohol. Amy takes her seat near the front of the class.

Sue   Amy, you're late to class today. What's that odor I smell?
Amy [defiantly]   I don't know!
Sue   I could send you to the office and let Mr. Braxton find out.
Amy [meekly]   Please don't. I'm sorry.
Sue [sternly]   Go ahead and start on this assignment. [handing her a copy.] However, I want to talk to you here right after your last class.
Amy [dejectedly]   Yes, Miss Suthard.

The last period has ended, and Sue is sitting at her desk grading papers as she waits for her conference with Amy. Twenty minutes after the end of the period Amy arrives and sits down in a chair next to Sue's desk.

Amy   You wanted to talk to me, Miss Suthard?
Sue   Yes, Amy, I do. Amy, I had your mother as a student in my night class last year. She and I became friends.
Amy   Yes, I know.
Sue   I want you to do well in my class and in school this year. However, I've noticed your poor attendance in the school records and, I'll be totally honest with you, I don't appreciate your coming to class under the influence of drugs or alcohol the way you did today. [Pause.]
Amy [hesitantly]   I have lots of friends, Miss Suthard, and they like to party a lot.
Sue [angrily]   That's not much of an excuse, Amy! Let me make this perfectly clear. If you come to class again under the influence, I'm going to send you to the office. Do you know what that will mean?
Amy [sheepishly]   Yes, they'll suspend me, and my parents will really be mad.
Sue   I decided to let you stay in class today for that very reason. However don't count on that next time!
Amy [quietly as she gets up to leave]   I'm sorry. It won't happen again.

***

Two months later Sue again drops by the office of the school nurse. Nancy looks up at Sue and smiles.

Nancy   Hi, Sue. How've you been?
Sue   Busy. It's fun but hectic.
Nancy   How are things going with Amy Martin?
Sue   Well she came to class one day about two months ago just reeking of alcohol. I had a conference with her afterward and really let her have it.
Nancy   Did it do any good?

Sue Yes it did. Overall her behavior has improved. She's had a few slips, but she's careful not to be obvious. I've noticed dilated pupils and poor focusing ability at times, but I really don't want to send her to the office. In my judgment she's better off in school than out. And as a matter of fact, Amy and I talk a lot now and have formed an honest and open relationship with one another. I talk to her like a Dutch uncle, but I think she trusts me. However, lately she has started acting very depressed, and she won't talk to me about it. She's become very sharp with me when I try to get her to open up. She refuses to do her work and keeps her head down on her desk. Something must be going on at home. Do you have any clues?

Nancy Not a one. As I told you, Amy doesn't confide in me anymore. I can tell you that your class is about the only one that she attends regularly. She's down here constantly for one illness or the other. Sometimes she does have a temperature but never anything serious. I think you may be the only one she relates to.

Sue [frowning] I was afraid of that. Well we'll just have to keep our fingers crossed for her.

***

Two weeks later Amy asks to talk to Sue after school. Amy sits down in a chair next to Sue's desk and begins to cry.

Amy [sobbing quietly] Miss Suthard, you're the only person I can talk to! I don't know what to do!

Sue [consolingly] I don't know whether I can help or not, Amy, but I'm a good listener.

Amy Do you promise not to tell anybody?

Sue Yes, I'll keep what you tell me in total confidence.

Amy [with strong emotion] Miss Suthard, I'm pregnant! It's been two months and I haven't had a period! What am I going to do?

Sue Have you told your parents?

Amy God, no! They'd kill me! You don't know how my stepfather can be! I just can't!

Sue What if I talked to your mother alone?

Amy No! She'd just tell Don, and then he'd get angry and hurt me! You promised!

Sue I know I did, and I won't talk to your mother if you don't want me to. But Amy, I'm sure that I could get her to keep the whole matter in confidence and help you if you'll just let me.

Amy No! Don would find out somehow! Don't talk to her!

Sue Okay. But what are you going to do?

Amy [weakly] I don't know.

Sue Are you aware of all of your options? Maybe you should go talk to Mrs. Rowley in the nurse's office.

Amy No! You're the only one I can talk to!

***

One week later, Sue is again having a closed-door conference with Amy in her room after school.

Sue Amy, we've talked about this every day after school for a week. We've explored all the alternatives. I still think you should let me call your mother.
Amy No! I've made up my mind what I'm going to do, but I'm afraid!
Sue What are you going to do, Amy?
Amy [calmly] I'm going to have an abortion.
Sue Have you really thought this over carefully?
Amy Yes. I know a girl that had to have one, and nobody found out about it. I know where she went to have it done. She said that it hurt a lot, especially afterward, but she's okay now.
Sue [sighing] Are you sure, Amy?
Amy Yes. But there's one problem. I don't have anyone to take me. I know it's going to hurt bad, and I need someone to take me. Will you take me, Miss Suthard?
Sue [hesitating] Why I don't know Amy, I—
Amy [pleading] Please, Miss Suthard! You're the only one who can help me! Please help me!

SPRINGFIELD HIGH SCHOOL
Cumulative Record

Name: Martin, Amy Leigh*

Address: 524 East Spruce St., Apt. 38B

Father: Donald M. Maze (Stepfather)

Mother: Dorothy Martin Maze

Siblings: Joseph F., Age 11
Deanna S., Age 2

Former Schools: Wilson Elementary
Jackson Middle S.

Date Entered SHS: 9/15/87

General Health: Fair

Home Phone: 375-4235

Occupation: Gas station attendant

Occupation: Clerk

*Student approved for free lunch

Handicaps: None

Date of Birth: 6/14/72

Age: 15

TEST RECORD

Intelligence Tests	Form	I.Q.	Date	Grade
Otis-Lennon Mental	Level 1H	111	10/14/81	3
Ability Tests	Level 3	108	10/20/85	7
	Level 4	98	10/18/88	10

ACADEMIC RECORD

Grades 1–6 (year averages)

	1	2	3	4	5	6
Citizenship	A	A	A	B	B	B
Lang. arts	C	C	C	C	C	C
Reading	C	C	C	C	C	C
English			C	C	C	D
Spelling	B	B	B	C	C	C
Writing	B	B	B	C	C	C
Social studies			B	B	C	C
Arithmetic	B	B	C	C	D	D
Music	B	B	B	B	B	B

Grades 7–9 (Year averages)

Grade 7	Grade 8	Grade 9
Eng. C	Eng. C	Eng. D
Geog. B	U.S. Hist. C	World Hist. C
Arith. D	Arith. D	Algebra F
P.E. C	P.E. C	P.E. D
Band B	Band B	Biol. D

PERSONAL AND SOCIAL DEVELOPMENT
CODE: 1 = SUPERIOR
          5 = UNSATISFACTORY

Grade	7	8	9
Emot. stab.	3	4	5
Initiative	3	4	4
Leadership	3	3	5
Social attitude	3	4	5
Integrity	3	4	4

QUESTIONS

1. What are the signs that indicate that a student has a drug or an alcohol problem?
2. How should a teacher intervene with a student who has a drug or an alcohol problem?
3. If you were Amy's teacher, how would you use the information presented in Amy's cumulative record?
4. It has been estimated that one million teenagers become pregnant each year. Should teachers play a role in responding to this problem? If so, what should they do?
5. Why does Amy confide in Sue and not in her other teachers? What are the characteristics of teachers whom students feel they can trust?
6. What should Sue do in response to Amy's request?
7. In what ways has Amy's home environment influenced her behavior in terms of drugs, alcohol, and sex?
8. What role does the peer group play in adolescent development, and how does it seem to have influenced Amy's behavior?
9. How effective are drug education and sex education programs? Would either have helped Amy?
10. At which stage of moral development does Amy seem to be operating? How could Sue take this into consideration in her efforts to try to work with Amy during her crisis?
11. At which level of Maslow's need hierarchy does Amy seem to be operating? At which level is Sue operating? How could Sue take this into consideration in working with Amy?
12. From a humanistic perspective, how does Amy perceive her life situation? Her self? How is the self-concept formed, and under what conditions does it change? What humanistic counseling techniques might Sue have used to help Amy?
13. What are the legal and ethical implications if Sue decides to take Amy to have her abortion without permission from her parents? Should Sue have violated her confidence with Amy and contacted Amy's mother? Did Sue get too close to Amy and not keep enough social distance from one of her students? Should Sue have involved the principal?
14. In light of the continuing increase in teenage pregnancies, should schools provide students with birth control information and materials? At schools that have initiated such programs, what have been the results?

CASE 19

RANDY'S INTERESTS

Overton Senior High School is located in an Eastern city of approximately 100,000 people. The black and white ratio is approximately 28–72, and there is a considerable amount of manufacturing and a low unemployment rate in the area. Overton High is new, well equipped, and both its college-prep and vocational education programs are strong.

Charles Dodson is in his tenth year of teaching and currently teaches advanced placement English. It is midway through the first semester and near the end of his fifth period eleventh grade class as he collects compositions from the students. The students were to think through their future vocational goals and defend their choices.

Charles   Okay, pass them up to Larry here in the front row. He'll collect them for me. [Pause.] I know this was a tough assignment. I certainly didn't think I was going to be a high school teacher when I was an eleventh grader. [Several students laugh.] My father thought that I should go into engineering and make my fortune. [Smiling.] But as you can see, I didn't do what my father wanted, I became an English teacher—I must admit at a somewhat lower salary than I would have made as an engineer. [The bell rings and Larry hands Charles the stack of compositions.] Okay, folks, that's it. See you tomorrow. [Charles looks at the composition on top and then looks for and locates one of the students leaving class.] Randy! Could I see you for just a minute?

Randy [moving over to Charles's desk]   Yes?

Charles   Randy, is this two-and-a-half-page paper yours? [Holding it up.]

Randy [looks at paper and then down at floor]   Yes, that's all I could think of.

Charles   Randy, I've talked to several students who told me how much this assignment made them think and read! I haven't looked through them yet, but I'll bet there isn't another paper here that's less than ten pages! Want to bet?

Randy   I just didn't know what to write about, Mr. Dodson! I don't have the slightest notion what I'm going to do after high school. How can I write anything when I don't know what I want to do?

Charles   Haven't you talked to your parents about this?

Randy   Not really. They've decided that I'm going to be a lawyer, but that's what they want, not me. We don't talk about it.

Charles   What do you think about being a lawyer?

Randy   Terrible! I don't want to spend my life exploiting people and ripping them off!

Charles   Have you tried to tell your parents how you feel?

Randy [cynically]   I'd have to get an appointment—then they wouldn't listen. [Pause.] Listen, Mr. Dodson, I don't know what I want to be, and I don't want to fight with them over it!

Charles   Must make it difficult to plan—to choose courses and apply for college admission.

Randy [with agitation]   Mr. Dodson, I don't care what I take or whether I go to college or not! I'm bored out of my skull with school! I'd drop out in a second if they'd let me!

Charles   Randy, I know you have to go to your next class, but I've got one thing I want to say to you. You're a bright guy—your grades are way too low for your ability. If you can just figure out where you want to head, well the sky's the limit. If you ever want to talk about it—

Randy [shaking his head]   Thanks, Mr. Dodson, but I don't think so. Right now I just want to be left alone. [The bell rings.] I'd better go.

Charles [sighs]   Okay, Randy. I'll talk to you another time.

***

Three weeks later Charles is given a message to call Dr. Martha Scott, Randy's mother, a professor of psychology at a nearby university. During his planning period, Charles places the call from the guidance office.

Charles   Is this Dr. Scott?

Dr. Scott   Yes it is.

Charles   Dr. Scott, this is Charles Dodson, Randy's A.P.E. teacher. I received a message to call you.

Dr. Scott   Yes, thanks for returning my call, Mr. Dodson. I am trying to set up conferences with Randy's teachers about his low grades. Mr. Scott and I are very disappointed. I wonder if we can put our schedules together?

Charles   Of course. Randy is very bright and has high potential as I'm sure you know.

Dr. Scott [somewhat coldly]   Yes, well we'd certainly like to find out why Randy isn't doing better in school. How would Wednesday after school in your room be?

Charles   That will be just fine, Dr. Scott. I'll see you then.

***

Charles enters the office of Beth Downs, who is in her first year as guidance counselor.

Beth Hi Charles. How are you?

Charles Fine, thank you. Beth, I have to prepare for a conference with a parent, and I'd appreciate your help.

Beth Sure. Who's the student?

Charles Randy Scott.

Beth [searches for and pulls out Randy's cum folder] Okay, here's his cum record. [Moves around and pulls up a chair next to Charles so they can look at the folder together.] Boy, look at these I.Q. scores!

Charles [staring intently at the scores] Yes, but notice how they seem to decrease as you go from third grade to the eighth grade. [Pause.] I notice the same pattern in his grades—from A's to B's in elementary and from B's to C's in high school. We have a clear case of underachievement here, don't we, Beth?

Beth No doubt about that.

Charles It looks like his difficulties started somewhere around the fourth grade. His mother's a professor, and his dad's a doctor, you know. I'll bet they started having less and less time for him along about that time.

Beth That could be true. [Looking at the cum folder.] What I don't understand is these citizenship and personal-social development grades. Randy has lots of friends and participates in several extracurricular activities. He seems to me to be quite well adjusted socially and is never a discipline problem. How is he in your class?

Charles He gets along well with others, and he's not a troublemaker—just bored and unmotivated. [Pause.] One thing's sure, Beth. He ought to be making straight A's.

Beth I sure can't argue with you there.

***

It is Wednesday after school, and Dr. Scott enters Charles's room. He gets up from behind his desk and offers her a seat. Dr. Scott is in her middle forties and is well groomed and "dressed for success."

Dr. Scott My husband wasn't able to come with me this evening. He had an emergency.

Charles I'm sorry to hear that, Dr. Scott. I was looking forward to meeting him.

Dr. Scott [officiously] That's part of the job, just as yours is helping students learn. I don't mind telling you, Mr. Dodson, that my husband and I are very upset with the school's lack of response to Randy's needs. Needless to say, we both value a college education greatly and, given Randy's abilities, we hope he'll seriously consider law school after graduation. But with the grades he's been receiving, we've become very concerned. Do you have any idea what's wrong, Mr. Dodson?

Charles [nervously] Well I've spent some time going over Randy's records with his counselor, Miss Downs, and they certainly indicate that Randy is quite bright. I'd even say gifted.

Dr. Scott [cutting in]   I would definitely say gifted, Mr. Dodson. I've seen his I.Q. scores too!

Charles   Yes, but that doesn't seem to be the problem. I've talked to Randy, especially about some of the work in my class, and he's just not motivated. He says he's bored.

Dr. Scott [aggressively]   And who's fault is that, Mr. Dodson? I don't mind telling you that I've long supported merit pay for teachers. I don't feel that Randy's teachers know how to motivate him—how to make the course material interesting. As a result Randy gets bored. The raw material is there. No one is drawing Randy out and getting him excited about learning!

Charles [conciliatory tone]   Well, Dr. Scott, to do that a teacher has to know something about a child's interests. I've tried to talk to Randy about his interests, and about all he's told me is that he's bored and doesn't care about school. He said he's not interested in college either.

Dr. Scott [aggressively]   See, you just made my point! Somebody has to care enough to take advantage of his potential. I can assure you that Randy has all the books and learning materials he needs at home. You should see what he has in his room! He doesn't even have to clean his room—our maid takes care of that. All he has to do is study, and we insist that our maid keep track of the amount of time he spends in his room studying before he goes out with his friends or watches T.V.

Charles   Well, Dr. Scott, what are some of Randy's interests? What kinds of hobbies does he have? What kinds of things does he have in his room? What books does he really enjoy reading? I've tried to find out, but—

Dr. Scott   Exactly! Those are the kinds of things his teachers need to find out and take advantage of. A colleague in the College of Education says that a good teacher shapes the curriculum to the child rather than the child to the curriculum.

Charles   Dr. Scott, I've tried to draw Randy out in conferences and classroom assignments and haven't really gotten anywhere. It would really help if you—

Dr. Scott [controlled anger]   Mr. Dodson, I've got to go now. I have a very important appointment. But let me tell you this before I go. Randy is going to go to college and make something of himself. My husband and I decided to talk to his teachers first to see if they are willing to help him and work with him. If not, I don't mind telling you that we are not without influence with members of the school board and intend to use that influence in Randy's behalf if necessary! I hope I have communicated clearly!

Charles [stunned]   Yes, well I—

Dr. Scott   Goodbye, Mr. Dodson. I have to rush.

***

It is the next day after school. As requested, Randy Scott sits in a chair in front of Charles's desk for a conference.

Charles   Randy, I wanted to talk to you today because—well I had a conference with your mother yesterday.

Randy [frowning]   Yes, I know. She and Dad are talking to all my teachers. They're really something when they start pushing!

Charles   Yes, well your mother is concerned about your grades. I am too. They really want you to go to college badly.

Randy [upset]   Well I told you that! Why do I have to decide about college now anyhow?

Charles [calming tone]   You don't, of course, even though you do have to make decisions about what courses you take. Those choices can affect your admission to college. [Pause.] However, the real issue is your being interested in any course you take, whether it's college prep or not. What I wanted to find out from your mother was what your real interests are, but I'm afraid I wasn't very successful.

Randy [still upset]   Why does everyone bug me about my interests, goals, and grades? They're my business! I'm doing just what I want to!

Charles [controlled]   But Randy, I think most people see you making C's when you could be making A's and they wonder why. More than that, they feel it's a waste.

Randy   Look, Mr. Dodson, that's their problem not mine. As far as I'm concerned, C's are passing, and that's all the work I want to do. Do I win a big prize if I make straight A's?

Charles   Yes, you get the college of your choice and perhaps a scholarship to go along with it. But if you're not interested in college, then I guess—

Randy   That's right, Mr. Dodson. What do I care about a scholarship? My parents have plenty of money to send me to any college I want to go to, which is none right now. Heck, I may want to be an electrician or carpenter when I graduate—I don't know. Why do I have to become a professional, like they're always saying? My parents are professionals and have lots of money, and I don't think they're very happy. [Short pause.] Isn't that what it's all about, Mr. Dodson, being happy?

Charles   Well, yes, I guess it is. But don't you think we make choices in life that—

Randy [interrupting]   The fact is, in the end we're all going to die anyhow, and life is too short not to be happy when you can. And I'd be a lot happier if people would stop trying to make me do what they want me to.

Charles   I guess that often happens when people care a lot, Randy. But tell me, what makes you happy now? I'd really like to know.

Randy   Mr. Dodson, life is a blast for me right now! I have lots of friends and we party a lot. I like fast sports cars, beautiful girls, and good music, and I'm not willing to give those things up for straight A's! [Pause.] Let me ask you something, Mr. Dodson. Does a college degree ensure success in life?

Charles Nope. But it sure increases the odds.

Randy Well, Mr. Dodson, I'm a pretty smart guy, and when it comes time for me to make a living, I'm sure I'll be able to figure out a way to do it. Until then I just want to enjoy life. The future will take care of itself.

***

Monday of the following week Charles meets with Betty Caster, head of the English department in her classroom after school.

Betty Charles, you are a good teacher, a concerned teacher, but you can't win them all you know.

Charles That's true. But Randy's case is a little hard to let go of. His parents are beginning to put on pressure at the school district level. We've already gotten phone calls from assistant superintendents asking about Randy.

Betty Yes I've heard.

Charles But that isn't my main problem, Betty. The kid is just so bright, and I guess that I hate to admit I can't get through to him. If I can't figure out how to motivate him, then how will I be able to handle other students like Randy that I have in the future?

Betty [thoughtfully] Well isn't there some way you can turn this around by capitalizing on Randy's interests?

Charles [smiling] I think you've got something there. But tell me, Randy says he's interested in cars, girls, and music. What do I do in my class to take advantage of his interests? What would you do about Randy if he were one of your students?

OVERTON SENIOR HIGH
Cumulative Record

Name: Scott, Randall
Address: 4221 Robin Lane
Father: Scott, Harry **Occupation:** Physician
Mother: Scott, Martha **Occupation:** Professor
Siblings: Pamela, age 12

Former School: Overton Junior High
Entered Overton: Sept. 1985
Home Telephone: (914) 387-1234
General Health: Good
Handicaps: none
Date of Birth: Sept. 14, 1971
Age: 16 years

TEST RECORD

Intelligence Test:

Group	I.Q.	Date	Grade
Kuhlman-Anderson, Form CD		9/17/79	Third
Verbal	143		
Non-Verbal	145		
Full	144		
Otis-Lennon Mental Ability Test-Intermediate	138	9/21/84	Eighth

	CA	MA	I.Q.	Date	Grade
Individual-Stanford-Binet (3d Rev.)	11-0	15-6	142	9/25/82	Sixth

(continued)

ACADEMIC RECORD

Record the year's average as A, B, C, D, or F:

ELEMENTARY

	Grade 1	Grade 2	Grade 3	Grade 4	Grade 5	Grade 6
English				B	B	B
Reading	A	A	A	A	B	B
Writing	A	A	A	B		
Spelling	A	A	A	A	B	B
Arithmetic	A	A	A	B	A	A
Social studies		A	A	A	B	C
Science and health		A	A	B	B	B
Music	A	A	A	B	B	C
Citizenship	A	A	A	B	B	C

JUNIOR HIGH SCHOOL

Grade 7
English C
English C
Geography B
Arithmetic A
P.E. C
Exploratory C
Per./Social Dev. C

Grade 8
English C
U.S. History C
Arithmetic A
P.E. C
Exploratory C
Per./Soc. Dev. C

Grade 9
World History C
Algebra B
P.E. C
Spanish B

SENIOR HIGH SCHOOL

Grade 10
English A
Biology B
P.E. C
Spanish C
Geometry B

Grade 11

Grade 12

QUESTIONS

1. What are the characteristics of students who are potential dropouts? Which of these characteristics does Randy display?
2. What does it mean to say that "a good teacher shapes the curriculum to the child rather than the child to the curriculum?" How might a teacher do this?
3. What are the differences between the intrinsic and extrinsic views of motivation? Which view is Dr. Scott taking when she says, "I don't feel that Randy's teachers know how to motivate him," or when she voices her support for merit pay for teachers? At what level of Maslow's need hierarchy is Randy operating? Randy's mother? Is there any way that Charles can take advantage of Randy's interest in cars, girls, and music to increase his achievement?
4. From the perspective of humanistic psychology, how does Randy perceive his world at home and school? How does he perceive himself (self-concept), and what are his ideals (self-ideal)? How is the self-concept formed, and under what conditions does it change?
5. How has Randy's home environment influenced his values and attitudes toward high achievement in school, the value of a college education, and a career as a professional? What is an underachiever, and why has Randy chosen to be one? To what extent have the schools Randy has attended contributed to his underachievement?
6. What is the best interpretation of the data in Randy's cumulative record at the end of the case? What does "gifted" mean, and do Randy's intelligence test scores indicate that he falls into that category? Is Charles's interpretation that Randy's I.Q. scores are decreasing correct? What differences exist between group and individual intelligence tests? What is the standard error of measurement of an intelligence test? How good a predictor is I.Q. of later success in life?
7. What are some of the most effective programs and procedures for helping students like Randy identify their vocational interests and aptitudes? What are some of the most valid and reliable vocational interest inventories that could be administered to students like Randy?
8. From the standpoint of communication and counseling procedures, what is the most effective way to communicate with Randy and his mother? Would techniques like those presented in Gordon's *Teacher Effectiveness Training* work in this situation?

CASE 20

AN HONEST DAY'S WORK

Mary Wilson is diversified cooperative training (DCT) coordinator at Jasonville High School which is located in a southern city of approximately 100,000 population. JHS is the oldest school in a college town and has traditional academic standards. The school serves a mixed student population of 55 percent white, 28 percent black, and a 17 percent mixture of a variety of different races and ethnic groups. Mary has 15 years' teaching experience mostly with eleventh and twelfth graders in the DCT program. It is January as she sits in the office of Sam Cook, an assistant principal who is serving as principal due to an illness.

Sam   Mary, you don't know how good it is to have a chance to talk to you. Life's been awfully hectic for me, and I know that you're constantly out visiting your kids' employers.

Mary   Yes, visiting employers is hard work and time consuming, but of all the vocational education positions I've held, DCT's the most rewarding.

Sam   Well I personally think that vocational education is important, and I know that it often gets lost in a college town like this. And DCT is a much better choice for a lot of our kids because it gives juniors and seniors on-the-job training as well as academic work.

Mary [smiling]   You've sold me, Sam! In fact I think I'll ask for a raise!

Sam [laughing]   Well if anyone deserves one, you certainly do. I hear that kids from your DCT program have received more honors and held more state offices than any other program in the state.

Mary [smiling]   I've heard that too! Too bad I'm not a coach.

Sam   You'd sure have a bunch of trophies in the trophy case if you were. How does your current group look?

Mary   Good bunch of kids—not my best, but good. Jenna Preston has been elected to a state office, and four or five others will receive state honors—which, by the way, brings me to the purpose for our meeting today. I want you to be sure and come to our annual end-of-the-school-year dinner to thank our employers.

Sam   Great! What do I have to do?

Mary You get to thank all the employers for hiring and working with the kids and also to announce the state awards and Jenna's election to office.

Sam Terrific! I assume that you have it all organized to make sure I don't mess up.

Mary [smiling] As big a ham as you are, Sam, I don't think there's any chance you'll disappoint an audience! But, yes, we'll have things all set up for you.

***

Mary is working in her office when the telephone rings. She picks up the receiver.

Mary Hello.

Dr. Martin Hello. Is this Mrs. Wilson?

Mary Yes it is.

Dr. Martin Mrs. Wilson, this is Kenneth Martin over here at Doctor's Hospital, and I'm calling you about Jenna Preston.

Mary Oh, yes, Dr. Martin. I didn't recognize you. Is there some problem with Jenna?

Dr. Martin I'm afraid so, Mrs. Wilson. I'm afraid we're going to have to let her go from her job because of theft. I'm sorry that I didn't get to talk to you about it sooner, Mrs. Wilson, but I didn't want to say anything until we were certain.

Mary [dismayed] I'm really shocked, Dr. Martin! Jenna Preston of all people! She's been elected to represent DCT next year. What on earth happened?

Mr. Martin Mrs. Wilson, we all know that you run a fine program, and of course we still want to participate in spite of this situation with Jenna. But her supervisor, Bill Johnson, told me earlier that he suspected she was involved in some thefts here; he just couldn't prove anything. He didn't want to say anything to you unless he could be sure. Bill was tied up today and I told him that I'd prefer to call you anyhow.

Mary Can you tell me what happened, Dr. Martin? I've got to explain this to my principal.

Dr. Martin Well first she stole a set of keys from Bill and took 20 dollars from a locker. When the person owning the locker came to Bill and he started looking around for his keys, Jenna innocently laid the keys on a counter and said, "Oh here they are." The other incident involved two rings taken from another locker. The next day Jenna actually wore them to work. When the owner of the rings asked her why she was wearing them, Jenna said, "I found them in the rest room." It was almost like she wanted to be caught.

Mary Well, Dr. Martin, I'm still in a state of shock. But I can certainly see why you had to take action. I'm going to tell Mr. Cook about this first thing in the morning. I apologize to you that one of my DCT students would behave that way. Thanks for letting me know.

***

The following morning Mary is sitting in Sam Cook's office.

Sam   Mary, I guess the thing that surprises me most is the fact that Jenna Preston of all people would behave that way. Her parents are divorced now, aren't they?

Mary   Yes, for over a year. I don't know whether there's any relationship or not. What should we do, Sam? We can't have a thief representing us as a state officer next year!

Sam   I agree. She'll either have to disqualify herself, or we'll have to call the state officials and do it for her. I'm sure it'll be less embarrassing for everybody if she agrees to do it herself.

Mary   That makes sense.

Sam   We also need to have a conference with Jenna and her mother here in my office. You're the DCT coordinator. What do you think we should do?

Mary   I'm not sure. On the one hand, I really think that Jenna is better off in the DCT program than in the regular academic program. On the other hand, I think that she ought to find her own next job instead of my doing it for her.

Sam   That makes good sense to me. Maybe Jenna's mother would agree to get counseling for Jenna. Mary, in terms of your schedule, when's the best time to hold the conference?

***

One week later Mary, Sam, Jenna, a tall thin blonde, and Jenna's mother are seated in Sam's office.

Sam   Mrs. Preston, I know how difficult this is for you and Jenna, but a meeting of all of us seemed to Mrs. Wilson and me the best way to handle things.

Mrs. Preston [with slight trembling in her voice]   If you hadn't called this meeting, Mr. Cook, I would have. First let me say that Jenna insists she did not steal those things at the hospital.

Jenna [aggressively]   That's true, Mr. Cook. They only have circumstantial evidence.

Mary   Then why would they accuse you, Jenna?

Jenna   Some of the people there, like my supervisor Bill Johnson, especially Bill Johnson, don't like me.

Mary   Why doesn't Bill like you?

Jenna   Well it's hard to say, but he came on to me and I made it clear I wasn't interested.

Mary   I've known Bill and his wife for a long time, and they're a happily married couple. I find it difficult to believe that Bill would make a pass at you! What did he say exactly?

Jenna   It wasn't what he said. It was the way he acted—always flirting. You know how men are!

Mrs. Preston [with strong emotion]   Yes and just because a couple seem happily married doesn't mean they really are! Believe me—I know!

Sam [assertively]   Just a minute now, folks! I don't want this to degenerate into a shouting match! [Pause.] Now, Jenna, let me ask you a couple of questions. First please explain to me what you were doing with Mr. Johnson's keys.

Jenna   I don't know! All I know is I found them!

Sam   Mr. Johnson told me that he didn't misplace them. He knew exactly where they were, namely in the right-hand pocket of his jacket, only 15 minutes before they disappeared.

Jenna   Well I don't know! All I know is I found them!

Sam   Okay. Now tell me about the two rings from the girl's locker.

Jenna   It's like I tried to tell everybody. I found them in the rest room!

Sam   Even if that's true, and the girl says she remembers putting them in the locker and does not even use that particular rest room, why did you wear them to work the next day?

Jenna   Well I didn't know who the owner was, and they were so pretty . . . [Begins to cry.]

Sam   Jenna, there are just too many holes in your story. Dr. Martin told me that they suspected you of stealing before but, since they couldn't prove it, they didn't say anything. [Jenna continues to cry.] Mrs. Preston, I strongly recommend counseling for Jenna to help her through this.

Mrs. Preston [aggressively]   No! I'm not interested in Jenna's receiving counseling! I'm fed up with counselors! They're useless!

Sam [calmly]   Then what do you think we should do to help her?

Mrs. Preston   The next time you have any problem with Jenna, call the police. I'm not sure now whether she stole those things or not, but you should tell the facts to the police and let them take whatever action they see fit! If Jenna is stealing, she'll have to learn to take the consequences!

Sam   Whatever you want, Mrs. Preston. However, there is one action that Mrs. Wilson and I feel that we have to take. Jenna is going to have to give up her state office.

Mrs. Preston [defensively]   Do whatever you think is right!

Sam   We also think that Jenna needs to find her own next job in the DCT program instead of Mary's finding it for her.

Mrs. Preston   I'm not sure that Jenna should stay in the DCT program.

Sam   We both feel very strongly that she should.

Mrs. Preston [looking at Jenna]   Perhaps there would be less temptation in regular classes.

Sam   If a person wants to steal, they'll find a way regardless of what classes they're in. Our job is to provide students with learning situations that are most likely to help them succeed in life. We believe that for Jenna that's the DCT program.

Mrs. Preston [sighing]   I guess you people are the teachers. Do whatever you think is best.

***

One month later Mary runs into Sam outside his office as she is passing by on her way to a meeting.

Sam   Hi, Mary. Where are you running to?

Mary   To another meeting. How are things going?

Sam [smiling]   Oh out of control, as usual. By the way, how are things with Jenna Preston?

Mary   Well she has a new job as salad girl at the Big Burger on Forty-Third Street.

Sam   Did she find the position herself?

Mary   Not really. I had to help her a bit.

Sam   Well I'd say that girl can use all the help she can get.

Mary [frowning]   One thing's for sure. Her mother's not helping any. She won't respond to my phone calls or my letters.

Sam   Given the way that she behaved at our meeting, I'm not surprised. Well hang in there, Mary!

Mary [smiling]   I'm sure trying, Sam!

***

The next week Mary stops in the Big Burger on Forty-Third Street to talk to Ray McBride, Jenna's supervisor.

Mary   Ray, how's Jenna doing?

Ray   As a salad girl she's about average. She does what she's told but shows no initiative. However, there's a problem.

Mary [frowning]   What's that?

Ray   Well since Jenna started working here, several employees have had personal items disappear. We've had some store supplies suddenly disappear too. We can't prove anything, but Jenna's our only new employee.

Mary [with strong emotion]   Oh, Ray, I hope that she's not responsible!

Ray [smiling]   Well like my mother used to say, "It'll all come out in the wash."

***

Two weeks later Mary receives a phone call from Ray McBride as she sits in her office. ˙

Ray   Mrs. Wilson? This is Ray down at Big Burger. I'm afraid I've got a little bad news.

Mary What is it, Ray?

Ray We caught Jenna Preston stealing last night. We began to watch her carefully, and last night we caught her putting a big load of hamburgers and buns in the trunk of her car. We fired her on the spot.

Mary Did you call the police?

Ray No; since she's one of your students we thought we'd call you before we did anything. To be honest with you, this kind of stealing by employees isn't all that uncommon. We just take it off our income tax as a loss.

Mary Well, Ray, let me talk to Mr. Cook and I'll get back to you. Thanks for letting me know.

Ray [laughing]   Yes, I'll bet I've made your day!

***

Later that same day after school Mary meets with Sam in his office.

Sam So they caught her red-handed?! I guess she didn't learn anything from what happened at the hospital!

Mary I guess not. I just don't know what to do, Sam. Should I tell them to go on and call the police? Should I drop her from the DCT program?

Sam Well, Mary, it's your program. I know you'll do what's best for Jenna and I'll back you whatever you decide to do. But one thing's for sure, we've got to try something different and apparently without the help of her mother. [Pause.] So what do you think, Mary?

Name: Preston, Jenna Ann
Address: 528 East Main St.
Father Ralph M. Preston* **Occupation:** Pharmacist
Mother: Ruth A. Preston* **Occupation:** Executive secretary
Siblings: Ralph M., Jr., age 20
Former Schools: East Elementary **Handicaps:** None
Carson Junior High **Date of Birth:** 10/2/72
Date Entered J.H.S.: 8/21/87 **Age:** 16
General Health: Excellent *Parents divorced

TEST RECORD

Intelligence Test	Form	Lang. I.Q.	Non-Lang. I.Q.	Total I.Q.	Date	Grade
California	Level 1H	121	119	120	5/6/81	3
Test of Mental	Level 3	119	117	118	4/30/85	7
Maturity						
(short form)	Level 4	111	115	113	5/4/88	10

ACADEMIC RECORD
(year averages)

Grade Level	1	2	3	4	5	6
Citizenship		5	5	5	5	5
Reading	4	4	4	4	4	A
English				4		A
Spelling		4	4	4	4	A
Writing	4	4	4	4	4	A
Social studies				4		B
Arithmetic	4	3	3	3	3	B
Science						B
Music	4	4	4	4	4	A

Key:

1. Child is working below grade level
2. Child is working below grade level, but is making progress
3. Child is working at grade level
4. Child is doing excellent work at grade level
5. Child is working above grade level

Grade Level	7	8	9	Grade Level	10
English	A	A	A	English	B
Social studies	B	B	B	Biology	C
Math	B	B	C	Gen. Math	C
Science	B	B	C	Phys. Ed.	C
P.E.	B	B	B	World Hist.	C
Exploratory	A	A	B		

QUESTIONS

1. What motives might Jenna have for stealing? How could her teachers gain and use insight into such motives?
2. How should Mary respond to Jenna's alleged theft from Big Burger? Should she drop Jenna from the DCT program?
3. Does Jenna's cumulative record present any clues as to why she might have begun to lie and steal?
4. At which of Kohlberg's stages of moral development does Jenna seem to be operating? How could Mary check to find out? What methods of discipline and moral education are most effective with people operating at Jenna's stage?
5. What are defense mechanisms from the perspective of psychoanalytic theory? Which defense mechanisms best explain the behavior of Jenna and her mother? Can lying and stealing serve as defensive and coping behavior?
6. Jenna's parents have been divorced for over a year. What effect can a broken home have on a 16-year-old female living with a single female parent? Could such a situation relate to Jenna's lying and stealing?
7. How might the principles of adolescent development help explain Jenna's behavior? How might the adolescent egocentrism construct, especially Elkind's notions of the imaginary audience and personal fable, relate to Jenna's seeming desire to get caught?
8. At which of Erikson's stages of personality development is Jenna operating? What is the principal developmental task of that stage, and how well does Jenna seem to be handling it? How well does she seem to have handled the developmental tasks of earlier stages?
9. What is the best interpretation of the intelligence and academic data presented in Jenna's cumulative record at the end of the case?
10. From a humanistic frame of reference, how does Jenna perceive her work situation and her position in it? How might these perceptions overlap with other aspects of her perceptual field, such as home and school? How might they relate to lying and cheating?

PART VI

CONDITIONS OF WORK CASES

CASE 21

NOT ENOUGH TIME

Claudia Smith is a black 22-year-old first year teacher at Jefferson Elementary School in a metropolitan area in the Northeast. Jefferson Elementary serves children whose parents for the most part work in the many factories and small businesses that surround the school. The school spans the first through fifth grades and has an enrollment of just over 750 students—45 percent of whom are black, 35 percent Spanish-speaking, 15 percent white, and 5 percent Oriental.

For the last five years, the area has been severely economically depressed, and unemployment and poverty have touched nearly half the families that have children attending the school. Recent data indicate that 80 percent of the students are eligible for the federally funded free lunch program. On the annual state-mandated test of basic skills for third graders, Jefferson students have typically scored below the norm. Among administrators and teachers in the city, Jefferson is generally regarded as a difficult teaching assignment. The school's 30 teachers regularly encounter problems in motivating and disciplining students whose home backgrounds tend not to provide the guidance and support most children need to succeed in school.

Claudia, who graduated with honors from the state university, teaches a combined second and third grade class at Jefferson. Though not a regular practice, the two grades were combined because there were not enough students at either level to support a separate position. While she had hoped to teach just the second grade, Claudia agreed to take the position when the principal, Alice Myers, assured her that she would have only second grade students the following year.

A few days after the Christmas break, Claudia and the other three third grade teachers at Jefferson—Martha Dole, Beth Hopkins, and Bill Miller—are meeting with Mrs. Myers to discuss this year's state assessment test of basic skills. It is 3:15 in the afternoon, and they are seated around a conference table in Mrs. Myers's office. Though students were dismissed ten minutes earlier, teachers are not allowed to sign out until 3:30.

Mrs. Myers I realize it's almost 3:30, so I won't take much of your time. We have just about two months between now and when the assessment test is given in March to prepare our third graders. As I'm sure you recall, last year's scores left a lot to be desired. [Referring to her notes.] Seventy-five percent of our students achieved mastery on all the reading objectives; the state norm was 87 percent. On writing we had 77 percent at the mastery level; the state had 93 percent. And we were even weaker in math. The state norm was 96 percent, and ours was 73. [Sighing.] It's clear that we have to do a lot of work between now and March.

Beth [after several moments of silence]   I don't mean this as an excuse, but we need to remember the kind of students we have. We're in a poor area of the city, and most of our kids are from families that don't really support education. Maybe we're doing the best we can, given our situation. It seems to me—

Mrs. Myers [interrupting]   It may not be easy teaching here, but I know of no reason why our children can't learn more.

Martha [interjecting]   That's right.

Mrs. Myers [continuing]   Ideas like that can become a self-fulfilling prophecy. If we *don't* believe the kids can learn more, they won't.

Beth   I understand that. I hear what you're saying. By the same token though, I don't think we should pretend we don't have problems. [Sarcastically.] There's no way in the world that we can be compared to a school out in the suburbs or a school in Elmtown, U.S.A.

Bill   Well, we don't want to get into a debate about what we can and cannot do. The fact remains that we need to do the best we can to prepare the kids for the test.

Mrs. Myers   Bill's right; we don't want to get into a debate. What I want to do is outline a few strategies to help our kids do the best they can on the test.

Claudia   That's what I want . . . just some ideas about what to do. With second and third graders in the same class, I've got my hands full trying to give both groups what they need. Sometimes I feel like there should be two of me.

Mrs. Myers   I admit, Claudia, you've got an extra challenge. And I want you to know that I'll do everything I can to help you out. [Clearing her voice as a signal that she is making a transition.] Now let me tell you what we will do with our third graders between now and March. First of all, I want each of you to devote time to teaching the objectives that are covered by the test. In case you don't have a copy of the objectives, here they are. [She passes out copies of a three-page handout with objectives in reading, writing, and mathematics.]

Claudia [hesitantly]   What do you mean when you say "teach the objectives"?

Mrs. Myers   What I mean is that you would actually teach those specific skills and give students a lot of drill and practice. Now the second thing I want you to do is to give students weekly tests based on those objectives. And I want the tests made up in the same format as the state's test. By the time March comes around our students will have had a lot of experiences with the same kinds of items they'll find on the test. [Pausing.] And the last thing I want you to do may be the most important. I want you to prepare our kids psychologically for the test. I mentioned the self-fulfilling prophecy before. Well, I want us to use it to our advantage. I want us to really build our kids up to take the test and [with gusto] to blow the top off of it. Let 'em know that we believe in them, and that they can excel.

***

After the meeting with Mrs. Myers, Claudia and Beth are walking out to their cars in the parking lot.

Claudia I think Mrs. Myers has some good ideas for getting the kids ready for the test in March, but I'm just not sure I can handle everything she wants us to do.

Beth The first year's kind of rough, isn't it?

Claudia That's really an understatement. I've never taught a combination grade class before. Plus I've got a lot of behavior problems in there. It seems like I don't have enough hours in the day with everything I have to do. It seems like I'm always exhausted. I'll be honest. I even thought about not coming back after Christmas. It felt *so good* to be away from here.

Beth Oh, Claudia, I didn't know it was getting to you like that!

Claudia I don't want a pity party, but I spend hours at home studying, planning, and calling parents. And then the paperwork; that's overwhelming! I've got papers to correct, grades to record, tests to grade, accountability forms for documenting the attainment of specific skills, report cards, notes to parents, midterm reports, and homework assignment sheets. It's almost like I'm being forced to make a decision between teaching my students or doing the paperwork. I can't do both.

Beth I agree that you've got to set some priorities.

Claudia It's really got to be the kids. They've got to be my priority. But then I can't let all the paperwork pile up; I'd lose my job. What I really need is a teacher aide.

Beth Have you asked Mrs. Myers about getting one? You know with both second and third graders in the same class, it seems like if anyone deserved an aide, it would be you.

Claudia [hopefully] You think so? That'd be great. Right now I feel like I'm trying to run a three-ring circus and I don't think I'm succeeding at it. [Becoming discouraged again.] And with this state assessment test on top of everything else, I don't know if I can make it.

Beth Oh you'll make it. Look, I've got some materials you can use to get your kids ready for the test . . . some worksheets based on the objectives.

Claudia Oh, Beth, that'd be wonderful. I can use all the help I can get. [Turning toward her car.] I'll drop by tomorrow and get them.

Beth Any time, Claudia. And remember, I'm right next door. Just give a yell if there's anything I can do.

Claudia I'll take you up on that. [Getting into her car.] See you tomorrow.

***

It is two weeks later, and Claudia is about to begin a reading lesson with 14 third graders at the back of her classroom. Her other 17 students, all of whom are second graders, are at their seats working on an assignment in their reading workbooks. They appear to be quite restless, and their seatwork is marked by an almost ceaseless amount of fidgeting and talk. Four students, in fact, are not doing their work. Instead they spend their time yawning, stretching, and gazing around the room.

The third graders sit in three rows of desks that span the width of the back half of the room. The desks occupied by the second graders are at the front half of the room and are arranged in four rows of five desks each. Claudia stands in front of her third graders, a position that allows her to monitor her second graders by looking to her left.

Claudia has just passed out copies of the basal reading series used by all third grade teachers in the city. Today's lesson, according to her teacher's manual, "introduces several new words that end in -ace and reviews skills related to base words and inflectional endings, inferences and conclusions, and punctuation and typographic clues."

Carlos [in a loud, angry voice] I didn't get no book.

Claudia [with frustration] Carlos, how many times have I told you not to yell out like that? Now we're short three books, so you and Wanda will have to share. [She motions for Carlos to slide his desk over next to Wanda's. Her attention is then momentarily diverted by two girls who appear to be squabbling over a pencil.] Brenda, keep your hands to yourself.

Carlos [making an ugly face] Ugh. I don't want to share with her. I want—

Claudia [angrily] Carlos! If you do that once more, I'm going to send you down to Mrs. Myers's office. [Directing her attention once again to the two girls.] Brenda and Carol, *sit down!*

Carlos Can I look on with Willie?

Claudia [with determination] I *told* you to look on with Wanda.

Carlos [grudgingly] All right. [He gets out of his desk and pushes it so it bangs up against Wanda's desk. At the sound, several second grade students turn and look toward the back of the room. Carlos then hops back into his seat. Claudia gives her student a stern look but does not say anything about his provocative behavior.]

Claudia All right, class. I want everyone to turn to page 21 and take a look at the picture on that page. What do you think the three boys are doing?

Several students in unison Running a race.

Claudia That's right. It looks like they're running a race. How many of you have been in a race? [Nearly every student yells out something related to his or her experiences with races.]

Claudia [gesturing for calm] All right. All right. Let's not get too excited. Do you think the boys are having a good time?

Class [in a spontaneous roar] Yes!

Claudia Yes, they're having a good time running the race. [Stepping over to the blackboard on the back wall and picking up a piece of chalk.] How do we spell the word *race?* [With great energy and a good deal of noise, several students begin to spell the word at various tempos. Claudia writes the word on the board and then draws a line under the *ace.*] Race. The boys are running a race. Who do you think will win the race? [Once again nearly every student blurts out something.] Well, when someone wins a race we say they win first . . . What do we say? Hector?

Hector They win first place.

Claudia Right, we say they win first place. [She writes the word *place* on the blackboard and also draws a line under the *ace.*] Now we're going to read a story about a boy and a girl who are in a very special kind of race. [She places the chalk back in the chalk tray and returns to her position in front of her third grade students. Suddenly she notices two second graders, a boy and a girl, pushing one another.] Michael! Gloria! Stop that right now. [She takes a few steps in their direction.]

Gloria [grumbling] That ol' boy took my eraser.

Michael Did not.

Gloria Did too.

Claudia [pointing her finger at Michael] Michael, did you take her eraser?

Michael I just wanted to erase my paper.

Claudia Give it back to her. If you want to use something, ask. Don't just take it.

Mrs. Myers [speaking over the PA system] Teachers, excuse the interruption, but I need to announce that compensatory education students will not meet with Mrs. Hernandez today. She is attending a district workshop. [During the announcements most students begin talking among themselves. Claudia motions for silence by putting her finger to her lips. Her gesture is relatively ineffective.] Also students who have the computer enrichment class today are not to go to the computer room. Your teacher is also at the workshop. Let me repeat. Compensatory education students and computer enrichment students, you will not have classes today. Just stay with your regular teacher. Thank you.

Claudia [with irritation] Boys and girls, how many times have I told you to keep quiet during announcements? Now how many of you have either comp ed today or computers? [About half her students raise their hands.] Well your teachers aren't here today, so you'll just stay here.

Several students [spontaneously expressing their disappointment]   Ah, no!

Claudia [to her second graders]   All right, I want you children to get back to work. We're going to check your work in just a few minutes. [She returns to the chalkboard at the back of the room and picks up the piece of chalk. She begins speaking to her third graders.] I'm going to have you read the story silently now. It's about a boy and a girl named Juan and Carmen. [She prints their names on the board.] You can see their picture on page 23. I want you to read the story and see if you can find the answer to these two questions that I'm going to put on the board. [She turns and writes on the board:]

1. How does Juan feel at the beginning of the story?
2. Why do Juan's feelings change?

Carlos [with disgust]   I can't read with her. [He scoots his desk away from Wanda's and sits there with a defiant look on his face.]

Claudia [calmly and evenly]   Here, you can read from my book. [She walks over and places the book on Carlos's desk. He snatches the book, flips it open to the correct page, and begins staring at the picture.]

Claudia   I want you to start reading now. [She points to the proper place on the page with her right index finger.]

Carlos [mumbling]   I am.

Claudia [to her third graders]   Read the story and see if you can answer the questions. If you finish before I'm done with the second graders, you can draw a picture of the race Juan and Carmen are in.

***

It is 3:10 later that day, and Claudia has just entered Mrs. Myers's office. She closes the door after her.

Mrs. Myers   Hi, Claudia. You said at lunch you wanted to see me today?

Claudia [collapsing with a sigh into an office chair across from Mrs. Myers's desk]   Yes, Mrs. Myers. Frankly I've had a really rough day.

Mrs. Myers [smiling]   You do look tired.

Claudia   Handling both second and third graders in the same class is really demanding. Trying to get my third graders ready for the state assessment test . . . it just doesn't seem like there's enough time to do everything. [Hesitating.] I . . . I think I need some help, or else I don't know if I can finish out the year.

Mrs. Myers [with concern]   What do you mean, Claudia? You told me Beth Hopkins was helping you, didn't you?

Claudia   Yes. She's been a real jewel. She's given me some materials to help the kids get ready for the state test. Plus she's someone I'm able to talk to.

Mrs. Myers   Sometimes that's the best kind of help we can get.

Claudia [with difficulty]   Well . . . I really wanted to ask about a teacher aide. I've got a lot of behavior problems in my class, and it seems like whenever I divide them up into any kind of groups I spend half the time keeping them in line. If I had a teacher aide to at least watch the group I wasn't working with . . .

Mrs. Myers   I really wish I could do that, Claudia, but there's no money for it.

Claudia [weakly]   Oh.

Mrs. Myers   Believe me, if I could swing it, I would. Now if you've got some behavior problems in there, send them to me. I know a lot of our students just don't have the self-discipline they should have by the time they're seven or eight.

Claudia [tiredly]   Well there's just a couple of kids in there that really run me down. And they seem to get the rest of the class going.

Mrs. Myers   Who are you talking about?

Claudia   Carlos Mendoza and Willie Williams are the worst ones. I didn't know third grade kids could be so nasty.

Mrs. Myers [chuckling]   Ah, I know them both. They've both got some real problems at home. You send them down to see me tomorrow. We'll have a talk.

Claudia [with a faint smile]   I'd really appreciate that, Mrs. Myers.

Mrs. Myers   Good. [Pausing.] There was something else I wanted to ask you about. Oh, yes, I remember. You told me at lunch that you don't have enough books?

Claudia   Right, the third grade basal. I'm short three books, and that always creates a hassle.

Mrs. Myers   Well I *can* do something about that. I'll call our area's curriculum coordinator and see if she can locate some more copies. That's part of her job. You can't teach without materials.

Claudia   I was wondering, could I meet with this curriculum coordinator? Maybe she could help me.

Mrs. Myers   Oh?

Claudia   I'm having a hard time following the objectives for the basal reading series. The same thing with the math series. They just don't seem to fit my students. They seem to be so structured, and it takes a lot of time for me to figure out the best way to use them.

Mrs. Myers   Well you know the reading and math series are required, don't you? With the way kids move around in this city, we couldn't have different books at different schools. [Pausing.] Is there some way you could modify the way you use the books?

Claudia   I don't think so. The second grade basal reader, for example. It's really hard to use with my Spanish-speaking kids. It presents over a dozen contractions that they just can't get. They find them impossible to deal with and remember. I don't know Spanish, but I've been told it doesn't have anything comparable to contractions. I've used all kinds of visuals, games, puzzles, and so on to get them across, but nothing seems to work.

Mrs. Myers Yours is not the first complaint I've heard about the basal. I just wish there was something I could do about it.

Claudia [glancing at her watch] I didn't mean to dump all this stuff on you at the end of the day, Mrs. Myers. I just wanted to be up front with you and see what kind of help I could get.

Mrs. Myers I understand.

Claudia [with emotion] I . . . I really need to make some changes. I can't continue like this. [She takes a deep breath.] Tell me, Mrs. Myers, what am I supposed to do if I can't get an aide and I'm forced to use a book that's not right for my kids?

JEFFERSON ELEMENTARY SCHOOL
Second–Third Grade: Miss Claudia Smith

	Grade Level	Total I.Q. Score*	Father's Education	Mother's Education
1. Arnold, Fred	2	98	Grade 12	Grade 12
2. Baranoski, Michael	3	87	Grade 8	Grade 9
3. Bland, Richard	3	110	Grade 7	Grade 10
4. Chen, Jau-Liang	3	90	Grade 12	Grade 12
5. Chow, Lisa	2	86	Grade 11	Grade 12
6. Crews, Sally	3	87	Grade 2	Grade 8
7. Diaz, Jose	2	76	Grade 4	Grade 9
8. Ellis, Jessie	2	134	Grade 8	Grade 8
9. Fox, Wanda	2	90	Grade 3	Grade 7
10. Garcia, Hector	3	79	Grade 6	Grade 8
11. Herring, Gloria	2	102	Grade 11	Grade 11
12. Jimenez, Lynn	3	110	Grade 9	Grade 9
13. Mendoza, Carlos	2	82	Grade 3	Grade 6
14. Lawson, Sylvia	3	91	Grade 12	Grade 12
15. Mason, Mary Ann	2	87	Grade 10	Grade 11
16. Mercer, Sherry	3	140	Grade 8	Grade 9
17. Nickerson, George	3	111	Grade 10	Grade 10
18. Pittman, David	2	81	Grade 11	Grade 10
19. Price, Randy	3	98	Grade 4	Grade 10
20. Purcell, Dan	2	131	Grade 12	Grade 12
21. Quinn, Heather	3	112	Grade 12	Grade 11
22. Ramos, Jorge	2	94	Grade 9	Grade 9
23. Randolph, Robert	3	97	Grade 10	Grade 10
24. Reed, Patti	2	104	Grade 12	Grade 11
25. Reynolds, Ann	2	88	Grade 7	Grade 8
26. Ryan, Michelle	3	107	Grade 9	Grade 10
27. Shaw, Mary Sue	2	86	Grade 8	Grade 8
28. Skinner, Brenda	2	109	Grade 9	Grade 9
29. Stewart, Carol	2	86	Grade 10	Grade 12
30. Tyler, Thomas	2	98	Grade 12	Grade 11
31. Williams, Willie	3	84	Grade 10	Grade 12

*Otis-Lennon School Ability Test, Primary II—Grades 2–3.

QUESTIONS

1. How might Claudia manage her time more effectively so that she wouldn't feel so overwhelmed by the requirements of the job?
2. Evaluate Mrs. Myers's approach to improving basic skill achievement at the school, that is, "teaching to the test" by teaching specific skills, giving students drill and practice opportunities, giving weekly tests, and preparing students psychologically to take tests.
3. How effective would the following approaches to instruction be for a teacher to use with a class of students at more than one grade level: individualized instruction, cooperative learning, peer tutoring, learning centers, and in-class grouping?
4. What relationships exist between the socioeconomic status and home environments of students like those in Claudia's class and student achievement? What are the most effective programs and techniques available to a teacher to compensate for home environmental differences? What is Project Follow Through and what Follow Through models have the most potential for Claudia's situation?
5. If Mrs. Myers had given Claudia an aide, how could Claudia use the aide most effectively? Could an aide have made home visits, for example? Could Claudia use parent volunteers to help her since money is not available for a paid aide?
6. What are Claudia's instructional objectives in view of the emphasis on the basic skills? State at least one such objective in each of the three areas of mathematics, reading, and writing. To what levels of Bloom's Cognitive Taxonomy do such objectives relate?
7. Mrs. Myers seems concerned about the "self-fulfilling prophecy" concept of Rosenthal and others. She suggests changing teacher expectations from negative to positive with regard to student performance on the state basic skills test, which she seems to equate with learning. Does Mrs. Myers have an accurate understanding of the "self-fulfilling prophecy" theory and research? How do teachers' expectations regarding student learning change? How is the teacher expectations construct different from the "teacher efficacy" and teacher "locus of control" constructs?
8. From a behavior modification perspective, how well does Claudia handle the classroom management problems of her second and third graders? What changes would you suggest she make?
9. What is the best interpretation of the data presented at the end of the case? What does it tell you about Claudia's second and third graders? In light of "self-fulfilling prophecy" research, should teachers be given such information about their students?

CASE 22

A QUESTION OF MERIT

Woodrow Wilson Junior High School is located in the midwestern city of Springville, has a population of 75,000. Farming, coal mining, and various light and heavy industries comprise the local economy. It is the last day of teacher preplanning prior to the opening of a new school year. All the teachers in the city school system are meeting in the Woodrow Wilson auditorium to participate in an informal workshop led by system administrators. The workshop covers everything from pupil attendance policies to the teacher retirement program. Of special interest is the new merit salary plan that the school board is implementing during the new school year after over two years of controversy and work.

Terry Wade, a seventh grade math teacher beginning his fifth year of teaching at Garfield Junior High School, does not see anyone he knows, so he takes a seat near the front of the auditorium between two strangers. As he sits down, the superintendent of schools, Dr. Chester Gunn, walks up to the lectern on the stage to begin the meeting.

Dr. Gunn Welcome, ladies and gentlemen, to the fourteenth annual citywide teachers' meeting and workshop. Teachers have indicated to me numerous times how helpful they find this orientation and updating meeting at the beginning of each school year. Of special interest this year is, of course, the new merit pay plan that we are putting into operation for the first time. I will introduce several people in a minute who will explain the various components of the plan. Of course, as in the case of any new plan, there are bugs that will have to be worked out. But with the cooperation of everyone involved, we'll be able to develop a system that identifies some of the fine teaching that goes on in this city. [Polite applause.]

Let me add that I think that our school board has taken a courageous step in developing a program to recognize meritorious teaching. Before becoming your superintendent, I had the privilege of serving as a vice president in the Acme Corporation, as many of you know. It was one of my pleasant duties in that position to administer the incentive pay program for the employees. That program was very effective and is still in operation today in almost exactly the same form as when I operated it 15 years ago. [Pause.]

In designing our program, we consulted with many experts and examined the latest research. As those who follow me will explain, the merit program consists primarily of three components. First, just as a good business is productive, our schools and teachers must also be productive. Our product, of course, is the learning of our students. Dr. Evans will shortly discuss our achievement testing program with you. We will be testing in every class at the beginning and at the end of each school year. Second your teaching will be observed at least twice during the school year by your building principal or assistant principal. Experts have helped us redesign our observation procedures as Mr. Rollie Johns will explain. [Pauses and clears throat.]

Finally each of you who wishes to be considered for merit will take the revised state teacher competency exam. Ms. Annette King is in charge of that testing and will shortly explain it to you in full. After their presentations, you will break down into small groups by grade levels for purposes of dealing with your questions.

***

It is the second day of classes the following week. Terry sits in the teachers' lounge during his planning period with five other teachers: Charles Everett (science), Tom Malloy (physical education), Mary Lasco (English), Sherry Woods (social studies), and Claude Billings (band).

Sherry [emotionally] I can't believe that the union caved in to the board's plan! All that talk of Gunn's about experts and research!

Charles There's no way you can measure good teaching objectively. The so-called experts can't even agree on what it is. Sure most parents and kids can name the best and worst teachers in a school, but they can't tell you why. It's mainly hearsay.

Terry In other words you can sort the extremes from the middle of the distribution but you can't do so on an objective basis.

Charles [laughing] Did I say that, Terry? Sometimes I worry about you math guys!

Sherry It's ridiculous to think that a high score on the state teacher exam means anything! I could name you several teachers who made high scores on it that are not good teachers!

Claude Yeah, Sherry, but how do you know they're not good teachers? Based on what?

Sherry Oh, Claude, I'm not sure, but it certainly is not based on anything objective!

Claude [laughing] I don't know about you, Sherry. First you and Charles say you can't tell what good teaching is and then you turn around and call some of us bad teachers.

Sherry [hitting Claude's arm with her fist and feigning frustration] Oh, Claude! You know I didn't name any names! Objectively I said!

Tom Well if they're going to measure achievement to see how much kids have learned, then I think they ought to let us pick what kids we have in our classes.

Sherry That's right, Tom. They've either got to let us pick or find some way to take into consideration the homes the kids come from. I swear, some of them could care less about school!

Charles [teasing] Now Mary there isn't saying anything and I know why.

Mary [smiling] Why, Charles?

Charles Because you've got all advanced placement kids, and they're going to make you look good.

Mary If you were as good a teacher as I am, Charles, you'd have advanced placement kids too.

Charles [laughing] Oh, brother! I set myself up for that one! [Everyone laughs.]

Claude What I can't figure out is how they think they are going to measure learning in things like music, art, and phys. ed. I've sure never seen an achievement test that could do that!

Charles Yeah, and I'll tell you another thing: They are going to use practically the same old rating instrument they've always used when they come in to observe us. It never has been worth a damn, and now all of a sudden it is good enough to make merit decisions based on only two observations!

Sherry [aggressively] The whole system stinks! It's supposed to reward and encourage good teaching, but what it's really going to do is turn more teachers off than it turns on! The teachers that think they should get merit and don't are going to give up and stop trying! A few are going to get merit, but a larger number are going to be punished! It stinks and we shouldn't stand for it!

***

The bell rings and everyone gets up to go to their next period class.

Sherry Gang, I'm having a party at my house Saturday night. You're all invited—BYOB. The main topic of conversation will no doubt be the merit plan. [Smiling.] Come join us and we'll organize a rebellion! [All nod and smile as they leave the room.]

***

As Terry enters the front door of Sherry Woods's beautiful upper-middle-class home, he sees a large number of teachers there from all over the city, drinking and talking.

Sherry [smiling] Terry, I'm so glad you could come! You didn't have much to say in the lounge last Tuesday so I really wasn't sure where you stood on the merit plan.

Terry   I don't see how it'll work either.

Sherry   Come on in and let me introduce you to some of the teachers from other schools. Several of the union officers are here including Frank Snyder, the president. Do you know Frank?

Terry   No, I've never met him.

Sherry walks Terry over to where Frank Snyder, a bald, heavyset man in his fifties, is talking to two young teachers, Jill and Toni Sue.

Frank [animatedly]   Our merit plan is one of those things you read about in administration textbooks—namely, what not to do! The thing went from the top down not from the bottom up. The board and the administration crammed it down our throats. The teachers are going to be evaluated by a plan that they had no real input into by administrators that they don't trust!

Jill   But, Frank, didn't the union agree to the plan?

Frank   Yes we had to. During the master contract negotiations, they tied the merit plan to salary increases. I guess you could say they bought us off and pointed out that they had the legal authority to implement a merit plan whether we liked it or not. Then they tied it to a salary package that gave nonmerit teachers a salary increase almost twice that of last year. The merit money was on top of that.

Sherry [interrupting]   Folks, before you go on I'd like you to meet Terry Wade, a math teacher from Garfield. Terry meet Frank, Jill, and Toni Sue. [Terry shakes hands all around. Sherry hands him a glass of punch and moves to greet another guest.]

Frank   Terry, we were discussing the new merit plan.

Toni Sue   Yes, and to go on, Frank [pause] I understand what the board did in tying the merit plan to big salary increases for everyone, but why didn't the union insist on helping design the plan?

Frank   We considered that, Toni, and I think that the real reason is that we don't really believe that teaching can be evaluated objectively and fairly. We decided to give them enough rope to hang themselves.

Jill [smiling]   In other words you let them develop the plan so you could shoot it down.

Frank   Yes and keep the bribe money to boot.

Jill   Pretty slick!

Frank   We were going to get merit whether we liked it or not! We knew it wasn't going to work the way they were going about it so we decided to let them pay the teachers for the privilege of hanging themselves.

Terry   Let's hope they don't hang any of us in the meantime!

Frank   The bottom line is that both the merit and nonmerit teachers are going to get more money, and we're in a good position to help the board look stupid. [Looking at Terry and smiling.] Terry, you're awfully quiet. What do you think about all this?

Terry   All I know, Frank, is that the administration didn't ask me what I thought about a merit plan.

Frank   That's part of their stupidity! I don't really believe that the rank and file teacher really opposes the idea of merit. But he sure wants input into how merit is going to be determined!

Terry   This is only my fifth year of teaching, but sometimes I feel like one of the kids. The administration decides what's best for me by passing school board policies just like they do for the kids. Teaching can sometimes seem like a thankless job because you get so little feedback. Even when one of your kids does well, you aren't sure if it's you, the home, or the kid's ability. Every now and then a parent or student will tell you something to let you know that you're doing a good job. I remember the summer that I worked at a construction job. It really felt good to see the product of your labor as you built houses. Maybe if we could build a really good merit plan, it might be helpful to teachers to give them regular feedback. But all the board seems to want to do is pass another policy and put a program in as quickly as possible.

Frank   You may be surprised to hear me say this, Terry, but I think that the fact that teachers have had to organize themselves into unions is a sorry state of affairs. But the very things you are talking about are the reasons we have to have them. Otherwise teachers are powerless peons who are treated no better than students. The administration sees itself as management and us as their skilled laborers. It's the only way we can get a share of the power.

In the other part of the living room, Sherry stands up on the built-up portion of the fireplace and asks for the crowd's attention.

Sherry   Let me have the floor for just a minute, and then you can all go back to partying! [Pause. Everyone stops talking and looks at Sherry.] Dottie and I just counted, and we have over 100 teachers here and at least one from every school in the city. [Exclamations of surprise.] I want to ask you a question and issue an invitation. I hope you don't get angry if I—well, actually the union leadership—put you on the spot. But we need to know. How many of you oppose the new merit plan? [Over 90 percent of the hands are raised.] Okay. Thank you. You've got a decision to make; Are you or are you not going to participate? [Pause.] Well a number of us are going to refuse to participate. If you decide to join us, we are going to have a nonparticipation party like this one at somebody's house every month. Dottie has agreed to host the next one at her house on October 1. [Applause.] Please tell the teachers at your school that they are invited. [More applause.] Now let's party!

* * *

It is the middle of November, and Terry has attended two nonparticipation parties. School has ended and Terry enters the doorway of the office of Tom Braxton, the building principal.

Terry You sent for me, Mr. Braxton?

Tom Hi, Terry. Come on in and have a seat. [Searches through a pile of papers on his desk and hands one to Terry.] Terry, I just wanted to officially notify you that I will be coming to your classroom the third and fifth periods tomorrow to officially observe your teaching in accordance with our new merit plan. You'll notice that the form has been signed by Sherry Woods, our union building representative. Everyone was given a copy of the observation instrument I'll be using which, with maybe a few minor differences, is the one we've always used. Do you have any questions about it?

Terry No, not really. Like you say, it's familiar: organization, discipline, knowledge of subject, quality of materials, rapport—

Tom [smiling] That's great, Terry! I think maybe you know it better than I do! [Pointing.] All you need to do is sign here to verify that we had this conference and that you agree to participate. [Terry hesitates for a few minutes, scans the paper as though he's reading it carefully, and finally signs.]

***

It is third period on the following day. Terry's eighth graders buzz with excitement as they see Terry dressed in suit and tie and watch Mr. Braxton enter the classroom, take a seat in the back of the room, and immediately begin to organize some papers. Johnny, in the front row, raises his hand.

Terry Yes, Johnny?

Johnny What's happening, Mr. Wade?!

Terry Mr. Braxton has dropped by this morning to observe my teaching. It's really important that you all ignore him and let him do his work. Just pretend that he isn't there and that it's just a regular class day.

Mitzi [without raising her hand] I really like your suit, Mr. Wade! [Everybody laughs and both Terry and Mr. Braxton smile.]

Terry Thank you, Mitzi. But now let's get right into math. It just so happens [begins to smile] that I've prepared a math game today that I think you'll all find fun. But most important, it'll give us a chance to apply what we've been learning the last few days. [Class buzzes with excitement.]

***

During the following week, Terry attends a nonparticipation party at a teacher's house. Terry is standing with a glass of punch in his hands as he talks to Sherry Woods, Charles Everett, and Jill Walls.

Charles Sherry, how do you think the teachers are split on the merit issue?

Sherry Frank has been counting heads and says its about 60–40 against.

Jill Boy, teachers sure cut their own throats, don't they?

Sherry By the way, Terry, I hear that Braxton came in to observe you last week. Doesn't he know you're not going for merit?

Terry [frowning] He really didn't give me much choice. He informed me when he was coming and about all I had time to do was salute.

Sherry [with rising anger in her voice.] He didn't ask you to sign anything? You're not going to let them know that you're going to refuse merit until they offer it to you! Now that's really slick! It'll be far more impressive if someone actually offered merit turns them down. [Terry says nothing but just smiles.]

Sherry [smiling] I'll be darned! Terry, you'd better watch yourself or you're going to be on the union executive committee before you realize what's happening.

Charles Well thank God someone around here has a plan! When I think of all the teachers and students that are going to be hurt when the merit ratings are finally announced—

Terry [frowning] Charles, I've been thinking about that. Do you really think that whether a teacher receives merit or doesn't receive merit when he's expecting to will affect what goes on in the classroom? A lot of teachers have been teaching their hearts out for a lot of years for very low pay. [Sherry, Jill, and Charles all look at one another and Terry with a puzzled look on their faces.]

***

It is late May of the following year as the school year is almost over. At the end of the school day, Terry has been asked to report to Tom Braxton's office. As he enters he notices five other teachers already seated in Tom's office. Tom motions to Terry to come on in and join them.

Tom [smiling] Now that Tom's here we can begin! Let me tell you why I really asked all of you here today. The Office of Testing and Evaluation has just completed its analysis of all the data for teacher merit for this school. Six of the teachers to receive merit are from Garfield! Can you guess which six it might be? Congratulations folks! [Begins to shake each teacher's hand.]

***

That same evening Terry sits at home alone with his wife, Marie. Frowning, he sips a cocktail as his wife drinks a glass of wine.

Marie But, Terry, why aren't you happy? You have just been recognized as one of the best teachers in the city.

Terry It's not that easy Marie! A lot, probably even the majority, of teachers think that the merit plan is bad!

Marie Don't you think you deserve merit, Terry?

Terry Well, yes, I do.

Marie Then what's wrong with the merit plan?

Terry [sighing] I don't know! I guess I'm really confused about it all right now. A lot of my buddies think I should turn down the merit money to make a statement. But now that I've been offered the money, which we need, and well, I guess the recognition, I'm not sure whether I want to turn it down or not. I'm in a no-win situation. If I don't turn down the merit I'm going to have a lot of people angry and disappointed with me. But if I turn the money down it's going to hurt us. Either way I lose!

Marie What are you going to do, Terry?

QUESTIONS

1. According to recent research and the opinions of educational leaders, what are the pros and cons of teacher merit pay plans?
2. Besides merit pay plans, what are other ways to reward and encourage good teaching?
3. How do you feel about teachers' unions? Do they add to or detract from the status of teaching as a profession? Explain your answer.
4. What are the positions of the National Education Association and the American Federation of Teachers in regard to merit pay plans? Do you agree or disagree with their positions?
5. If you were Terry, would you accept or refuse to accept the merit money? Explain your answer.
6. What are the differences between the intrinsic and extrinsic views of motivation? One of the fundamental assumptions on which the merit pay concept rests is that it will affect the way a teacher behaves in the classroom. From an extrinsic viewpoint (operant conditioning), the assumption would be that the money would serve as a reinforcer. Terry argues against this when he says, "A lot of teachers have been teaching their hearts out for a lot of years for very low pay." Is he right? Does the intrinsic view of motivation support Terry's view?
7. What is effective teaching? Can it be measured objectively? Are there behaviors that all good teachers exhibit? For many years research has been conducted with observational instruments that are used to systematically record teacher and student classroom interactions. This important research area is identified by different labels, such as "teacher behavior research," "process-product research," "teacher effectiveness research," and "systematic observation research." Do the research findings in this field hold any implications for the merit pay evaluation model that Springville is trying to implement?

8. How valid is Springville's view that student achievement tests be used as a measure of student learning? How much danger is there that such tests will become Springville's educational goals? What levels of Bloom's Cognitive Taxonomy do achievement tests measure? How valid is Sherry's argument that students' home backgrounds influence how well the students perform on achievement tests? Can achievement tests measure student performance in subjects such as music, art, and physical education?

9. What does it mean to say that teaching is a profession? Is Frank right when he says, "The administration sees itself as management and us as their skilled laborers?" How is the position of the teacher as a professional different from other professionals, such as physicians, dentists, and attorneys, who operate a private practice and charge professional fees for their service?

10. How valid and reliable are observational rating instruments like the one Tom Braxton used to observe Terry? How valid and reliable are national and state teacher competency and certification exams?

CASE 23

DOES IT GET ANY BETTER?

It is the first day of the second semester at Hanover High School, and almost 2,000 students wait restlessly in the cold auditorium for the principal to begin the assembly that will kick off the new semester. Of the 75 or so homeroom teachers present, about half are on their feet actively monitoring students' behavior. The remaining teachers are about evenly divided between those who use the time to catch up on paperwork and those who sit doing nothing.

Hanover High is situated in a poor high-crime area of a major midwestern metropolis. Nearly 60 percent of Hanover's students are black; 30 percent are Spanish-speaking; and the remaining 10 percent are white. About 70 percent of the students come from families that are on some form of public assistance, and 85 percent are eligible for the federally funded free lunch program. During the first two decades following its construction in 1935, Hanover had a reputation for providing a good education for the children of immigrant, blue-collar families. Since the mid 1950s, however, the area served by Hanover began to pass through the irreversible stages of urban decline. Today the school is considered one of the worst in the city. The results of annual standardized tests, for example, regularly place Hanover students in the lowest percentiles for reading, writing, and mathematics.

Hanover High is a dreary looking, three-story yellow brick building that covers half a city block. The building's exterior hints at the fact that the school is only marginally successful at providing students with the kind of education they need. Several windows on the first floor have been boarded over, the school's engineer having decided that he could no longer afford to have his crew replace countless broken panes of glass. The only open area around the school is a gravel lot, once the sight of a warehouse. With no athletic playing field, the football team must practice at a city park several blocks away. The battered green doors leading into the school are covered with various graffiti that have been spray painted or carved or scratched into the wood by anonymous students over the years.

While the school's custodial staff does a good job of keeping the inside of the school clean, the hallways nevertheless are dark and dreary. Noticeably absent in the corridors are brightly colored displays highlighting students' work, upcoming holidays, or student activities. Across from the main office are two large display cases. At most schools such cases would present proud evidence of student accomplishments. At Hanover High, however, they are empty.

As John Harrington, a 37-year-old social studies teacher, stands in the auditorium aisle keeping an eye on his three rows of restless sophomores waiting for the assembly to begin, he strikes up a conversation with Jan Anderson whose freshmen are seated behind. Jan is 21 years old and just took the place of Hazel Worthington, who retired at the end of the first semester.

John Welcome to Hanover High. [He extends his hand.] I'm John Harrington, and I'm in the social studies department. I've been here for ten years, and I don't think I can remember one of these assemblies beginning on time. But, then, no one ever said teaching was going to be stress free, did they? [He laughs heartily and then turns away for a moment to motion a student to take his seat.]

Jan is tall, well dressed, and looks older than 21. She graduated last June with honors from the state's major public university. Her student teaching experience, eight weeks at a high school affiliated with the university, was very positive. She had one of the school's best English teachers as a cooperating teacher. Jan received very strong recommendations from her and from her university supervisor.

Jan [smiling] I'm Jan Anderson, and I've taken Mrs. Worthington's place in English. Last semester I was a full-time substitute over at Wacker High, but when Mrs. Worthington's position came open, I applied for it. [With a sigh.] Working with different classes every few days didn't give me a feeling of accomplishment.

John [chuckling] Well I don't want to be discouraging, but you may not find things much different around here. It's an accomplishment if you can just get through the day. [He nods his head toward the stage where the principal, Mr. Prokop, is adjusting the microphone.] Delays like this are typical. The kids really aren't that bad. But you'll find that this place is not at all organized, and we teachers don't get the kind of support we need.

Jan [with concern in her voice] What kinds of things are you talking about?

John [with evident anger] What it all comes down to is time. We don't have enough time to give these kids the attention they need. I'm sure you've noticed your schedule doesn't include a planning period. I ask you, how can we be expected to teach 125 to 150 kids who read anywhere from the second grade level to the tenth grade level if we don't have time to prepare?

Jan [frowning and nodding her head in agreement]   It sounds like an impossible task.

John   You're darn right. And teacher aides, there's another thing. According to Chapter 1 of ECIA [Educational Consolidation and Improvement Act], schools like Hanover are supposed to have aides.

Jan   Really? Why don't we have them?

John   You can't guess? Money. The idiots downtown at the board somehow screwed up on their application for federal funding, so you and I miss out. I think if Prokop would lean on them downtown though, we'd get aides. But he's afraid to make waves. I think his goal is to become a district superintendent some day.

Jan   Have the teachers ever banded together and pressed Prokop to get the aides? [Hopefully.] It seems like we could do something to improve our situation.

John [laughs]   From time to time, old-timers like myself will give him a little hell about one thing or another. [Shakes his head with resignation.] But there's not much we can do. He just listens and says he knows how we feel and that he'll look into it. [Shrugs his shoulders.] But nothing ever happens. Both he and the people down at the board know that teachers don't have the time to organize and push for better working conditions. We're too busy trying to keep our heads above water as it is. And let's face it, a lot of teachers are burned out. When they first started teaching, they tried to change things. But they learned that the system just doesn't, or can't, respond. So they do the natural thing and—[He is interrupted by Mr. Prokop's request for quiet so the assembly can begin.]

Mr. Prokop   I want to welcome all Hanover students, faculty, and staff to a brand new semester. I know this will be a marvelous semester for us all. We have the greatest students in the city and—[He is cut off by several loud whistles and cheers.] And we also have the city's best teachers. Our teaching staff has been strengthened greatly by two new teachers who have just joined us: Ms. Jan Anderson in English and Mr. Roy Parkins in mathematics. Would you both please stand so we can see you? [Jan and the other new teacher stand up, acknowledging the polite applause.] Welcome to Hanover High. I and the administrative staff will do all we can to ensure your success in the classroom. [Clearing his throat.] Now let's take a look at the new semester.

***

The following morning Jan arrives at school 45 minutes early in order to arrange her room. Her second floor classroom is in a section of the building added on during the mid-1950s. Though clean and functional, the room lacks any spark of creativity, anything that might invite students to learn. The walls are an innocuous shade of light green. New blackboards line the front and rear walls, and three rows of fluorescent lights give the room an almost distracting brightness. About 30 moveable desks are spread around the room in no particular pattern. She begins by moving the desks into five neat parallel rows. Though she has often imagined herself teaching students who sit clustered in several small, intimate groups or in one large circle, she now thinks she'll have fewer discipline problems if students sit in traditional rows.

Once the desks are rearranged, Jan quickly tapes four motivational posters on the walls. Her favorite shows a black runner and a white runner exchanging a baton during a relay race. In bold white letters, the poster asserts that "Teamwork Pays Off."

With 20 minutes remaining before her first period class, remedial freshman English, begins, she starts to count the literature books in the wooden cabinet at the back of the room. If she has 62 books, each student in her third and seventh period classes can be issued a book. To her surprise she learned yesterday that a chronic book shortage forces many Hanover teachers to distribute books at the start of each period and then collect them at the end.

Just as Jan finishes counting the books and releases a long sigh prompted by the realization that she has only 35, Mrs. Porter, the teacher across the hall, enters.

Mrs. Porter [smiling]   Hi there. I'm Edith Porter, junior and senior English. How's it going?

Jan [hesitantly]   Well I'm not sure. I just found out I don't have enough books for each student to check one out. (Jan walks up to Mrs. Porter and takes her proffered hand.)

Mrs. Porter [warmly]   Well don't let that get you down. As long as we have one classroom set, we figure we're doing pretty well.

Jan   But how can you assign homework? Plus it seems the kids would get the message that they're not very important if their school can't even give them books.

Mrs. Porter   I hear what you're saying, but remember, the kids are the ones who lost the books in the first place. Most of 'em have little or no respect for school property. You can give a student a book today, and nine times out of ten tomorrow it'll be gone.

Jan   Well I guess it could be worse. [Motioning toward the stack of books at the back of the room.] At least I've got *some* books.

Mrs. Porter [with concern]   I don't blame you for being upset. But I think you'll find it will work out all right to keep the books in your room. I admit I can't help you with the books, but please let me know if there's anything else I can do to help. I know it's hard to come into a new school in the middle of the year.

Jan [hesitantly]   I'm not sure how to put this. But yesterday during the short periods I gave most of my classes a simple little vocabulary test. Only ten words . . . spell them and use each one correctly in a sentence. [Sighing.] Well last night I corrected their papers and found that more than half of them failed. [She pauses and then shakes her head in discouragement.] Here I thought I'd start off real positive—give an easy little quiz so everybody'd get an A. I had this pep talk all ready about being a winner and staying on top. [Looking straight at Mrs. Porter and with a serious tone.] You know, I think most of my students need remedial help.

Mrs. Porter [with force and determination] Absolutely. What you're saying is true of about 90 percent of the classes in this building. Our kids need remedial help, and we don't have the training, time, or materials to give it to them. [She shrugs her shoulders.] Actually a lot of our students have learning disabilities, and a few I'm sure are even mentally retarded. We need more special education teachers. The two who are assigned to Hanover have got all the kids they can handle. So the ones they can't take are in our classes. [With irritation.] It's called "mainstreaming."

Jan Yeah, I read about that in college. [Thoughtfully.] You know the frustrating thing is that I think I could give my students the remedial help they need if I just didn't have so many. Five classes with at least 30 kids per class just isn't realistic.

At this moment two boys breeze into Jan's classroom and take their seats near the back of the room. Jan smiles at them and says good morning. They smile awkwardly and return the greeting.

Mrs. Porter Well I'd better get on back across the hall. Duty calls. What period do you have lunch? Mine's sixth period. Maybe we could visit some more. I've got some tips on grouping and budgeting your time that might help.

Jan I'd like that. [Checking her schedule in the open notebook on her desk.] I should remember an important thing like when I have lunch. Yesterday I was so busy I didn't even stop for lunch. Here it is. Oh, good, it's sixth period.

Mrs. Porter Great. I'll meet you here at the end of fifth period. I'll show you where the teachers' lunchroom is. It's not the easiest place to find.

***

About ten weeks later, Jan and her fellow teachers are in the lunchroom entering grades in students' report cards which are spread out, according to homeroom, on top of the lunchroom tables. Students were dismissed at 2:00. The room is quite noisy and full of bustle as the teachers race to get all their grades, total absences, and any appropriate comments entered by the 3:30 sign-out time. Occasionally a homeroom teacher, his or her grades already entered, calls out the name of a teacher who has yet to enter grades for students in that homeroom.

Jan leans over one of the tables, scanning Mr. Wilson's report cards for one belonging to Julius Dismukes. Her pen is poised ready to insert a D, six absences and five cuts, and a terse "needs to try harder." Suddenly she notices that Roy Parkins is standing right next to her, also searching for a report card.

Jan Hi, Roy. How's the other new kid on the block?

Roy Jan, I don't think I've seen you since that first day when Mr. Prokop introduced us. I'm doing okay, how are you?

Jan [tiredly] I don't know about you, Roy, but this has been a whirlwind marking period. [She finds Julius's report card and enters the appropriate information.]

Roy I know what you mean. [He pauses for a moment in his search for a report card.] The record keeping is just unreal, isn't it? I thought this was the computer age.

Jan Well you know all those computers downtown wouldn't have anything to process without the input of foot soldiers like us. What I find really drags me down is grading student papers. I come early, stay late, and work on the weekends, and I'm still never caught up. [With a display of mock agony on her face.] There's nothing like 75 compositions to ruin a weekend.

Roy Wow I'm glad I'm in math. Give me problems at the end of a chapter to correct any day. That's rough. How do you do it?

Jan Not easily, I'll tell you that. [With reflection.] I really like the kids here, and I think I'm doing a good job. But the workload is overwhelming. I wonder if it ever gets any better. Maybe I'm trying to do too much.

Roy Have you thought about applying for a transfer?

Jan [with a surprised look on her face] Oh, no. I wouldn't want to do that. That'd be like admitting I can't do anything to improve the situation. [She pauses.] I don't feel that powerless . . . yet, anyway.

Roy [thoughtfully and with empathy] Well you know, Jan, there are a lot of things around here that nobody could change—not even an act of Congress. So don't burn yourself out trying to do the impossible.

***

It is three weeks later, and Jan is in Mr. Prokop's office at his request. Jan is seated, businesslike, in an office chair just across from Mr. Prokop's big oak desk. It is the end of the day, and without the usually boisterous students in the hallways, the building is unnaturally quiet.

Mr. Prokop [clearing his throat] Well let me thank you for stopping by before you sign out. I just wanted to find out how things have been going for you during your first couple of months here at Hanover.

Jan [hesitantly at first] I'm glad you asked me that—

Mr. Prokop [interrupting] I think it's really important for principals to be in touch with their teachers—all of them. Also I think teachers need feedback from their principal. I think that's really important.

Jan [nodding] Yes it is. I—

Mr. Prokop [interrupting again] Let me start by saying I think you're doing a fine job, Ms. Anderson. You came in here in the middle of the year and just got right with the program. All your reports have been turned in on time. Your grades for last marking period were ready on time.

Jan   Thank you.

Mr. Prokop [leaning forward in his chair]   Now I do have a request to make of you, and I wouldn't ask this if I didn't think you could handle it. Mrs. McPherson, as you probably know, is going on maternity leave. She's the one who handles the honors day assembly at the end of the year. I'd like you to take the assembly this year.

Jan [sighing]   I don't know. What about the person taking Mrs. McPherson's place?

Mr. Prokop   Well the board's just sending us a substitute for the rest of the year. I don't think it would be fair to ask that person to take the assembly.

Jan [becoming irritated]   I don't see how I can take on another thing, Mr. Prokop. You build me up by telling me I'm doing a great job, and then you give me part of another teacher's load.

Mr. Prokop [defensively]   I didn't mean to upset you.

Jan [with a quivering voice]   You began by telling me you want to know how things're going. Well let me tell you. I never thought teaching would be like this. [Speaking more rapidly.] I've got over 150 kids, no planning period, and not enough books. None of us in the department have the aides we should have. And a lot of my kids need remedial help that I'm not trained to give them. Plus I've got some kids that I'm sure have learning disabilities. [She pauses and takes a deep breath.] I mean, frankly I'm having trouble keeping my head above water.

Mr. Prokop [with concern]   I'm sorry you feel that way, Ms. Anderson. I admit we do have some problems here. But we're doing as much as the board will allow us to. [Shrugs his shoulders.] My hands are really tied. Every week I'm after someone down at the board to improve things here, believe me.

Jan [slowly]   I know you've got your frustrations too, Mr. Prokop. I'm sorry I got upset. It's been an especially long, hard day.

Mr. Prokop   I understand. We all have those days. Look, let me see if I can get one of the other teachers to help you with the assembly. How does that sound?

Jan [weakly]   Well all right.

Mr. Prokop [stands up smiling and shows Jan to the door]   I really appreciate your efforts. I really do. Don't worry now. Get a good night's rest. Things will get better.

***

The following morning Jan is chatting with Roy as they both climb the stairs to their classrooms.

Roy   I don't blame you for being mad when he asked you to take the honors assembly. [He gestures emphatically with his free left arm.]

That's his style—shower you with compliments and then pile on the extra work. He can't do that, though, with a lot of the older teachers. They just tell him where to get off. I think he's afraid of some of them.

Jan [sighing]   I'm just not sure what to do. I keep telling myself if I can just hang in there, summer will be here soon. Maybe things'll be better next year. Oh I don't know. Maybe I wasn't cut out for teaching. Maybe I should just resign and go into something else. I'm still young. What do you think?

Roy   Boy, I'm surprised to hear you talking like that. You must really be upset. [Pausing.] I wish I could tell you what to do, Jan, but I can't. That's a decision you've got to make on your own. Maybe you ought to wait and give it some thought over the weekend.

HANOVER HIGH SCHOOL

Schedule of Classes for Jan Anderson,
Room 260, Second Semester

Period	Time	Subject	Grade	Enrollment
HR	8:05–8:30	Homeroom	9	36
1	8:35–9:30	Remedial English	9	32
2	9:35–10:30	Study hall		122
3	10:35–11:30	Regular English	9	32
4	11:35–12:30	Remedial English	10	35
5	12:35–1:30	Lunch		
6	1:35–2:30	Remedial English	10	36
7	2:35–3:30	Regular English	9	30

QUESTIONS

1. To what extent is Mr. Prokop responsible for conditions at Hanover High School? What are some ways that a principal can support his or her teachers?
2. What is the purpose of Chapter 1 of the Educational Consolidation and Improvement Act? How effective is this program?
3. What is "teacher efficacy," and how does it apply to Jan and Roy? Neither have tenure. What is tenure and how might it relate to teacher sense of efficacy?
4. From the standpoint of motivational theory, what needs seem to be operating in the cases of Jan and Mr. Prokop? For example, at what levels of Maslow's need hierarchy do they seem to be operating? How might Jan use such information in dealing with Mr. Prokop?
5. Do you believe that Jan might be trying to do too much during her first semester at Hanover High? In what areas might Jan cut back in order to make her job more manageable? What suggestions do you have for the beginning teacher so that the first year of teaching might not be so overwhelming?
6. What impact does the surrounding environment have on the climate at Hanover High? What effects does poverty have on learning? What steps can teachers take to minimize the negative effects that poverty might have on schooling?
7. How would you describe teacher morale at Hanover High? What factors seem to contribute to teacher morale? What factors lessen morale? How do you think the principal, Mr. Prokop, affects morale? What is frustration, and how do you think it affects teacher behavior?
8. What should Jan do? Should she apply for a transfer? Should she try to improve conditions at Hanover? If so, how?
9. What effect, if any, do you think Hanover's multicultural student body has on teachers? What are some of the special concerns of teachers in multicultural settings? What are the characteristics of teachers who can effectively work with students from subcultures other than their own?
10. What kind of remedial methods and materials do you think Jan would find helpful? What kind of support services would help her and other Hanover teachers?
11. What is teacher burnout, and how does it relate to stress? What are the sources of stress in Jan's situation? What can teachers do to cope with stress? What can Jan do in her situation?
12. What is locus of control? How does this construct relate to Jan's situation? What elements in Jan's situation can she change and not change?

CASE 24

VALUES IN THE WORKPLACE

Bill Normandy is 32 years old and has four years' experience as an art teacher. Since he wishes to pursue a graduate degree at a nearby university, Bill interviews for a job in the small town (population approximately 2,000) of Farmington. Farmington High School is about 60 percent white, 30 percent black, and 10 percent Hispanic and draws students from a primarily low-income, semiskilled labor population in the southeastern portion of the United States. Bill's job interview is conducted in the office of Jim Rawlings, longtime principal and local good old boy. John Dunn, the assistant principal, also sits in on the interview.

Jim   Yes this building's an old one, Bill, but our maintenance staff has taken mighty good care of it. Also I think that the folks who built school buildings back around World War I had a pride in their labor that you don't often see in today's buildings.

John   Isn't that the truth! All you have to do is look at the way some of the newer buildings in University City have held up—University High, for example.

Jim   Boy, that's for sure. I feel sorry for ole George Aarons, the principal over there. He probably spends more time on the phone to the building maintenance division than anyone else. I hear one of his boilers went last week. [Pause.] Well, Bill, I'm sure you didn't come here to listen to us brag about our old building. [Laughs.] Jim and I have gone over your credentials and believe that you are exactly what we're looking for.

Bill [smiling]   Well I'm glad to hear that!

Jim   However, this is a small town and a small school, Bill, and you need to understand that.

Bill   I grew up in a town not much larger than this in the Midwest. There were only 60 students in my high school graduating class.

Jim   That cinches it—you're our man. [Pauses and looks serious.] There is one problem though. You're going to have to teach a couple of classes out of field. We don't like to have to ask you to do it, but there's no other way. Mrs. Fielding, the art teacher before you, had to do the same thing.

Bill [frowning]   What would my load be?

Jim Well you'll teach three art classes, two classes in painting and pottery, and a photography class.
Bill [interrupting] A photography class?
Jim Yes. I notice from your credentials that photography is one of your hobbies.
Bill That's true, but I never thought that I'd get a chance to teach it!
Jim I'm sure that you'll enjoy it then! However, the difficult part is that you'll have to teach eighth grade language arts and the yearbook class.
Bill The yearbook class!
Jim Yes, well, I guess it would be more accurate to call it journalism. However, with your photography skills and an experienced student staff left over from last year, it should be fun for you.
Bill Boy, I don't know. Two classes out of field—
Jim Eighth grade language arts shouldn't be a problem either. Mrs. Fielding had it all laid out before she left. The curriculum and materials are all cut and dried. All you have to do is follow them. She did the same thing with the yearbook class. You just have to keep the students organized so they meet the deadlines. They do all the work. After all it's their yearbook, and the other kids are really going to give them a hard time if they don't come out with a good one.
John We know how tough it is to teach out of field, but Jim and I are working on your position so you can become full-time art.
Jim We've just got to find a way to shake a few more dollars out of the board so they'll give us another English teacher.
Bill Well, gentlemen, I'll give it my best shot! Thanks a lot for asking me!
Jim [smiling] Our pleasure. We look forward to working with you.

***

Bill walks to the art room after receiving directions from the school secretary. He is shocked as he enters the art room: There are garbage, trash, dirt, and roaches everywhere. The room is in complete disarray and appears to have been so for some time. As Bill contemplates the scrubbing and cleaning it will take to get things in order before school begins, he is joined by a middle-aged woman.

Sarah Hello there! I'm Sarah Downing, the music teacher. I'll bet you're the new art teacher.
Bill Yes I am. I'm Bill Normandy. [Pointing at the art room.] What on earth happened here? Was this room hit by a bomb?
Sarah [in a secretive, hushed manner] Well, Bill, I just met you and I really shouldn't gossip, but we are going to be working together. I'm afraid that your predecessor became rather bitter and angry and decided to leave the room like this to get back at the school.
Bill [shocked] Mrs. Fielding?
Sarah Yes. I'm afraid with all this cleaning you won't have much time

to get your plans and materials ready. So Mary didn't end up getting back at the school after all. She's only hurt a fellow teacher.

Bill   Can't I get some help from the custodial staff?

Sarah   Yes but you'll end up doing most of it yourself. Our custodial staff is slow and always busy, if you know what I mean. Talk to George down in the boiler room. Maybe he'll be able to get you some help.

Bill   If Mrs. Fielding left her room looking like this, where do you suppose she left her plans and materials? In some file cabinets some where?

Sarah   No. I think this is the only room and storage space Mary had.

Bill   Since I'm taking over her art classes, her language arts class, and her journalism class, I'd sure like to get the lesson plans and materials Mr. Rawlings mentioned during my job interview.

Sarah   Bill, as mad as she was when she left, I really can't imagine her leaving anything behind! You may want to talk to Roy Moore, the English teacher. He's in 211. If she left any plans for language arts or journalism, Roy would know about them.

***

Bill sticks his head in room 211 and sees a white-haired man in his early sixties putting books in a closet.

Bill   Are you Roy Moore?

Roy [looking up]   Yes I am.

Bill   I'm Bill Normandy the new art teacher. Could I talk to you for a minute?

Roy [smiling, walking over to Bill and shaking his hand]   You sure can. I'm glad to hear that they found a replacement for Mary Fielding.

Bill   Thanks. [Frowning.] But I'm afraid that I'm a bit upset at the moment. That's why I wanted to talk to you.

Roy [sitting down.]   Have a seat, Bill. How can I help?

Bill   Well I just talked to Sarah . . . I'm afraid I can't remember her last name. The music teacher.

Roy   You mean Sarah Downing.

Bill   Yeah that's it. It seems that Mary Fielding left the art room in a mess, and I was asking Sarah about Mary's lesson plans and materials. Sarah said she didn't think she left any.

Roy   That's right.

Bill   Well, you see I have to teach Mary's eighth grade language arts and journalism classes, and Mr. Rawlings said that all I had to do was follow Mary's plans, that everything was all laid out—

Roy   I'm afraid that Mr. Rawlings is wrong. Mary was mad when she left and took everything with her.

Bill   Oh boy! Now what am I going to do?!

Roy   Don't worry, Bill. I'll help you all I can. [Walking over to the closet and picking up a book.] Here's the book that Mary used in language arts.

Bill Thanks.

Roy There's also a workbook that goes with the text. I'll bring you a copy from home.

Bill Great! Did she use a book in journalism?

Roy Yes. I'm sure I have a copy of it at home too. Also, just ask if you have trouble making out your lesson plans. [Pause.] I'm afraid though that there's very little money for materials and supplies.

Bill I was afraid you were going to say that! By the way, what kind of kids can I expect in journalism? Experienced?

Roy I'm afraid not. You see, Mary lost her job because of the yearbook. The work that needed to be done in April and May to get the yearbook out just wasn't done. To be honest with you, the kids in her class just didn't care, and deadlines weren't met.

Bill Oh boy!

Roy Probably 50 percent of the kids in journalism were D–F students in other classes. I'd be surprised if the ones you get this year are any different. Mary felt that both the students and the administration let her down. I think it's safe to say that she was bitter when she left.

Bill I'm sure I'm going to be sorry for asking, but can you tell me what kind of students I'm likely to get in my art classes?

Roy Well, I remember Mary saying that she had over 30 students in her painting and pottery classes. She always complained that she got a mixture of advanced and beginning students and that there was neither space nor materials for them.

Bill That does me in! None of this sounds like the situation that Mr. Rawlings described. [frowns.] But I'm not a complainer or a quitter, Roy.

Roy I'm sure it'll get better, Bill!

***

It is the first day of classes. Bill has spent the entire preplanning period cleaning and scrubbing his room. The last period ended one-half hour ago, and Bill has been sitting just outside Jim Rawlings's office waiting his turn to talk to him. Jim finishes with another teacher and motions for Bill to come into his office.

Jim Have a seat, Bill, and make yourself at home.

Bill Thanks, Mr. Rawlings. [Pause.] I need to talk to you about my classes.

Jim Sure, Bill. Go ahead.

Bill Do you remember when I interviewed with John and you? [Jim nods.] One of the things we talked about was that teaching two courses out of field wouldn't be difficult because Mrs. Fielding left her plans and materials for me to use.

Jim Yes, that's right.

Bill Well, Mr. Rawlings, she didn't leave anything. She left the art room in a real mess and took everything with her.

Jim [frowning] She did? That really surprises me. I thought that Mary was more of a professional than that.

Bill I suppose the hardest part is the yearbook class. Practically all the students in there are new, and most are slow learners.

Jim Bill, believe me that John and I had no idea that Mary left things in such a mess!

Bill Well, Jim, that's not all. My painting and pottery classes are over-crowded, and there aren't enough supplies. As if that isn't bad enough, I met with my photography class the last period and found out that the kids weren't aware of the paper and film costs that are involved. They thought the school would furnish them.

Jim Now they know better than that! We've never furnished those supplies!

Bill So, Mr. Rawlings, I find myself with five new classes without any plans or adequate materials. That just doesn't seem like the situation we discussed at my interview.

Jim [smiling] Bill, John and I had no idea that things would turn out like this! It's a little bit like a football team expecting an easy game and then suddenly finding itself behind at the end of the first quarter. Unexpected things happen. But with you at quarterback, Bill, I've no doubt that the superior team will turn the game around and win it going away!

Bill Well you know I'll give it my best shot! But the job just isn't what I expected!

Jim [smiling and enthusiastic] I know you will, boy! I told John after your interview, "That kid's a winner."

Bill Well, thanks, Mr. Rawlings. I—

Jim [in a serious tone] Bill, I'm awful glad you dropped by today. It saves me from hunting you up.

Bill You wanted to see me?

Jim Yes. I need your help in a big way! I know after all that's happened that it's awful for me to ask but, frankly, I don't know who else to ask bail me out.

Bill What is it?

Jim Well, Bill, Mr. Moore, the English teacher, isn't in the best of health. I guess that's to be expected at his age. Anyhow, at his doctor's advice, he has to give up the school paper. This is a small school, Bill, and you're the only one that can take it over. Will you help us out?

Bill Well, gosh, Mr. Rawlings, can I have a little time to think about it?

Jim Bill, someone needs to begin meeting that class tomorrow, and I'd take it as a special favor if you'd at least begin meeting it for me.

Bill Well, okay. I guess I can do that since it's during my planning period.

Jim [smiling] Bill, you don't know how much I appreciate this! We don't have much money and precious few teachers, but John and I are going to do our best to get you a better schedule next year. We're going to do our best to get another English teacher in here to take over both the yearbook and the school paper. Then you can just concentrate on the art program.

Bill That'd be great.

Jim I'll tell you what. You like football don't you?

Bill Yes I do. Very much.

Jim How'd you like to attend the football games and make a little extra money at the same time?

Bill How do I do that?

Jim I could put you in charge of the concession stand at the football games. The kids really do all the work. All you have to do is organize it and check in and make sure things are going okay from time to time.

Bill Well I've never done anything like that before.

Jim I know that a little extra money always comes in handy, and the kids really appreciate teachers who get involved with them like that.

Bill I guess I could give it a try!

Jim Bill, you're a good man! It's a delight to work with a young man who is so professional!

***

It is November of the same year, and Bill runs into Roy Moore, the English teacher, right after the last period ends.

Roy Why, hi there, Bill! I haven't seen you in a long time! How have you been?

Bill [smiling] Do you really want to know?

Roy [in a serious tone] Why sure, Bill. Aren't things going well for you?

Bill I hate to lay my troubles on you, but I really don't know who else to tell.

Roy [sitting down in a classroom chair] Fire away!

Bill Well, besides my two art classes and my photography, language arts, and yearbook classes, I now have the school paper.

Roy I guess that's partly my fault, Bill. I have done the school paper for over 10 years and told Jim that I wanted out or else I was going to look for another position.

Bill You don't have medical problems?

Roy [smiling] Not that I know of! Is that what Jim told you?

Bill Yes. [Pause.] Oh, well, I've managed to combine both the yearbook and most of the school paper staff into one class that meets the same period. But, Roy, practically all these kids are beginners, and we've missed our first three deadlines.

Roy I know what you're going through, Bill. It was like that for 10 years. I had enough.

Bill Rawlings also put me in charge of the concessions stand at the football games. Trying to stock the concessions stand is worse than trying to get out the yearbook. Can you believe that the supplier closes at 4:00 P.M.? There's no way I can teach my classes and get there before they close.

Roy Oh boy!

Bill Roy, I just don't have any time to do anything! I find myself spending every evening and weekend at school doing yearbook and school paper work. I spend the leftover time grading papers.

Roy If you keep this up, Bill, you're eventually going to crack!

Bill You haven't heard it all! I have to take the GRE for admission to graduate school at the university. I haven't had any time to study for it. They sent me a bad batch of clay for my art classes, and the county coordinator sent me a letter asking me to set up a mini-course in computer graphics. There's just no time to plan and organize my courses. And I know I'm not doing a good job.

Roy Bill, why did you say "yes" to all these things? You've gotten yourself in over your head. You've got to learn to say "no." Enough is enough.

Bill Rawlings is a hard man to say "no" to. But he promised that he and John Dunn would work out a good schedule for me next year. [Pause.] If I can survive this one!

Roy [sternly] A word of advice, Bill. If you don't have that in writing, don't count on it.

* * *

It is May of the next year, and Bill is finally ending his first school year at Farmington High. The school day is over, and Bill is seated in Jim Rawlings's office trying to keep his emotions under control.

Jim How can I help you, Bill?

Bill John Dunn just gave me my class assignments for next year.

Jim Yes?

Bill Mr. Rawlings, I have the same load I had this year! You promised me—

Jim I know I did, Bill. John and I really worked hard on the school board, but they just wouldn't budge! No money for another English teacher. That puts both of us in a bind. Don't think I don't know what kind of job you've done for us this year! But you know, there's a school board election coming up, and if we're lucky, we'll get a board that's a little easier to work with.

Bill [with strong emotion] Mr. Rawlings, I just can't go through another year like this one. If my assignment stands as it is, I may have to look for another job!

Jim Bill, that would disappoint me greatly. You're a good teacher, and John and I both had such high hopes for you. Why don't you take a couple of days and think it over before you do something we both might regret. Art positions aren't that easy to come by these days. Give me a call on Friday and let me know what you have decided, okay?

FARMINGTON HIGH SCHOOL
Schedule of Classes for Bill Normandy

Period	Time	Subject	Grade	Enrollment
HR	8:05–8:35	Homeroom	9	35
1	8:40–9:35	Study hall		131
2	9:40–10:35	Art graphics (photography)	9–12	24
3	10:40–11:35	Art (painting, pottery)	9–12	29
4	11:40–12:35	Lunch (planning)		
5	12:40–1:35	Art (painting, pottery)	9–12	33
6	1:40–2:35	Journalism (yearbook, school paper)	11–12	31
7	2:40–3:35	Language arts (remedial)	8	34

QUESTIONS

1. Would you like to work for a principal like Jim Rawlings? Why or why not?
2. How can teachers avoid being taken advantage of by administrators?
3. Imagine that you were in Bill's teaching position. How would you deal with Jim and John?
4. Should Bill look for another job? If he returns to Farmington High School next year, could he improve his working conditions in any way?
5. At which of Kohlberg's stages of moral development does Jim Rawlings seem to be operating? Bill?
6. What is stress in teaching? What stressors are operating in Bill's case? What are the most effective ways of dealing with stress?
7. What does it mean to call teaching a profession? In what ways does Bill's job resemble a profession and in what ways not? How is Bill's job different from that of a physician or attorney in private practice?
8. What are the differences between the intrinsic and extrinsic views of motivation? What are the intrinsic rewards in teaching? What should a prospective teacher find out about the extrinsic aspects of a teaching situation before accepting a position?
9. What communication techniques are available to Bill to use in communicating with Jim and John? For example, would the techniques of sending "I-messages" and using "active listening" from *Teacher Effectiveness Training* work? If Bill decides to stay, what kind of "no lose solution" (from TET) might he try to work out? What aspects of his job situation should he try to eliminate as he bargains and in what order of priority?
10. What are the real disadvantages of teaching out of field? What is the best way to try to cope with such a situation?

CASE 25

THE POWER STRUGGLE

Eastridge High School consists of a large modern structure located in a metropolitan area of over one million people. It serves a student population that is 55 percent Hispanic, 30 percent white, and 15 percent black. Jerry Eddy is a 38-year-old English teacher with 15 years' teaching experience. It is the first day of classes of a new school year, and Jerry drops by the room of a beginning teacher, Jim Young, before the first period begins.

Jerry Hi Jim! All ready for your first year?

Jim [smiling and getting up from his desk]   Hello, Jerry. I guess I'm as ready as I'm going to be. Bring on the juniors!

Jerry That's right. You're mostly going to be teaching English 11, aren't you?

Jim Yeah, and I think I have everything ready to go, at least for the first grading period. By the way where is the faculty meeting going to be held?

Jerry In the auditorium.

Jim I was really impressed with Mr. Owens when he interviewed me.

Jerry Yes, Chet's quite a principal. I think that he's the best I've ever worked under.

Jim Really? Some people, especially in the English department, don't seem to like him.

Jerry I guess he's one of those people you either love or hate. In the three years that he's been principal, he's made a lot of improvements. He's cleaned up the halls, put the athletic program in proper perspective, and made people accountable. He doesn't put up with teachers ducking out early, arriving late, or taking long breakfast or lunch breaks.

Jim So that's why some of the teachers don't like him.

Jerry Yes, but I'll tell you one thing. The kids love him. He knows virtually every kid's name, no mean trick in a school this size, and he's aware of what's going on in the classrooms. He has this habit of walking unannounced through classes and sometimes even takes them over.

Jim Wow! I'm glad you told me about that! That must be a bit unnerving.

Jerry Yes, you always know where you stand with old Chet. [Pause.]

I think one of the most important decisions that Chet made was to appoint Don Pope chair of the English department over Jane Sable.
Jim I guess Jane didn't like that much, right?
Jerry Right. Jane's a really competent teacher, but she's a very negative human being. I think Chet realized that Jane would be hell to live with as a chair. In the two years that Don has been chair, he and Chet have become very close. I think Chet's developed a lot of respect for Don's personal and professional integrity. He's given Don more and more responsibility and has made him his confidant. They both put the education of the students first and don't mind being unpopular with people whose feathers get ruffled.
Jim Is Jane one of those people?
Jerry Yes. Jane and her little clique of four or five in the English department hate their guts!
Jim Boy, this is going to be an interesting first year of teaching!

***

It is still the first day of classes. The first faculty meeting of the year was held in the auditorium and is followed by a meeting of the English department in Don Pope's classroom. Don sits at his desk and presides over the meeting. Jane Sable and her friends sit in chairs closest to the desk. Jerry and Jim, fast becoming friends, sit together in chairs near the back of the room.

Don Therefore I think it's time that we take a new and hard look at our English curriculum both in terms of scope and sequence. To get the ball rolling, I'm going to appoint a committee of five to address these matters: Mary Conswello, Jerry Eddy, Michael Kane, Sally Blair, and Jane Sable. [Pointing.] Jane?
Jane Don, I don't want to serve on the curriculum committee.
Don When I talked to you this summer I thought you agreed to.
Jane I did. But I've given it a lot of thought, and I feel we have a pretty good English program the way it is. If it's not broke, don't fix it.
Don Well I think that the least we can do is ask the committee to examine the matter and bring back recommendations to the whole department for action.
Jane [slightly trembling with anger] I don't know who's supposed to benefit from all this! Somebody's friends, I suppose!
Don [angrily] I think you'd better explain what you mean by that!
Jane What I mean is this. By the time you and your committee finished studying the rooms and teaching schedules in the English department, you ended up making totally unbelievable and inappropriate changes!
Don Course and room changes that the committee agreed were best for all!
Jane It hardly seems equitable when a person takes years to build up

a course and puts her life's blood into it and then has it taken away! And as for my room—

Don [interrupting] It was the committee's feeling and mine that courses and rooms are not privately owned by anybody, and that everybody should have a chance to teach those courses they're prepared for and would enjoy teaching!

Jane I had to teach a long time before I earned the right to teach my advanced placement courses, and other people should have to pay their dues too!

Don [calming down] That's one way to look at it, Jane, but it's not the only way.

Jane I'll tell you one thing, Don! I'm going to protest all this to Mr. Owens!

Don That's your right, Jane, but if you think Mr. Owens doesn't know all about it, you're mistaken.

***

Three days later Jane and five other teachers are seated in Chet Owens's office after school.

Jane [angrily] And now, Mr. Owens, on top of everything else, he's setting up a scope and sequence committee! I wonder how he's going to use that against us?!

Chet [calmly] Now, folks, let's act like professionals. Mr. Pope has explained to me his reasons for what he's doing. I fully agree with him.

Jane [with controlled hostility] You do? I guess that doesn't surprise me! You always back him no matter who he hurts! Excuse us for taking up your time, Mr. Owens! [Stands up to leave.]

Chet [forcefully] Jane, you're an excellent teacher, and no one is trying to hurt you. I'm sure when you've had time to think things over you'll realize that a department chairman has to consider what's best for the entire department.

Jane [storming out in a huffy manner with the others following] I just hope that there is an English department left after Mr. Pope finishes wrecking it!

***

A year has gone by and it is the beginning of the next school year. Over the summer Chet Owens died, and Charles Holt replaced him as principal. Jerry Eddy once again stops in Jim Young's classroom before school begins.

Jim Hey Jer'. How're you doin'?

Jerry [smiling] I know what you're going to say: We've got to stop meeting like this at the beginning of each school year.

Jim Yes, I think you started a tradition.

Jerry [seriously]   I sure hope that the department meeting this year is better than it was last year!

Jim   Yes, I was just thinking about that and Mr. Owens's funeral before you came in. What do you think of Mr. Holt? Do you think he'll back up Pope the way Mr. Owens did?

Jerry   I don't know, but we'll soon be finding out.

Jim   How's that?

Jerry   I just talked to Bill Rion in the hall. He's union rep again, you know. Well it seems that while Owens was dying in the hospital, Jane Sable and company were filing a union grievance against Pope to protest the room and schedule changes that he made.

Jim [whistles aloud]   What do you think Holt will do?

Jerry   Don't know, Jimbo. One thing he's done already I don't like.

Jim   What's that?

Jerry   Have you met the new blonde English teacher, Diana Holt, who will be joining us this year?

Jim   You aren't going to tell me that they're related?!

Jerry   She's his sister-in-law.

Jim [throwing up his hands]   This place is crazy! That's nepotism!

Jerry   I'd say so. How's he going to evaluate her fairly for merit?

Jim   It beats me! How?

Jerry [laughing]   With great difficulty! [Pause.] All I know about Holt is that he's an ex-coach and a counselor who knows very little about the power struggles that have gone on in our English department. He's different from Mr. Owens. His method of dealing with people seems to be to listen to everybody and try to make everybody happy.

Jim   That'll be a good trick with our English department!

Jerry   True. It may also mean that he'll cave in to whoever is most aggressive and talks to him last.

Jim   And that is most likely to be sweet Jane. Right?

Jerry   You've got it.

***

Don Pope presides at the English department meeting in his classroom after school. Jane and her friends sit up front again.

Don   Although she has already been introduced to us at the general faculty meeting, I'd like all of us to get to know the newest member of our English faculty a little better. Diana, won't you tell us a little about yourself.

Diana [in an overbearing manner]   Yes, thank you, Don. Well, first, I guess it's no secret that I'm Charles's sister-in-law. In case you're wondering, there are both advantages and disadvantages to that situation. [Smiling.] It makes it very difficult to have friends among the troops since anything I hear I may have to end up telling Charles. However I'm sure you'll find me a friendly and likeable person once you get to know me.

Don [thoughtfully and carefully]   I'm sure we will Diana. [Sees Jane's hand up.] Yes, Jane?

Jane   Don't you have an announcement, Don?

Don [angrily]   I'm running this meeting, Jane! I'll make announcements when I see fit! [Pause.] Since you've so rudely brought it up [passing out papers to everyone], I just got word before the meeting that Mr. Holt upheld the grievance that some members of our faculty filed this summer about class schedules and rooms. I know this messes up all your planning and in some cases will cause a lot of hardship, but I had very little control over it.

Jane [angrily]   Might I point out that you're the one who made the changes to start with! It strikes me that you're the one who *created* the problem in the first place!

Diana [standing up to leave]   I can't believe such unprofessional behavior. I refuse to attend a meeting where adults behave like such babies! [Leaves.]

Don [shouts]   That's it! That's all of this I'm going to tolerate! Meeting adjourned!

***

It is one month later. Jim runs into Jerry in the hallway between classes.

Jim [excitedly]   Hi, Jer'. Are you going to sign the petition?

Jerry [with surprise]   What petition?

Jim   I've finally scooped you! The petition to make Jane Sable department chair!

Jerry   Oh, God, no! Tell me it isn't so!

Jim   It's so, all right. And I hear from Rion that Pope just might resign.

Jerry   Old Jane Sable might have a surprise coming if he does.

Jim   What's that?

Jerry   Holt might name Diane department chair instead.

Jim   Oh, boy! Do you really think so?

Jerry   Why not? She already has the best teaching schedule and room in the department!

Jim   That's true, and old Sable was apparently too afraid to say anything about it!

Jerry   Now Rion tells me that Holt has nominated her for merit pay based on his own totally unbiased evaluation. Now I ask you: Is it inconceivable that he would name her department chair and point out that she's the best person for the job since she's not a member of either department clique?

Jim   That's too much! Jerry, I've got to go. We've got to get together and talk all this over! We've got to do something! Can you come to my house tonight after dinner?

Jerry   Sounds good. See you then.

***

That same evening Jim and Jerry sit in Jim's living room drinking beer.

Jim   What are we going to do, Jer'? We've got to do something! Do you think we should circulate a counterpetition endorsing Pope as chair?

Jerry   Gee, I don't know! That's risky.

Jim   Maybe the two of us should go in and talk to Holt—tell him that we support Pope.

Jerry   Maybe we'd better go see Pope first before he gets fed up and resigns. Can you imagine either Sable or Holt as department chairs?

Jim   That would be a fate worse than death all right!

Jerry   Maybe we should try playing games and go talk to Diane. Maybe we could get her support on Pope's behalf.

Jim   At least we might get some clue as to whether or not Holt is considering her as department chair. [Pause.] But just the mere thought of asking her for anything leaves a bad taste in my mouth.

Jerry   I know what you mean! Anything we do is a big risk, Jim. Maybe we should just do nothing and let the chips fall where they may. Remember. You don't have tenure yet!

Jim   I've got to do something, Jerry, or I won't be able to live with myself. [Pause.] And to think that I thought teaching was about students' learning.

Jerry   [laughing]   Quit trying to get us off track! What do you think we ought to do?

Preamble to Petition Circulated at Eastridge High School

We, the undersigned, while recognizing the leadership efforts and sincerity of the current chair of the English department, feel it is time for new leadership. We strongly petition and recommend to our principal that he appoint Ms. Jane Sable as chair of the English department at Eastridge High School.

QUESTIONS

1. What are the characteristics of an effective school principal? How does he or she support the classroom teacher?
2. What is curriculum scope and sequence? How should scope and sequence be determined?
3. What kind of activities can teachers become involved in to promote the overall status of the profession?
4. Do power struggles such as the one at Eastridge High have an impact on students in the classroom? Explain your answer.
5. From a social psychology perspective, what is power? What different kinds of power do Chet Owens, Jane Sable, Diana Holt, and Jerry Eddy have? How is power lost and gained? What are cliques, and how do they relate to power?
6. What is teacher morale, and what are the sources of high and low teacher morale? How is it measured? How might the English department power struggle at EHS influence teacher morale? Does high or low teacher morale actually influence teacher effectiveness in the classroom?
7. At what levels of Maslow's need hierarchy do Jerry, Jim, Jane, Don, Jane, and Diana seem to be operating? At what need level can teachers begin "to consider what's best for the entire department" and look beyond their individual or clique needs?
8. What is nepotism? In what ways can it be detrimental?
9. What are conflict, conflict management, and assertiveness training? How might they apply to this situation?
10. At which of Kohlberg's stages of moral development do Jane, Don, and Jerry seem to be operating? How does upward stage movement occur according to the principles of moral education?

PART VII

ADDITIONAL CASES

CASE 26

STANDARDS, STIGMA, MATURITY, AND MOTIVATION

Jan Smith, an attractive first grade teacher, is in her second year of teaching. She is completing her first year at Lincoln Elementary School. She and her husband, Ben, moved to the community in the fall. Ben had completed his law degree and wanted to practice in a small town. Lincoln School serves a small, lower-middle-class community in a midwestern state. Jan sits waiting in the office to talk with Mr. Johnson, the elderly principal who has been at Lincoln 22 years, since it was built. Mr. Johnson finishes his phone call and turns to Jan.

Mr. Johnson [leans forward]   Jan, you really fit in here! Young teachers sometimes have problems since we're set in our ways here. [With emphasis.] However, I've really been pleased with your teaching! And I mean it. I'm not just saying it to make you feel good. The other teachers have been pleased too. Especially the other two first grade teachers. They tell me that you've given them some new ideas and that the three of you have worked like a team.

Jan [smiling in a warm manner]   Thank you, Mr. Johnson. I love teaching, and Miss Grayson and Mrs. Wilson have really helped me a lot. They tell me what they are doing and explain why but still give me freedom to teach my way.

Mr. Johnson [leans back and becomes businesslike]   I wanted you to know that we appreciate your teaching, but I also wanted to go over this May 10th promotion list you sent to the office. I see you promoted every child.

Jan [frowning and with emphasis]   Is there anything wrong with promoting everybody?

Mr. Johnson [businesslike but warm]   No not necessarily. But I do wonder if it's wise to promote Randy Duncan. I think Randy would be hopelessly lost in the second grade. He wouldn't be able to keep up, and he'd take up so much of his teacher's time that it wouldn't be fair to the other students. I looked at his classroom performance, and it matched the impression I had formed by watching him on the playground.

Jan [speaks slowly, thoughtfully]   I know there will be some difficulties if we promote Randy, but I don't want to penalize him unjustly. You see,

285

Mr. Johnson, I'm really concerned about this. Maybe because I had a bad experience last year.

Mr. Johnson What happened?

Jan [sighs, then continues slowly] Last year I taught in a school where the policy was to retain first graders if they couldn't read. I was really in turmoil since I had just graduated and could still remember reading that teachers should only rarely retain kids. And then only if the retention is clearly to the kid's benefit. Kevin was very, very big for his age. He came from a family of repeaters. Some older brothers and sisters had repeated grades. He was slow all year, even with all the extra help I gave him. I sent many letters to his parents asking them for a conference, but they never once replied. It was almost as if Kevin's failure were expected—at least they were sure willing to accept his poor performance.

Mr. Johnson Did you ever call them on the phone or go see them?

Jan No.

Mr. Johnson What kind of work did Kevin's parents do?

Jan [speaks slowly and thoughtfully] His father was a janitor at the university, and I think the mother was a checker at a supermarket.

Mr. Johnson What finally happened?

Jan [shakes her head negatively] Well, my principal looked at Kevin's work, his achievement test scores, and so on and told me to retain him. I wrote the parents telling them that I was afraid I would have to hold Kevin back. Still no reply. I was forced to retain Kevin in the first grade. Earlier this year I received a letter from Kevin's new teacher, who is a friend of mine. She told me about his poor attitude and classroom behavior. [With emphasis.] At least last year he was cooperative and wanted to learn! [Shakes her head and bites her lip.] She says he is much bigger than the other kids and sticks out like a sore thumb. In fact, she says she's heard some first graders say things like, "There goes that stupid Kevin Thompson! He flunked first grade." When I got that letter I felt like I had branded Kevin for life. Since then I've read a lot about the bad effects that retention can have. [Firmly.] And I'm convinced that it's poor policy.

Mr. Johnson [sympathetic, but businesslike] Jan, I know how you feel. I still remember the first student I had to retain. And maybe Kevin should have been promoted. But you must remember that each child has to be considered individually.

Jan Well let's talk about Randy. [With exasperation.] Why would it be good to retain him?

Mr. Johnson Randy is the smallest boy in your room and from watching him on the playground, I know he has very poor coordination. He also seems to stay by himself, and he apparently has no close friends or social skills. I think he's immature. Children who are behind other pupils physically and emotionally as well as academically often profit from retention.

Jan [as she tears a Kleenex in two] But Mr. Johnson, I learned in college that repeaters make less academic progress than a promoted child of comparable academic ability.

Mr. Johnson [talks with a mixture of anger and uneasiness] Jan, this is different. This is the real world. It's not a theoretical case study. College professors don't have to deal with students who can't learn and their parents. We have to uphold standards. Unearned promotions cause students to develop unrealistic beliefs about the relationship between hard work and success. We have to face up to reality.

Jan But doesn't repeating first grade tell a child that he's inferior? [She adds earnestly.] It also seems to me that some students would never reach a minimum level and never leave the first grade if we hold to our standards!

Mr. Johnson [in a placating tone]   Jan, I'm not saying that all children need to be retained. But when a young first grader doesn't learn to read and is also physically and socially immature, I think we have no choice. Some kids are motivated by being retained, and it gives them a second chance to learn the material. We just have to be careful and see to it that retention doesn't become a stigma.

Jan [argumentatively and with emotion]   It's hard for me to see how Randy will be motivated by spending the first two months of school next year going through readiness activities. What he needs next year is for the second grade teacher to start him in the reading primer so he can learn to read! He's ready to start the primer. If he repeats the first grade, he'll be bored during readiness activities and fall behind when academics begin. It seems such a waste. He knows what sounds are about. He's ready to read.

Mr. Johnson [firmly]   Some low achievers like Randy do profit from retention. I want to observe him in the classroom and see how he gets along when he works on his own. Then I want to see him in his reading group. [With some authority.] We'll get together next week and make a final decision. In the meantime think things over carefully. Don't let last year's experiences blind you. Look at the case objectively.

(Developed and filled in by teacher on each child, partly from cumulative record data)

Pupil: Randy Duncan
Birth Date: 9/15/82
Age: 6
Metropolitan Readiness Test: Absent
Peabody Picture Vocabulary: Scored in the very low, normal range

	Grading Periods			
	1	2	3	4
Language arts	U	U	N	U
Spelling	N	U	U	N
Math	N	N	N	N
Science	S	N	N	N
Social studies	S	S	S	S

(Grading scale: E = excellent, S = satisfactory, N = needs improvement, U = unsatisfactory)

Parent conference notes

Saw Mrs. Duncan on 10/4/88. She remarried (Mr. Duncan) a year ago. She works at an insurance office as a secretary and is two months pregnant. Mother reports that Randy talks about the coming baby a great deal. Randy has an older sister in the fourth grade. Mother doesn't seem greatly interested in Randy.

Comments

Grading period 1—Quiet, immature, very small, cries easily, excessive baby talk.

Grading period 2—Sweet, cooperative child, just can't read. I thought he had a learning problem but he scored low normal on the Peabody test.

Grading period 3—Cooperative, very immature, still some baby talk, not good at sounds. He is showing some progress, has finished the second preprimer, will probably finish the third preprimer before school ends. However he won't get to the primer.

QUESTIONS

1. What kinds of evidence should be considered in making promotion-retention decisions?
2. What is the case for Randy to be promoted and to be retained?
3. In general what does the research on promotion and retention say about their effects on student learning and emotional development? How well do the findings of this research fit Randy's case?
4. If, from an operant conditioning perspective, retention is viewed as punishment, how effective is punishment in increasing the learning of a six year old? What is "stimulus generalization" or "spread effect" due to punishment, and how might it apply to Randy's case if he is retained? What behaviors of Randy's do Jan and Mr. Johnson wish to increase? Could such behavior be shaped regardless of whether Randy is promoted or not?
5. From the viewpoint of teacher expectancy theory (self-fulfilling prophecy research) or labeling and stereotyping research from social psychology, how might retention affect Randy? What expectations might Randy's teachers and peers have about him, and how might this affect his behavior?
6. From a humanistic framework, how might retention affect Randy's self-concept? What relationships exist between self-concept and school achievement?
7. What does immaturity mean from a developmental viewpoint? Mr. Johnson says that Randy is "physically and socially immature." Is there evidence that retention or promotion helps or hinders such children? Are there other aspects of Randy's development as a six year old that Mr. Johnson and Jan should consider in making their decision?
8. What are educational standards and how are they determined? What relative value should elementary schools place on the needs of the child, the acquisition of subject matter, and upholding the norms of society as goals? Does either a "social promotion" policy or a strict retention policy raise or lower standards and eventually either cheapen or increase the value of a diploma? Does having high standards mean that some students must fail? How are educational standards communicated to students and parents?

BRETT THE BRAT

It is almost 9:00 A.M. on a cool October day in New England. Suzanne Landers, a pretty, slender young 21-year-old woman with long, ash-brown hair is seen approaching the Elm Street Elementary School. Miss Landers is a senior in elementary education at the state university located in this small upstate, rural community with a population of 7,600 people. She is to begin today an eight-week internship with Mrs. Mayes, a third grade teacher who has been with the school for 23 years.

As Suzanne nears the school, she pauses for a moment to observe her surroundings. The freshly painted, two-story elementary school with white columns was built in 1936. It sits on a slight rise on a well-land-scaped lawn.

Suzanne half runs up the steps and enters the front entrance. She proceeds to the office where she is met by the school secretary.

Mrs. Adams [cheerfully] Good morning. May I help you?
Suzanne Yes, I'm Suzanne Landers. I'm going to intern under Mrs. Mayes this fall. Could you tell me where her room is?
Mrs. Adams Yes, I'll be happy to. [She comes to the door and holds it open for Suzanne to pass through.] Mrs. Mayes's room is on the second floor. I'll take you there.

***

The rooms that line the hall are decorated with posters, pictures, and heavily decorated bulletin boards. The furniture is old but not shabby. In each room the students are busily working at their desks as their teacher moves about the room from student to student. As they climb the stairs to the second floor, Suzanne and Mrs. Adams talk quietly.

Mrs. Adams This is a nice school to work in. The kids really respect the teachers. We don't have very many problems here—our principal won't put up with any troublemakers for long. [She concludes proudly.]
Suzanne [somewhat puzzled] It certainly is quiet. Somehow, I expected a little more activity.

Her voice trails off as Mrs. Adams stops at Room 114. They stand quietly as Mrs. Mayes, the third grade teacher, acknowledges their presence with a nod. Everything is quiet as Mrs. Mayes gazes around the room filled with 35 young children seated at their desks in long horizontal rows. She gives a warning look to her students and brings her fingers to her lips in a "shush" gesture before she walks to the door to greet Suzanne and Mrs. Adams.

Mrs. Mayes [pleasantly]   You must be Miss Landers from the university. I expected you earlier, but I guess you had no way of knowing our daily schedule. [Then to Mrs. Adams.] Thanks Claire. [Mrs. Adams smiles and leaves.]

Suzanne [with a nervous laugh]   I'm sorry to be late. I thought I'd get a ride, but at the last minute I decided to walk, and—

Mrs. Mayes [briskly]   Let's go back to the children. [She pauses and says matter-of-factly.] I think it's customary for you interns to observe for a few days before you take the class. Is that right?

Without waiting for an answer, Mrs. Mayes directs her attention back to the class where there is a disturbance. She snaps her fingers twice in an attempt to get order but is unsuccessful. She steps back into the room and sees two boys punching each other. She moves quickly to separate them.

Mrs. Mayes [firmly as she pulls the boys apart]   Boys, boys, this must stop. Now! I won't have this! [The boys briefly struggle to free themselves, but Mrs. Mayes has them in a firm grip.] Now tell me what happened!

Joe [plaintively]   Mrs. Mayes, I didn't do anything. Brett tripped me as I started to go to the pencil sharpener.

Mrs. Mayes nods, releases her hold, and motions Joe to his seat. She turns her attention to Brett, now squirming in her grasp.

Brett [grinning]   Mrs. Mayes, I didn't mean to trip him. He just stumbled over my foot and—[Mrs. Mayes yanks his collar angrily.] Hey don't do that! [He draws back his arm as if to strike her, but is stopped by her menacing look.]

Mrs. Mayes   Brett, I've told you before about fighting in school. Come with me, young man. [She takes him by the arm to lead him to the front of the room.]

Brett [twisting away from her]   I told you! Don't do that. [He begins to flail out against Mrs. Mayes, and one or two blows fall on her arms. Mrs. Mayes succeeds in grabbing his arms and holding him securely. She maneuvers to the intercom and presses the button. The class is in silence as she speaks into the intercom.]

Mrs. Mayes [with authority]   It's Brett Browning again and he's fighting in class. Ask Mr. Thompson to come down please. [Turning to Brett.] Brett, how many times do you have to be spanked before you learn not to fight in school?

A few minutes later, Mr. Thompson, the portly 53-year-old principal, appears at the door and motions Mrs. Mayes, still holding Brett, to accompany him. Mrs. Mayes moves to leave, and she motions Suzanne to take over in her absence. Suzanne looks after her, shrugs her shoulders imperceptibly, and moves to the front of the room facing the subdued students.

Suzanne [hesitantly]   Boys and girls. I'm Miss Landers, your intern teacher this fall, and I'll be with you until January 16th. I, ah [pauses with uncertainty] I don't have anything planned, so why don't we just chat for a few minutes until Mrs. Mayes and Brett return, okay? [Her friendly smile seems to break the ice and the children begin to talk all at once.]

Jo Ann [a pert little 8 year old in the front]   Brett's going to get another spanking. He's not nice.

Tom [a tall boy in the back]   Brett gets a spanking 'bout every day.

The other children nod and smile in affirmation as though they are pleased. Mrs. Mayes then appears at the door, and Suzanne walks toward the back of the room and takes a seat to observe, sighing with relief.

***

Mrs. Mayes and Suzanne sit talking quietly together at the end of the school day.

Mrs. Mayes   I'm sorry that you had to see Brett's terrible behavior on your very first day, but I must admit, it's typical for him! He's an impossible child! [She makes a deprecatory gesture.]

Suzanne [with interest]   Can you tell me a little more about him?

Mrs. Mayes [offhandedly]   Oh he's bright, there's no doubting that. That may be part of his problem. He's a smart aleck. [She continues.] I heard about him when he was still in the first grade. He could read before he started school, and he'd laugh out loud when other children mispronounced words. Mrs. Johnston, his first grade teacher—she's one of my best friends—said he was unpopular mainly because the other kids resented his always correcting them. He seemed to delight in making the others feel inferior.

Suzanne   Does he still do that to the other kids?

Mrs. Mayes [with heat] Constantly! He belittles the others, even the really good students. Yet when *he* makes a mistake, he can't stand criticism. If another child points out his mistakes, Brett gets absolutely rigid, glares at him, and yells, "Liar!" [She nods her head.] And before you know it, Brett has found some way to physically attack the other child. Once he's got it out of his system, he just grins and tries to look innocent. He's hopeless.

Suzanne [caught up in the conversation] Do you usually send him to the principal?

Mrs. Mayes Well frankly I've gotten to the stage where I just want to get him out of the room. At the beginning of the year, I must have spanked him every day. Now he's gotten so bad—you saw him hit me today—that I can't cope with him. [With finality.] I'd much rather have the principal deal with Brett. He's the only one who can handle him.

Suzanne What about sending Brett to a school counselor?

Mrs. Mayes [laughing] Oh, are you idealistic! Let me tell you about Brett. His father's a dentist, and his mother holds a master's degree in sociology. They've given that kid everything. He had a chemistry set when he was four. And they made a three-room playhouse with miniature furniture at the back of their house just for him. The whole town was amazed at the money that cost! [Thoughtfully.] But at the same time, his parents really don't pamper him. I've even seen his father jerk him out of his seat for acting up in a restaurant and spank him hard in front of everyone. [Firmly.] Brett doesn't need a counselor—he's not emotionally disturbed. He's just a hateful, ill-tempered little boy who needs to know he can't get away with murder. [She adds.] You saw how quiet the other children were with Brett out of the room. If you're smart, you'll follow my advice and let him know you mean business right from the start.

Suzanne [hesitantly] Mrs. Mayes, my teachers stressed over and over again that we should not physically punish kids, that we should—

Mrs. Mayes [interrupting Suzanne's point] Yes, I've heard all that before. [She pats Suzanne's hand as she gathers some papers and a class roll from her desk.] Miss Landers, I suspect you have a lot to learn. [She takes Suzanne's arm to guide her toward the door. Suzanne, with a puzzled, intense look on her face, walks slowly along beside Mrs. Mayes.]

***

It is the morning of Suzanne's first day of intern teaching. For the past week she has been observing in the back of the classroom.

Suzanne bustles nervously around the room, stopping occasionally to straighten a picture on the bulletin board or to align the venetian blinds. Mrs. Mayes is at the back of the room grading papers. She glances up from time to time and smiles to herself.

The bell rings, and as the children begin to enter the classroom, Suzanne takes her place close to the door, smiles, and begins to greet them by name.

One student [whispering to another]   Look, Miss Landers is going to teach us today. Isn't that good? I like her. She's pretty. [Seeing Mrs. Mayes in the back of the room, she cuts off the conversation and goes to her desk.]

The children take their seats quietly and sit whispering together. Several of them smile warmly at Suzanne. They all look up hushed and expectant as she begins to speak.

Suzanne [brightly]   Good morning boys and girls. Today is the first day I'm going to be with you as your teacher. I was busy all last week learning your names and the schedule, but I'm still a little shaky. You'll have to help me out. Will you? [She smiles at the children, and they return her smile and nod their heads in affirmation.] All right, children, let's begin our spelling lesson.

***

It is later that morning. Suzanne appears poised and confident as she concludes the spelling lesson and directs the children to prepare for reading from their basal texts. The children are cooperative and relaxed, and without a murmur they smoothly make the transition from their work in spelling to reading. They now sit quietly with their reading books open, awaiting Suzanne's instructions.

Suzanne   I'm pleased to see such good scores on your spelling tests this morning. Now let's turn our attention to our story, "They Didn't Believe Jake." I want you all to read the whole story silently.

The children seem absorbed by the story. Suzanne walks slowly around the room, pausing from time to time to interpret a word or phrase. Finally all the students finish the story, and Suzanne, standing by the window, begins to talk about it.

Suzanne   Sometimes parents just don't seem to believe what their children say. Have you ever had *your* parents not understand what you say or what you feel? [There is a loud chorus of yeses.]
Suzanne [continuing in a friendly, conversational tone]   Let's read between the lines in our story. I mean, let's imagine what Jake must be feeling when nobody believes him. It's not written down, but we can put ourselves in Jake's place, can't we?
Ann [eagerly]   I think Jake must have been sad, and maybe he cried.

Brett [from the back of the room] That's stupid! Boys don't cry! [He laughs loudly in derision; a few other boys laugh too.]

Suzanne [surprised at this first outburst of the day from Brett] Brett, you have a point. Perhaps boys don't cry as much as girls do, but Ann might be right, too.

Brett [persisting] Ann's a crybaby. She thinks everyone's a baby like she is. [Under his breath.] She's stupid!

Suzanne [ignoring his last comment] What do some of the others think Jake must have felt? Yes, Charles. [She nods to a bespectacled little boy in the front row.]

Charles Jake thought they didn't trust him. I'll bet he wouldn't tell his parents any more things after that.

Suzanne [nodding] Yes, I can see how Jake might do just that.

Brett [without waiting for recognition blurts out] Jake would feel mad at his parents. And he'd just tell them he didn't care what they felt. If they didn't believe him, he'd just tell them they were dummies!

Sally [shaking her head] You're not supposed to call your Mother and Daddy dummies.

Brett [loudly] That's silly. If they're dummies, they're dummies. [His voice rises on a shrill note. Suzanne is nonplussed by this final outburst. She stands almost helpless for a minute, obviously puzzled at what it do next.]

Mrs. Mayes [angrily rising to her feet at the back of the room] Well I've heard enough, young man. [She grabs his arm and jerks him toward the door.] This has gone quite far enough! You need a good paddling for this. [She jerks him a step further.] Come along right now. You're going to the principal with me. [Brett pulls back, but Mrs. Mayes forces him to accompany her.]

* * *

It is late afternoon of the same day. The children have gone, and Suzanne stands pensively at the window. She looks up as Mrs. Mayes enters the room.

Mrs. Mayes I'm sorry about having to take over this morning, but I felt that things had gone too far.

Suzanne That's all right. [Hesitantly.] I was caught off guard, I guess.

Mrs. Mayes [with some kindness] You should never have let it go so far. [Then firmly.] Now do you see what I mean by firmness with Brett? The only thing he respects is a good paddling.

Suzanne [earnestly] It's just not my way, Mrs. Mayes. I don't like the thought of hitting a child.

Mrs. Mayes Then tell me, my dear, how else could you have handled it?

ELM STREET ELEMENTARY SCHOOL
Cumulative Record

Name:	Browning, Brett Jeremy
Address:	224 Maple Drive
Father:	Browning, Robert Brett
Mother:	Browning, Doris J.
Siblings:	None

Home Phone:	734-0738
Occupation:	Dentist
Occupation:	Sociologist

Former School:	
Date Entered:	8/30/86
General Health:	Good
Handicaps:	None
Date of Birth:	7/24/80
Age:	8

TEST RECORD
Intelligence Tests

	MA	I.Q.	CA	Date	Grade
California Test of Mental Maturity:				5/14/87	1
Language	8–11	133	6–9		
Non-Language	8–9	129	6–9		

ACADEMIC RECORD

Grade Level	1	2	3	4	5	6
Citizenship	1	1				
Reading	5	5				
English						
Spelling		5				
Writing		5				
Social Studies						
Arithmetic	5	5				
Science		5				

KEY:
1. Child is working below grade level
2. Child is working below grade level, but is making progress
3. Child is working at grade level
4. Child is doing excellent work at grade level
5. Child is working above grade level

QUESTIONS

1. Mrs. Mayes says that Brett does not need to see a counselor. Do you agree? How might a counselor work with Brett?
2. Should Mrs. Mayes have taken over when Suzanne was undecided about how to respond to Brett's outburst? How do you think Suzanne would have handled Brett's behavior if Mrs. Mayes had not intervened?
3. What are the pros and cons of using corporal punishment to influence behavior? What does educational research say about the effectiveness of corporal punishment?
4. From an operant conditioning viewpoint, what undesirable behaviors is Brett emitting and why hasn't Mrs. Mayes's attempt at punishment decreased them? What reinforcer(s) is maintaining Brett's behavior? Pinpoint desirable, competing behaviors that Suzanne can reinforce to replace the undesirable behaviors. What role has Brett's peers played in reinforcing his undesirable behaviors?
5. From an observational learning perspective, what aggressive models has Brett observed? What vicarious reinforcement has Brett received? What observational learning procedures are available to Suzanne for changing Brett's behavior?
6. At what level of Maslow's need hierarchy is Brett operating? At what levels are Mrs. Mayes and Suzanne operating? What are boredom and frustration from a motivational theory standpoint? How might these constructs relate to Brett's high I.Q. and aggressive behavior?
7. From a humanistic perspective, what is the self-ideal and how does it differ from the self-concept? How does Brett's self-ideal explain his reaction to criticism? How are the self-ideal and self-concept formed, and under what conditions do they change?
8. What factors in the home environment contribute to Brett's behavior? Specifically how could Suzanne involve Brett's parents in helping her deal with his behavior?
9. What is a gifted child? Is Brett gifted? What are the characteristics of gifted children, and why do gifted children sometimes become bored and frustrated? What can be done in such cases?

CASE 28

THE ETERNAL TRIANGLE: TEACHER, PUPIL, PARENT

Joan Purcell, a 27-year-old fourth grade teacher, has taught at Mt. Summit for five years. Mt. Summit is an exclusive elementary school in a west coast community of 400,000. The children who attend Mt. Summit come from upper-middle- to upper-class professional homes. Joan and the fifth grade teacher, Mary Steinkle, are sitting in Joan's classroom discussing an impending teacher-parent conference.

Joan [wrinkles her face as she nervously looks at her watch and sighs] Ten minutes after 3:00, they'll be here in 20 minutes.
Mary Good grief, Joan. You're blowing this thing out of proportion. I know you don't hold many teacher-parent conferences but—
Joan [in exasperation] But Tim's mother is *only* an officer in the PTA, and his father is *only* one of the most influential lawyers in town. And I have to tell them that I think they're placing too much emphasis on Tim's grades.
Mary [her surprise is evident] Say, I didn't know you had a problem with Tim. I don't know him well, but he seems like a polite, compliant kid. When you said you had a conference with the Bailey's, I thought they were coming in for a friendly visit. They come to all PTA meetings, talk a lot, and seem to be interested in school. I thought—
Joan No, I called them and asked them to come in for a visit.
Mary [hesitantly] What's the problem?
Joan Well you put your finger on it a moment ago when you described Tim as a polite, compliant kid. The point is he's too compliant. I think he's a frightened little boy who works too hard for high grades because his whole self-concept is tied to marks. A good mark is his only proof of being a good, worthwhile person.
Mary [apologetically] Gee, I'm sorry for being so flippant. You aren't going to have an easy conference. [She adds.] How did you draw these conclusions about Tim?
Joan First because of Tim's clinging dependency on me. During the first few days of school when I gave class assignments, he would constantly come to my desk for clarification and assurance. "What do you want us to do, Miss Purcell? Where can I find the answer? Is this right?"

He constantly wanted me to approve his work. [She admits.] At first I was flattered by such heavy reliance. It's nice to be needed. But gradually it occurred to me that his dependence was just too much—it wasn't normal!

Mary Why did you wait until now, in April, to talk with the Baileys?

Joan Well I thought I could deal with Tim in the classroom. In fact [she smiles broadly] I did succeed somewhat in getting him to work on his own.

Mary How?

Joan I wanted him to rely on me less so I shifted our meetings to his seat. When he came up to me, I'd send him back to his desk and immediately follow him and thank him for being in his seat working on the problem. At first it didn't work. I'd help him at his desk and then leave, but he would be right back at my desk a few minutes later, and we'd have to go through the whole process again.

Mary How did you solve the problem?

Joan I learned that after I helped him at his seat, I needed to keep him there. So I'd tell him something like, "Well, now we've worked the first one; you work on the next three and I'll be back in ten minutes to go over them with you." Then I'd come back in a couple of minutes and praise him for being in his seat.

Mary [teasingly] Hey, you're a behavior modifier! That guy at school must have made some impression on you. What else did you do?

Joan [with a flushed face] Oh not much. I gradually delayed going back to his desk for 15 minutes and then 30 minutes. I also forced him to check his own work before I graded it. I wanted him to express his feelings about his own work. I wanted him to learn that his work can be good before I put a red A on it. I've seen progress in his private relations with me, but in public contacts in front of the class he's still the same frightened, compulsive kid with a strong need to comply.

Mary [puzzled] What do you mean?

Joan When I ask Tim a question in class, I feel like a traffic light. He examines my face intently looking for clues about how to respond. If I nod my head or signal approval in any way, he answers very fast and loud. But at the slightest sign of disapproval, he changes the direction of his answer. The sad thing is that he acts this way even when he's answering questions that have no right answers. I remember one day I asked him if he would like to be an astronaut. As he was describing how much fun it would be, I shook my head slightly at a student sitting behind him who had his hand up. After I shook my head, Tim suggested that the job might get boring after a while. [She pauses, then adds earnestly.] I think he's paying too high a price for his grades. He'll do anything to get them. It's all he thinks about.

Mary Why did you call his parents?

Joan I'm trying to help, but I think Tim's parents contribute to the problem. My guess is that they stress school too much and don't tell him he's good unless he he does something well.

Mary You'd better be careful. How are you going to bring that up in the conference?

Joan I don't know. I just plan to talk about his compulsive behavior in class and hope that we can get to the home some way. I'm just going to play it by ear.

Mary Play it by ear! You'd better think about this some more. How come you're so sure that his parents act that way?

Joan I'm not sure. It's just a hunch, but I've had a few conversations with Tim about what he likes to do at home. And let me show you this. [She hands a sheet to Mary.] A few days ago I had the children do this sentence completion interest inventory that I made up. I'm not really qualified to interpret these things, but I do know Tim's answers aren't like other fourth grade boys' answers.

Mary [briefly glances at the sheet and hands it back to Joan]   I don't put much stock in these things, and I don't think you should either. Say, it's 3:30. I better clear out of here. You'll see me first thing tomorrow. I want to know what happens. Good luck!

***

Ten minutes later Mr. and Mrs. Bailey arrive. Their attractive physical appearance and expensive clothing give them a strong presence, and Joan feels like a nervous child.

Joan Good afternoon, Mr. and Mrs. Bailey. I'm glad we have this chance to visit and talk about Tim.

Mr. Bailey [quickly] What's wrong with Tim, Miss Purcell? Has he done something wrong?

Sentence Completion Interest Inventory

Name: *Tim Bailey*

1. My father likes me best *When I bring home an A paper and when I finish my homework.*

2. My mother likes me best *When my room is perfectly straight.*

3. I feel proudest *When I get all A's.*

4. When I finish school I want to be _____

5. My favorite hobby is *reading.*

6. When I go home in the afternoon I like to *Finish my homework.*

7. My worst fear is *Get poor marks.*

8. People are happiest _____

9. My friends *are quiet.*

10. My favorite school subject is _____

11. School is *Hard.*

MT. SUMMIT ELEMENTARY SCHOOL
Cumulative Record

Name: Bailey, Timothy L.	**Home Phone:** 844-8464	**Former School:**
Address: 529 Booth Avenue	**Occupation:** Lawyer	**Date Entered:** 8/29/86
Father: Bailey, Thomas J.	**Occupation:** Housewife (holds	**General Health:** Excellent
Mother: Bailey, Ruth	teaching certificate)	**Handicaps:** None
Siblings: None		**Date of Birth:** 9/1/80
		Age: 9

TEST RECORD

Intelligence Test

Intelligence Test	Grade	CA	MA	IQ	Date
California Test of Mental Maturity	1				9/15/86
Language		6-0	6-0	100	
Non-language		6-0	6-8	113	
		6-0	6-4	106	

Achievement Test	Grade	Reading	Word Meaning	Spelling	Paragraph Skills	Arithmetic	Word St. Vocab.
Stanford Achievement Test 5/10/67	1	2.5	3.0	2.7	2.2	3.1	3.0

ACADEMIC RECORD

Record the year's average as A, B, C, D, or F

	Grade 1	Grade 2	Grade 3	Grade 4	Grade 5	Grade 6
Reading	A	A	A			
English			A			
Writing	A	A	A			
Spelling	A	A	A			
Arithmetic	A	A	A			
Social studies			A			
Science and health			B+			
Art	A	A	A			
Physical education	B	C	C			
Music	B+	A–	B+			

QUESTIONS

1. Do you see any relationship between Tim's sentence completion interest inventory and his behavior in Joan's class? How valid and reliable are such instruments?
2. What relationships exist between the home environment and student achievement in school? What parenting behaviors contribute to overachieving, dependent behavior like Tim's?
3. From the standpoint of humanistic psychology, what are the self-ideal and self-concept? Describe Tim's self-ideal and self-concept. How are the self-ideal and self-concept formed, and under what conditions do they change?
4. What is an overachiever? From the perspective of motivational theory, what is fear of failure, and how well does this construct describe Tim's behavior?
5. What behavior modification techniques has Joan used to try to shape Tim toward more independent behavior? How might she use "schedule stretching and reinforcer fading-in and fading-out" techniques to try to move Tim toward even more independent behavior?
6. How can Joan communicate with Tim's parents so they do not become threatened or defensive? Could she use techniques like those described in Thomas Gordon's *Teacher Effectiveness Training?* Are there other communication or counseling techniques available to her?

CASE 29

THE CHEATERS

The student body of Lincoln Junior High School is gathered in the school auditorium for the orientation assembly at the beginning of the school year. Lincoln is located in a small, middle-class residential community in the Midwest. The principal goes to the podium. After welcoming the new students and introducing some of the faculty members, he starts in on his orientation speech.

Mr. Pierce Honesty is the best policy. This school has stood for this ideal for 60 years, just as Lincoln himself stood for it 100 years ago. We have never had any serious incidents of dishonesty here at Lincoln Junior High School, and we hope that the new students this year and the old, too, will hold to the responsibility that those before you have held to.

***

Mrs. Lewis, who is in her third year of teaching, is giving an examination in her American history class. Some of the students grimace as they read the multiple-choice questions. Mrs. Lewis walks up and down the aisle.

Mrs. Lewis You have three minutes 'til the bell. Please put your papers on my desk as you leave.

Students work on intensely. The bell rings. The students get up and gather their books. They leave the room after putting the tests on the front desk, grumbling and shaking their heads.

One student to another Where did she get those questions? She never tests on what she talks about in class!

***

It is the end of the first grading period. Mrs. Lewis sits at her desk averaging grades. Some of the students have very high test grades and very low quiz and homework grades.

Mrs. Lewis [to herself] This just can't be possible. How could these students be doing so well on tests and so poorly on homework and snap quizzes? [She flips to another class section in the grade book, comparing the grade differences.] In my other sections, there aren't half as many A's on this test. Could this section be cheating?

***

The next day in class, Mrs. Lewis is reviewing the test. She has not handed back the corrected test papers and is asking the questions orally to quiz each student.

Mrs. Lewis Who was the governor of New Amsterdam at the time that the British took it over and made it New York? John?
John Uh . . . I don't know.
Mrs. Lewis You got it right on the test.
John I guess I just forgot it.
Mrs. Lewis Well, Jim. What about this one? Who was the original founder of Georgia?
Jim James Oglethorpe.
Mrs. Lewis Fine. And Joey, name the first permanent white settlement in New England and give its founding date. [Silence.] Well Joey?
Joey Uh . . .
Mrs. Lewis [firmly] Can't you remember? You had the right answer on your test paper.
Joey [nodding] No. [The bell rings and students leave.]
Mrs. Lewis [to herself] That's interesting. Some of the kids who got good grades on their tests can't remember the correct answers now. During the next test I'll just have to watch closely.

***

Three weeks later Mrs. Lewis is giving another exam. Facial expressions and students' movements are like those at the first test. Mrs. Lewis is proctoring closely. There are no signs of cheating anywhere.

Mrs. Lewis [to herself] I just can't understand it. How can their grades be so high if they don't cheat. They can't remember the correct answers the very next day!

***

Some of the students from the American history class are sitting around a booth at a drive-in restaurant. John and Joey are sitting on one side of the table. Another boy, Sam, is seated across from them.

Joey Brother, old lady Lewis had me sweating in American history today!

John That was a close call. I can't figure it out. Do you think she was wise to us and didn't give back the papers so she could see if we really knew the answers?

Sam I answered my question right. That should have thrown her off a little even if she did suspect, and I don't think she did.

Jim, a well-built athlete, enters, walks over to the boys at the table, and sits down.

Jim Hi! How's it going? Wasn't that history class last period tough? [They nod.] I really lucked out on that answer. I only made a C on the test and I studied for three hours. I can't understand it.

John Yeah, we were having lots of trouble too until we discovered something. Should we tell him?

Joey Sure.

Sam Why not? He's good at keeping his mouth shut.

John Well it's this way, man. Sam's sister, Linda, had Mrs. Lewis for this class last year. She saved all her tests instead of turning them in at the end of the year because she knew that Sam was going to take it this year.

Joey It's been an easy ride ever since. Mrs. Lewis hardly changed the tests at all.

John Do you want to be in with us on it? It's only us and a couple of other guys.

Jim Well I don't know; I'll have to think about it. It sounds pretty easy, but I sure wouldn't want to get caught! Well, see you all tomorrow. I'll tell you then. [Jim gets up and leaves; the boys continue talking.]

***

Later that afternoon, Mrs. Lewis is in the main office looking in her mailbox. A fellow teacher also enters to look for her mail.

Mrs. Lewis Madge, do you have a minute?

Madge [nodding] Sure. What is it?

Mrs. Lewis I think that there's been a group of students cheating in one of my history classes. Do you have any special way you handle cheating? [Earnestly.] I'm really bewildered; this has never happened to me before.

Madge I've never had to deal with the problem. I won't cross that bridge until I come to it. [She laughs to herself and leaves the office.]

Mrs. Lewis Well thanks anyhow, Madge.

Mrs. Lewis looks down at her mail and sees a note among the letters that says:

Mrs. Lewis,
Could we see you today in your room about 20 minutes after school is out? It is important. Thank you.

Jim Tanner
Susie George
Mark Synder

Mrs. Lewis hurries out of the office and down the hall to her classroom. The three students who signed the note are sitting there. Mrs. Lewis listens to the students tell about the cheating.

Jim So, Sue, Mark, and I thought it would be best to come to you about it. We all studied hard for that test and only made C's because the curve was set so high. We don't think it's right that those guys should be able to cheat and set the curve.
Susie It's just ruining our grades and lots of other kids', too.
Mark Isn't there something that you can do, Mrs. Lewis?
Mrs. Lewis I can start by thanking the three of you for trusting me enough to tell me this. I'll see what I can do before tomorrow.
Jim Well thanks a lot. We just thought it was best to come straight to you. See you tomorrow.
Mrs. Lewis Okay. Goodbye.

***

The next day near the end of the American history class, Mrs. Lewis finishes her lecture.

Mrs. Lewis Oh one more thing before the bell rings. Will John Bunch, Joey Simmons, Sam Krieger, Kent Largo, and Paul Nisner please remain a minute after class. I need to talk to you.

The bell rings. The class gets up, collects their books, and all leave but the five boys. They move up to the desks in front of Mrs. Lewis's desk. Sam is visibly nervous, the others are "keeping cool."

Mrs. Lewis I've noticed, boys, that you're doing very well on your tests but failing your homework assignments and quizzes. I suspected cheating, but I only found out for sure yesterday. Do you have anything to say? [All sit in silence.] I really don't know what to do. [Pauses, sighs.] One thing's for sure, I'll have to tell your parents. I'll probably make up a new set of tests and give the whole class a retest. Suspension seems in line, but I'll have to talk to the principal about that. I'm really disappointed in all of you. I'll talk to you boys tomorrow.

The boys get up without a word and leave. Mrs. Lewis sits down at her desk and sighs.

Mrs. Lewis [to herself]   What can I do? Give them all F's, call their parents in for conferences, go to the principal? How can I handle it? They said my tests were too hard, but that doesn't justify cheating. Nothing does!

Subject: American history

* = student who cheated
† = student who informed

Month: _____
Date: _____

Names	Quiz	Test	Home-work	Quiz	Test	Home-work
Adams, Jeffery	B	B	C	C	C	B
Ashly, Richard	D	D	D	D	F	D
Atterbury, Jamie	C	C	B	C	C	C
Bailey, Jimmy	B	C	B	C	C	A
Black, Timmy	A	A	A	B	A	A
Bunch, John*	D	A	F	F	A	D
Dale, Wendy	C	C	B	C	B	C
Ernst, Timmy	C	C	C	C	C	C
Faraway, Rick	A	B	A	A	B	A
Farmer, Patty	C	C	C	C	C	C
George, Susie†	B	C	B	C	C	B
Gilbert, Shannon	A	A	B	A	A	A
Haines, Betty	B	B	B	B	C	B
Hubert, Ellis	C	D	C	D	C	D
Jackson, April	F	D	F	D	D	F
James, Mary	C	C	C	C	C	C
Johnson, Joe	D	C	D	D	D	C
Krieger, Sam*	D	B	D	F	A	F
Kristy, Linda	B	C	B	B	C	B
Largo, Kent*	F	B	F	D	A	F
Litchfield, William	C	C	C	C	C	B
Martin, Carl	B	C	B	C	C	B
Moore, Cathy	D	D	C	C	D	C
Mottola, Diane	C	C	C	C	C	C
Murry, Calvin	C	D	D	D	D	D
Nisner, Paul*	F	A	F	F	A	D
Nopworth, Greg	D	D	F	D	D	D
Page, Carolyn	B	C	B	C	B	B
Pellis, Robert	C	C	B	C	C	C
Quincy, Burt	A	B	B	B	B	B
Rawis, Philip	F	F	F	D	D	D
Simmons, Joey*	F	A	D	F	A	D
Synder, Mark†	B	C	C	B	B	B
Tanner, Jim	C	C	C	B	C	C
Tompson, Virginia	B	B	B	C	B	B
Vickers, Sally	C	D	C	C	C	D
Wells, Cris	B	C	B	B	C	B
Wilson, Sara	C	D	C	C	D	C

QUESTIONS

1. What options are open to Mrs. Lewis as she responds to the fact that five of her students cheated? Discuss the advantages and disadvantages of each. Which options would contribute most to the growth of the five guilty students? The least?
2. Should Mrs. Lewis gather additional information before deciding how to deal with the cheaters? What information should she gather, and how should she use it?
3. Why did Jim, Susie, and Mark tell Mrs. Lewis about the cheating? Why do you suppose Jim decided not to cheat?
4. Have any of Mrs. Lewis's evaluation procedures contributed to the cheating situation? What does the student mean who says, "She never tests on what she talks about in class!" What is content validity in testing, and how does it relate to this situation?
5. Has Mrs. Lewis contributed to the cheating situation by letting her students keep their tests after they are returned and then by not changing the items on future tests? If Mrs. Lewis wishes to develop a test item pool, should she collect the tests from the students after she has gone over them or is there educational value in letting the students keep old tests? Is it reasonable to expect Mrs. Lewis to develop all new tests each year?
6. At which of Kohlberg's stages of moral development do the cheaters seem to be operating? What about the students who reported the cheating to Mrs. Lewis? What moral education techniques or values clarification techniques might Mrs. Lewis use in this situation?
7. What role do the home environment and adolescent peer groups play in forming students values regarding cheating? If Mrs. Lewis decides to involve the students' parents in this situation, what approach might she use? Should she deal with the situation confidentially or publicly? Should she deal with it herself or take the matter to the principal or other school administrator?
8. How might research and theory on attitude formation and conformity help explain the cheaters' behavior? How do attitudes change?

CASE 30

TEACHER TO TEACHER

Mr. Williams, the principal of Edgemont Junior High School, anxiously looks at his desk calendar and mutters to himself, "New teacher orientation day. I hope I survive." Abruptly he crushes his cigarette in the big oval ashtray and smiles broadly as Mrs. Sharp enters the room.

Ann Sharp has taught in Edgemont, a small town of 20,000 in a midwestern state, for five years. Mr. Williams is pleased to have her at Edgemont Junior High; he knows that she is a good teacher. Each year several parents call him requesting that their son or daughter be placed in her social studies section. Students consistently describe her on evaluation forms as a fair, considerate teacher and a "cool head."

Bill Good morning, Ann. It's good to see you this morning.

Ann Good morning, Bill. I wanted to get a copy of the hall and lunch monitor assignments so I can let the new recruits know when they have duty.

Bill [pointing] They're on the bottom shelf behind you—underneath the fire regulation pamphlets.

Ann Got them. [She pauses.] Say, could you come in and say a few words to my group this morning?

Bill No, I'll do my talking this afternoon when I speak to all the new teachers. I prefer to have a small group of new teachers meet with one experienced teacher before I speak to them. This way the new teachers have a chance to ask questions about things that really interest them. New teachers often feel foolish asking the principal about—

Ann [interrupting] You mean they don't ask you about the things that really bother them?

Bill [nodding] Precisely.

Ann I agree. I remember four years ago when you talked to us. I was afraid to ask you my real questions.

Bill Such as?

Ann Well, like: How much paper can I use? How does the duplicating machine work? How do I get movies and filmstrips? What are you going to look for when you come into my classroom? What do you think a good teacher is?

Bill Good, you get the idea. I want them to get answers for those questions.

Ann Tell me anything about the three new social studies teachers I'll be working with in orientation. Last night I looked at their placement folders. They all looked like the same person! You know it's hard to tell about a new teacher until you actually teach with her. They all had good marks in school. They all had A's in student teaching. And their letters of recommendation read like carbon copies.

Bill I know. [He adds wryly.] Almost all the applicants have earned A's in student teaching. Cooperating teachers become so involved with their student teachers that they feel a B or C is a sign of their failure as a cooperating teacher. [In exasperation.] These people are graded artificially high, and there's no way to tell high-potential teachers from low-potential teachers.

Ann Then you don't remember anything about them?

Bill Let's see. No, nothing in particular, except maybe Cynthia Clove. During the interview she seemed to put on airs; but that's probably just me.

Ann [with a puzzled look] What do you mean put on airs?

Bill Well she seemed afraid to talk about herself or what she felt. She constantly referred to what one of her professors had said about ability grouping or what some textbook said about retaining students. She never voiced her opinion. It was almost as if she didn't have opinions of her own. It was like she was role playing—like she was playing the role of a concerned teacher. But as I said, it was probably just me or a bad day for her. You better get going. It's time to meet the troops. [Smiling.] Tell it like it is.

Ann See you later.

***

Ann finishes her 30-minute orientation speech and is greeted by three enthusiastic, almost indistinguishable voices, June Morton, Cynthia Clove, and Betty Jordon, three recent graduates from the state university.

Cynthia Ann, you really made us feel welcome!

June Thanks for letting us know what's expected here. I'm glad you gave us both the good and bad news.

Betty If the other teachers are as frank and helpful as you are, this is going to be a good school for me.

Ann [smiling] Thanks a lot. I'm glad we can work together. We've gone over the stuff I wanted to talk about. Any questions? [Earnestly.] Anything goes. [The girls lower their heads, shuffle their feet, and furiously scribble on their note pads.] Take a minute or two and write down your questions, and then we'll read them all. Maybe two or three can be answered at one time. [After a two-minute pause.] Okay—read your questions and I'll take notes.

Cynthia [hesitantly]   If you think students are cheating, how do you handle it?

June   Why do students cheat?

Betty [with eager anticipation]   What enrichment materials can we use with our fast students?

Cynthia   How do you know if the kids really like you? [With feeling.] When kids are truant, who do we call?

Betty   What's a good way to start off class on the first day to get a serious but relaxed atmosphere?

Cynthia   How do you keep from getting bored in the classroom doing the same thing every day?

June   How do we involve parents in the school program?

Betty   How closely do we have to follow the curriculum guide?

Cynthia   When the curriculum supervisor comes, what will she want to see?

Ann   Well that's a good list of questions. Let's start with the first two. Betty and Cynthia were concerned about student cheating—

Cynthia [interrupting]   I'm not really concerned. I'm just interested in getting more effective techniques. In college we were taught to reinforce behaviors incompatible with those you want to decrease . . .

***

That afternoon in the principal's office, Bill Williams and Ann Sharp review the orientation program.

Bill [warmly]   I was really pleased with the orientation program this afternoon. I felt like I was talking with, not to, the new teachers.

Ann   You did a good job. I think the teachers respect you and are glad to be working with you.

Bill   Well if I did a good job it was because you and the three other orientation teachers did some good spade work in the morning session. How did it go?

Ann   Very well. They really responded to my opening remarks, and June and Betty became involved in the question and answer period.

Bill   What about Cynthia?

Ann [frowning]   I'm worried about Cynthia. I was bothered by her reaction during the discussion. She'd half-listen to me or one of the other teachers responding to her question. Then she'd quickly answer her own question, insisting that it wasn't really important, just something she wanted to toss out so she could get someone else's opinion. She kept a little distance between herself and the discussion. She seemed afraid to really talk. [With concern.] Bill, I hope your comments didn't bias me, but I think she's going to have problems in the classroom. She's concerned or worried about teaching. But she can't admit it.

***

One month later the curriculum supervisor [making her first visit to Cynthia's room] enters the class and takes a seat in back as Cynthia begins her presentation.

Cynthia Now I want you to read Chapter 15 by yourself without any noise or moving around. You have 20 minutes to read pages 110 to 125 about how a bill becomes a law. When you finish we can talk about it.

Four students approach the desk. Two need to go to the rest room, and the other two need to go to their lockers. Cynthia gives them all permission to leave, and they depart noisily. Randy, a student in the middle of the room, waves his hand furiously until Cynthia spots him.

Cynthia [harshly] Well, Randy, what do you want?
Randy Mrs. Clove, I read this last night.
Cynthia Well read it again or just relax. Keep quiet and let the other students work.

Randy frowns, lowers his head, and eventually turns to look out the window. Finally he begins to write his initials on the desk. Moments later Cynthia hurriedly approaches him.

Cynthia Randy, what are you doing?
Randy Nothing. I didn't have anything to do and—
Cynthia [with exasperation] You never have anything to do, do you? Can't you sit in a seat for 10 minutes and not bother anyone? Watch the clock for 10 minutes!

Randy watches the clock for 10 minutes and then, unnoticed by Cynthia, finishes writing his initials on the desk. Two students carefully observe Randy as he places the finishing touches on the initials. Both then begin scribbling on their desks with a pencil. Cynthia looks up as the two students finally return from the rest room. She notices that it took them 15 minutes, but she doesn't say anything. She looks at the class and notices several students with their heads on their desks.

Cynthia Well now that we've finished reading, let's see what we know—
Class [in chorus] We need more time! Not yet!
Bill [a large student sitting in the rear of the room shouting out] Hey I know. Let's pass a law. We can set up committees and do the whole bit.
Cynthia Perhaps we can do that next week, but first we'd better learn how to pass laws. Besides we're already two units behind in the book. Now who can tell me how a bill gets on the calendar? Ruth, [one of her best students, who is sitting in the front row] can you answer that?

Cynthia thumbs through to the answer section in the teacher edition and looks for her next question as she half listens to Ruth's answer. When Ruth finishes, Cynthia immediately looks at Jim.

Cynthia Jim, can you tell me . . .

***

Later that evening at home Cynthia washes dishes and her husband, Tom, reads the sports news at the kitchen table.

Cynthia [angrily] Tom, I have never been so humiliated in all my life. Doesn't that supervisor know I've only been teaching four weeks? What can you expect from kids like these anyway? They don't care about school or anything else for that matter. I think the principal gave me the hardest kids in school to teach.
Tom Well, hon, what did the supervisor criticize? What did she say?
Cynthia Oh she criticized everything.
Tom Like what?
Cynthia I can't remember specifics. She, uh . . . uh . . . I don't know. Sometimes I don't think I want to be a teacher.

***

Two days later in the principal's office, Bill Williams and Ann Sharp discuss Cynthia.

Bill Now that you've read the curriculum supervisor's detailed account of what went on in Cynthia's room during her visit, what do you think?
Ann It matches pretty well with my impression. Cynthia's never been in my room to see me, so we haven't had time to really talk. However, her room is directly across the hall from mine, and I stop in almost every morning to exchange a few words. I always get the same story: "Everything's fine, no problems at all!" [Firmly.] But everything's not fine. During the last two weeks, I've been interrupted by noise and confusion coming from her room. The only day in the last few days her kids have been quiet was when the curriculum supervisor visited. [She adds.] Even with her door closed, you can hear everything. It's getting difficult for me to control my class, and other teachers in our wing have started to complain.
Bill I have had a couple of calls from parents saying that Cynthia's been extremely critical of their kids, but I didn't pay much attention until I received the supervisor's report, and now you tell me—
Ann [interrupting] I'm sorry. I should have mentioned it to you, but it's only been really bad for the last five or six days. I hoped that she'd come and talk to me. I thought that would be better; but obviously she's not going to come to me. Bill, as her orientation teacher, I think I should be the one to talk to her. But how can I help her examine the situation openly when she's so defensive?

QUESTIONS

1. Review the questions that June, Cynthia, and Betty pose to Ann. Can you answer such questions?
2. What kinds of feedback (i.e., data) would help Cynthia become more effective in the classroom?
3. How might Cynthia have responded more appropriately to Randy during their brief exchanges?
4. Why do teachers so rarely observe one another teach and, even more rarely, give one another constructive feedback? How might the conditions under which teachers work be altered in order to promote such interactions?
5. What are the real concerns of beginning teachers like June, Betty, and Cynthia? How do these concerns differ from those of more experienced teachers?
6. From a motivational or psychoanalytic perspective, what is defensive behavior? How does it relate to insecurity, rigidity of response, angry threats, and use of punishment? How well do these constructs explain Cynthia's behavior?
7. What systematic observation instruments are available to observe teacher-pupil interactions in the classroom? Could such an instrument be used to observe Cynthia's interactions and help change her classroom behavior?
8. What counseling techniques can Ann use to hold a nonthreatening and productive consultation with Cynthia about her teaching?
9. From a humanistic viewpoint, what relationships exist between threat and perception? Between fear of failure and defensive behavior? How are the perceptual field and self-concept formed, and under what conditions do they change?

Appendix A

SMALL-GROUP DECISION MAKING

The purpose of this appendix is to provide college instructors with a practical format for using the case material in this book. Most of the procedures we describe have been used in teaching college courses for many years.

One way to use the cases in the book is as evaluation devices. A format such as the following may be used.

Directions: Read the case entitled _____ on pages _____ in *Case Studies for Teacher Decision Making*. Then follow the instructions listed here. Quality, not quantity, should characterize your answers.

1. Briefly analyze in psychological terms the problems faced by the teacher. Use only as much psychological theory as you need to fully cover the problem, and use only one theory if possible.
2. Cite behavioral evidence to support the application of each of the theories that you have used. Be sure to indicate what you are supporting with each behavioral event that you cite.
3. State and number the courses of action that the teacher should take to deal with the problem. Each course of action you suggest should be operational and feasible and should be consistent with your analysis on a point-by-point basis. The courses of action should fully cover the problem as you have analyzed it. Do not switch theories as you move from the analysis and support to the courses of action.

The papers can be scored in terms of such criteria as those discussed in Chapter 2 of this book. For example: (1) the number of analytic statements that are stated in correct psychological terminology as well as the total number of such statements; (2) the number of analytic statements that are clearly and objectively supported by the appropriate evidence; (3) the consistency, feasibility, and operationality of each course of action suggested. Each criterion can be scored using a five-point scale, and a total score can be computed.

The cases in this book can also be used as an integral part of small-group decision-making activities (SGDM), which is described here.

Problem Identification   The instructor can either select a case from *Case Studies for Teacher Decision Making* for the students to use, or the students may read the cases and identify those that are of most interest. In the latter situation, the students can write the names of three cases in rank order on a 3×5 inch card, and the instructor can then sort the students into small groups of six to nine based on their having selected a common case. If the instructor chooses the cases, he or she can assign the students to small groups using a table of random numbers or allow the students to choose whom they wish to work with. If the instructor does the selecting, he or she will have to decide whether the entire class will work on the same case or whether different cases will be assigned to different groups.

Instructor's Role   Once the students are divided into groups, the instructor must determine the extent of his or her own involvement in each group's decision-making activities. In SGDM the instructor usually becomes a resource person and does not become a group leader. Instead he or she moves from group to group and often sits on the fringe waiting until asked to make a contribution or until the group is moving in an unproductive direction. At other times the instructor sits in his or her office and waits for the group to ask for help.

The instructor does structure the group activities in at least two important ways: by establishing a due date for the group product (usually a group paper) and a procedure for evaluation of the product. The group process could be evaluated by either the students or the instructor, but it is our experience that this hampers a free and productive exchange of ideas by the group members. The criteria used for evaluating the group product are those presented in the introduction to the book, and further information is presented later in this appendix.

In SGDM each group works together as a unit until it is time to crystallize their oral or written product. Members of the group usually divide up the labor in terms of gathering data (reviewing the literature, interviewing teachers, etc.), and use each other (and the instructor if they desire) as sounding boards for their ideas. A group consensus is not necessary however. At the point of preparing a product for evaluation, if individuals and subgroups within a group differ from the rest of the group in the way in which they analyze and reach a decision, they are free to prepare a separate product. In the case of a group or subgroup product, all the members of the group or subgroup receive the same evaluation.

Case Analysis and Decision Making   Undergraduates in teacher education courses are usually told to focus on a given case from the standpoint of the teacher's role. They should focus on such things as what the teacher has done to help or hinder the situation, and what the teacher can do about the situation. Graduate students, however, are sometimes asked to focus on a problem situation from the standpoint of a consultant advising the teacher in the problem situation. This means, of course, that they must not only develop strategies for teacher behavior but must develop strategies for dealing with the teacher as well. Undergraduate teacher education students, on the other hand, are generally told to assume that the teacher will put into operation any courses of action that they decide upon and not to worry about strategies for getting the teacher to change his or her behavior.

In an educational psychology course, the students are generally asked to analyze a case from the frame of reference of relevant psychological theories, principles, and concepts. In a philosophy course, philosophical frames of reference are used, and in other kinds of education courses, still other frames of reference are stressed. The instructor may either direct the students to use a particular theory (e.g., operant conditioning) or let them choose the theory that they feel best fits the case.

Whatever the course content (and hence the frames of reference) applied to a case, the point should be made that there is no one correct way for a case to be analyzed. A theory or set of principles fits a case if the students show that it does. This means that they must state the theory or theories that they feel apply and then interpret the case in terms of the theory. As they do this, they can indeed show that the theory fits the case by citing evidence, such as cum record data, what people say and do, and so on. Notice how this was done using three different frames of reference in the case of "Joe Defies Authority" in Chapter 2.

An individual or a group may, of course, apply more than one theory or set of principles to a case. Doing so may involve the problem of mixing basically incompatible theories. In SGDM the students are free to mix theories and principles as long as they show how they go together. The instructor must point out to the students that teachers tend to think in terms of an organized set of personal beliefs—therefore, theories and principles that are substituted for a belief system should be organized so that they are meaningful. The SGDM process permits the student to look at a case from a new frame of reference (a scientific one) instead of the framework of personal beliefs that he or she might ordinarily use.

It is important to stress to the groups that there is no correct decision. Decisions are simply courses of action that follow from the analysis of the case. Different frames of reference may produce different courses of action for the teacher to take in dealing with a given case. Hence a theory is the correct one for the student to use in analyzing a case if the student shows that it fits by citing evidence, and a decision is correct if it is consistent with the frame of reference applied.

The best test of a decision would be to execute it and examine its consequences. This may be possible if the students have access to live teaching situations. For example, after working with situations like those in this book, the instructor might arrange for a real teacher to describe a case that he or she is currently facing. The students could gather data by interviewing the teacher, by observing in the classroom, and so on. After analyzing the data and mutually arriving at a decision with the teacher, they can let the teacher test the courses of action chosen. A next step, of course, would be to actually put the students in teaching situations and let them blend theory and experience themselves. The students can continue to meet in groups to receive help with whatever problems concern them or are identified by the use of videotape or some other means. Resource people (reading specialists, psychologists, special education specialists, etc.) could be invited to attend group sessions when the need arises. It might be pointed out that such small-group activities make real sense for teachers on the job as continuous in-service training activities.

Initiation of Analysis   In SGDM students do not usually start off analyzing a case in terms of a scientific theory. They usually begin by using their own personal belief system as a frame of reference and by stating the problem in layman's terms. The instructor sometimes has to help them get started by saying such things as, "How could you say the same thing in psychological terms?" or "What do you mean when you talk about needs?" The instructor may have to suggest that a group begin by answering the questions at the end of each case or questions that the instructor develops. Such questions should be viewed as starters or discussion stimulators.

Cycling and Extending   The entire SGDM process, from choosing the case to be analyzed to submitting a product to be evaluated, usually takes about eight one-hour class periods. Distributed practice seems better than massed practice in terms of scheduling the course meetings, and students usually have to meet outside the class as well. The SGDM cycle can be repeated for the rest of the semester or combined with other procedures. As has already been mentioned, it can move progressively from written materials to real-life experiences. Moving from written cases to filmed cases to videotaped real teaching situations to observing real teaching situations to actually engaging in teaching would be one such series of transitions.

Evaluating SGDM Papers   In analyzing and reaching decisions about a given case, students eventually have to deal with the following questions:

1. What, in the language of the theory you are employing, is the nature of the situation faced by the teacher?
2. Can you state the theory or set of principles that you have applied? Is it backed by research?

3. Can you cite evidence from the case to support the application of each of the theories or principles that you have applied?
4. Can you suggest operational and feasible courses of action that the teacher can take to deal with the situation? Are they consistent with the theory that you have applied? Have you considered both long-range and immediate courses of action?
5. How could the teacher check to make sure that the courses of action you have suggested are working?

SGDM products, whether group or individual, usually take a written form. The instructor generally scores such papers in terms of criteria that are communicated to the students before they begin their group activities. For example, the instructor might hand students a sheet containing evaluation criteria such as the following.

Objectives

1. Analyze the case in psychological terms and objectively support your analysis with evidence from the case.
2. Present a decision for the teacher to execute that is consistent with the analysis, feasible to execute, and operationally stated.

Evaluation Criteria

1. *Application of appropriate psychological theory to case analysis*
   A. Theory must fit the situation. Use only one theory if possible.
   B. All facets of the situation must be covered—hence, it may be necessary to use more than one theory.
   C. Theories or sets of principles used must be clearly identified and used correctly. Use the language and concepts of the theory for purposes of analysis.
2. *Objectivity of Analysis*   All key contentions in the analysis must be supported by evidence from the case that is objectivity cited. Behavioral events in the case are best reported as quotations or in as objective terms as possible. Do not try to paraphrase or summarize the evidence, and do not use inferences from the evidence to support your analysis unless the inferences are clearly labeled as such and are the only support available.
3. *Consistency Between Analysis and Decision*   Divide your paper into two parts and label them "Analysis" and "Decision." There should be an almost point-by-point consistency between the two. Do not analyze a problem in humanistic terms, for example, and then suddenly shift to an S-R model in arriving at a decision. The decision should logically flow from the analysis. It is best to indicate right in the paper the way in which you see the decision flowing from the analysis rather than leaving it up to the scorer.

4. *Feasibility of the Decision*   This criterion includes whether the decision you are suggesting is reasonably practical in the school situation described in the case. Demands on teacher time, abilities, cost, and so on must be considered. You should consider the question, "Will the decision work in the context of the situation being analyzed?"

5. *Operationality of the Decision*   The decision should be operational enough so that a teacher applying the decision can see the steps involved in putting it into operation. Be specific and spell out clearly how the teacher should deal with the situation. You *do not* need to worry about how to get the teacher to follow your advice. You may assume that the teacher will automatically do so.

6. *Organization of the paper*   Deduction will be made if the paper is not footnoted or does not have some kind of bibliography if you use sources *other* than the text. A good paper will have the following organization:

A. The paper will be divided into analysis and the decision, and the two parts will be clearly labeled.

B. The overall problem should be stated in psychological terms in the first paragraph or two.

C. Each key psychological contention should then be objectively supported, one by one, with evidence from the case.

D. A consistent, feasible, and operational decision that follows on a point-by-point basis should come next under "Decision."

E. The paper should be neatly typed, double-spaced, and the rules of spelling and grammar observed. The paper should be 8½ × 11 inch standard-size typing paper, and the paper should not ordinarily be longer than 10 pages, exclusive of title page and bibliography.

Statement of Personal Theory   We state in Chapter 1 of this book that students and teachers tend to interpret problem situations in terms of their own set of personal beliefs. A process such as SGDM involves students' learning to look at situations in terms of a research-based frame of reference. The instructor may decide that it is desirable to let the student analyze a case in terms of the student's own personal theory. This means, of course, that the student must realize that he or she has a set of beliefs about the world that influences his or her behavior. The student must be aware of these beliefs and define key terms before being able to communicate them to others. One way to begin is to ask the student to answer the questions indicated in the "Teacher Beliefs and Educational Research and Theory" section of the first chapter of this book.

Such a task can be quite painful and is subject to all the usual problems involved in any type of self-report activity. However, if students can succeed in stating their theories, they can then take the next step of comparing and contrasting their beliefs with research-based theory and principles. Perhaps they can then modify some of their own beliefs or at least feel better about the ones they hold. Finally, the students can examine the classroom implications that follow from their theories.

For example, an educational psychology instructor might give the student instructions for a term project such as the following.

1. Identify the psychological theory that you actually use, consciously or unconsciously, when you teach or think about teaching. Talk your psychological beliefs over with others, including your instructor. You might begin by answering the questions in the first chapter of this book in the section entitled, "Teacher Beliefs and Educational Research and Theory."
2. Identify the psychological theory that best approximates your own theory. The library may be of some help here. State the theory, proposition by proposition, and describe any relevant research that has been done in testing any of its hypotheses. State the references that you use.
3. Compare and contrast, point by point, your theory with the psychological theory that you have identified.
4. Indicate modifications, if any, in your own theory as a result of your research and reasons for making and rejecting changes in your theory.
5. Indicate in operational terms the implications of your theory (as you finally resolve it) for your own teaching and that of others.

Appendix B

THEORY GUIDE

We have already mentioned that our expertise is in the areas of educational psychology and curriculum and instruction. As a possible aid to instructors of courses in those two areas, this appendix offers a theory guide that presents our view as to what theories and sets of principles we believe are most useful for analyzing and making decisions about the 30 cases in the book. It was from this guide that we generated the "starter" or "stimulus" questions at the end of each case. Of course, just as two officials in an athletic contest might call the same play differently, we do not present this as the correct or complete list of theories to apply to each case. It merely represents our "judgment call." Also, we hope that experts in other fields such as philosophy of education, social foundations of education, educational administration, and so on, will construct a similar list for their own fields.

The theory guide is organized as follows. Content areas, subtopics, and specific theories are presented from the fields of educational psychology and curriculum and instruction. Following each are the numbers of the cases that in our opinion lend themselves to analysis using that content or theory.

Educational Psychology

1. Developmental Psychology 8, 26
   A. Adolescent development 18, 20
   B. Language acquisition 9
   C. Drug and sex education 18
2. Learning Theory
   A. Operant learning (including behavior modification) 1, 8, 11, 15, 16, 17, 21, 26, 27, 28
   B. Observational learning 1, 2, 12, 16, 27
3. Cognitive Theory
   A. Meaningful learning (Ausubel) 2, 9
   B. Information processing theory 2
   C. Metacognitive theory 2
   D. Field dependence-independence 1, 7
4. Gagné's seven types of learning 9
5. Instructional Objectives and Goals 1, 2, 3, 4, 5, 6, 10, 13, 21, 22

A. Cognitive taxonomy (Bloom et al.) 2, 7, 10, 22
B. Affective taxonomy (Krathwohl et al.) 2
6. Classroom Questions 5, 6, 10
7. Teacher behavior and effectiveness 5, 6, 10, 22, 30
8. Classroom Management Models
   A. Teacher effectiveness training (Gordon) 13, 19, 24, 28
   B. Kounin's classroom management model 6, 10, 12, 14
   C. Reality therapy (Glasser) 13
   D. Assertiveness training 25
9. Personality theory
   A. Psychoanalytic (Freud) 11, 20, 30
   B. Erikson 20
10. Motivational theory 8, 10, 11, 12, 14, 28, 30
    A. Maslow 1, 2, 3, 15, 16, 17, 18, 19, 23, 25, 27
    B. Intrinsic versus extrinsic 1, 6, 12, 13, 17, 19, 20, 22, 24, 28
    C. Attribution theory 11, 23
    D. Stress and burnout 12, 23, 24
    E. Efficacy 23
    F. Morale 23, 25
11. Humanistic Psychology 1, 16, 17, 18, 19, 20
    A. Rogers 30
    B. Self-concept theory 15, 16, 17, 18, 19, 26, 27, 28
    C. Values clarification (Simon et al.) 2, 3
12. Moral development (Kohlberg) 3, 18, 20, 24, 25, 29
13. Teacher expectancy theory (Rosenthal) 2, 10, 13, 14, 16, 21, 26
14. Social Psychology 17
    A. Group dynamics 1
    B. Conformity 3, 29
    C. Social norms 8, 18, 26
    D. Cooperation versus Competition 14
    E. Role theory 18, 22, 24
    F. Power 25
    G. Attitude formation and change 29
15. Exceptionalities (including giftedness) 14, 16, 19, 27
16. Home and Parent Influence and SES 4, 5, 6, 7, 11, 12, 13, 14, 15, 16, 18, 19, 20, 21, 23, 27, 28, 29
17. Measurement and Evaluation Principles 1, 2, 4, 5, 6, 7, 8, 9, 10, 14, 17, 19, 22, 29
    A. Intelligence and achievement theory and measurement 14, 15, 19, 20, 22
    B. Aptitude/Treatment interaction (ATI) 7

Curriculum and Instruction

1. Curriculum
   A. Goals and objectives 1, 2, 3, 14
   B. Content of the curriculum 2, 3, 19
   C. Influences on the curriculum 2, 3
   D. Curriculum scope and sequence 25

E. Back-to-basics 4, 21
F. The curriculum and individual differences 1, 14
2. Teacher Use of Time 6, 7, 23
3. Teacher Attitudes 13, 16
4. Individualized Instruction 1, 7, 11, 14, 21
5. Grouping (Tracking) 1, 11, 14, 21
6. Small Group Instruction 1, 5
7. Peer Tutoring 23
8. Teacher-Student Feedback 1, 2, 3, 5, 6, 10, 13
9. Student-Teacher Feedback 1, 2, 3, 5, 6, 10, 13
10. Seatwork 5, 6
11. Teacher Use of Praise 6
12. Instructional Materials 1, 9
13. Classroom Management
   A. Withitness 5, 6, 10, 17
   B. Ripple effect 6, 10, 13, 17
   C. Momentum 1, 6, 10
   D. Student attention 1, 6, 10, 13
   E. Conflict resolution 1, 2, 3, 6, 10, 12, 13, 16, 27
   F. Overlapping 5, 10, 17
   G. Group climate 1, 6, 13
   H. Preventing management problems 1, 5, 6, 10, 13, 17, 21, 27
   I. Dealing with management problems 1, 6, 10, 13, 16, 17, 21, 27
   J. Punishment 13, 17, 27, 29
   K. Classroom roles 5, 13, 17
   L. Misbehaving students 10, 13, 17, 27
   M. Unresponsive and withdrawn students 15
   N. Group dynamics in the classroom 1, 10, 13
   O. Desist strategies 5, 6, 13, 17, 27
14. Motivating Low Achievers 1, 12, 23
15. School Improvement 4, 13
16. Multicultural Education 12, 13, 23
17. Teaching as a Profession 22, 25, 30
18. Conditions Under Which Teachers Work 13, 21, 23, 24, 25, 30
19. Working with Parents 3, 15, 28
20. Rights of Students 18
21. Rights of Teachers 3, 18, 24

14.22